THE
ART OF
OBJECTS

The Addison-Wesley Object Technology Series

Grady Booch, Ivar Jacobson, and James Rumbaugh, Series Editors
For more information check out the series web site [http://www.awl.com/cseng/otseries/].

The Component Software Series

Clemens Szyperski, Series Editor
For more information check out the series web site
[http://www.awl.com/cseng/csseries/].

THE
ART OF
OBJECTS

Object-Oriented Design and Architecture

YUN-TUNG LAU, Ph.D.

ADDISON–WESLEY

Boston   San Francisco   New York   Toronto   Montreal
London   Munich   Paris   Madrid   Capetown
Sydney   Tokyo   Singapore   Mexico City

Many of the designations used by manufacturers and sellers to distinguish their products are claimed as trademarks. Where those designations appear in this book, and we were aware of a trademark claim, the designations have been printed in initial capital letters or in all capitals.

The author and publisher have taken care in the preparation of this book, but make no expressed or implied warranty of any kind and assume no responsibility for errors or omissions. No liability is assumed for incidental or consequential damages in connection with or arising out of the use of the information or programs contained herein.

Java™ and Enterprise JavaBeans™ are trademarks or registered trademarks of Sun Microsystems, Inc., in the United States and other countries.

The publisher offers discounts on this book when ordered in quantity for special sales. For more information, please contact

Pearson Education Corporate Sales Division
One Lake Street
Upper Saddle River, NJ 07458
(800) 382-3419
corpsales@pearsontechgroup.com

Visit AW on the Web: www.awl.com/cseng/

Library of Congress Cataloging-in-Publication Data

Lau, Yun-Tung, Ph.D.
  The art of objects : object-oriented design and architecture / Yun Tung Lau.
      p. cm. — (The Addison-Wesley object technology series)
  Includes bibliographical references and index.
  ISBN 0-201-71161-3
    1. Object-oriented methods (Computer science)   I. Title.   II. Series.

  QA76.9.O35 L39 2000
  005.1'17—dc21   00-056924

ISBN 0-201-71161-3
Text printed on recycled paper
1 2 3 4 5 6 7 8 9 10—MA—0403020100
First printing, October 2000

To Monica, Fa, and Mo

Contents

Preface

Object-oriented programming relies on programming languages. However, the concepts of objects transcend any specific programming languages. Many design patterns offer efficient modeling of static and dynamic object relationships. They can be used as the building blocks for sophisticated software systems. Similarly, at a system level, object-oriented architecture provides a lucid, high-level description of interconnected objects.

Tools may change. Programming languages may go out of favor. Yet the foundation of object design and architecture, and the art of applying it, will remain sound for a long time.

This book systematically presents the basic concepts of objects and practical object design patterns (both static and dynamic). It helps readers to gain a deep understanding of the patterns, allowing them to find design solutions quickly. In addition, the topics are forward looking, encompassing persistent objects, distributed objects, interface design patterns, XML (eXtensible Markup Language) object models, Web applications with thin clients, and so forth. Going beyond the design level, the book discusses object-oriented architecture, covering clients/servers, multi-tier systems, federations, agents, and others.

The Unified Modeling Language (UML), especially its graphic notation, is used as the primary means of presentation. The contents are independent of specific programming languages, making the book a general-purpose reference. However, many exercises do relate to certain languages (mostly Java). They help bring the readers closer to implementation and foster a concrete understanding of the underlying concepts. In addition, a wide range of real-world case studies and examples help elucidate these concepts and their practical application.

I did not use UML to specify all the details of an object design. For example, the UML Object Constraint Language is not used. In my opinion, source code with adequate inline comments is the best place to document the detailed logic of object behaviors.

This book can be used as a textbook for university or industrial training courses, or as a reference book for courses on object-oriented programming languages. This book is also suitable as a reference for mid- to advanced-level software professionals and graduate students. Many exercises are derived from actual projects. They expose readers to the full complexity of real-world systems.

Organization of the Book

This book has nine chapters, including several integrated case studies throughout the book. Chapter 1 describes the basic concepts in object-oriented programming, which include object, class, association, aggregation, servant class, and inheritance. It also introduces some basic notations of UML.

Chapter 2 discusses the common patterns in static design. The focus here is on the static relationships between classes. The dynamic or time-dependent behaviors are left to later chapters. I systematically present simple and complex patterns. They allow object designers to design with patterns rather than with individual classes.

I note that the distinction between analysis and design is vague. Analysis is more on understanding the concepts in an application domain and investigating the requirements. Design is more on finding a solution and verifying that the solution fits the requirements. With a concrete understanding of the object concepts and the relationships behind the static patterns, one would naturally apply object analyses and designs in an iterative fashion. The ultimate criterion for an appropriate object design is its fitness to the requirements.

In Chapter 3 I first present the basic concepts on database management and persistent objects. I then discuss different strategies to make objects persistent, particularly those involving object-oriented databases and relational databases. I also examine object-relational mapping in detail and give a comparison between the two types of databases.

Chapter 4 introduces some advanced topics in object modeling. They include abstract classes, multiple inheritance, interfaces, inner classes, collections, packages, and components. These are extensions to the basic object concepts. I also discuss the reverse engineering of object designs and the identification of irreducible patterns, which is presented in Chapter 2.

Chapter 5 describes modeling the dynamic behavior of objects. I discuss use case analyses and object sequence diagrams. I also introduce the important concepts of client/server and distributed objects. For distributed objects, I cover interface definition, and the Common Object Request Broker Architecture (CORBA) standard and its operational mechanisms.

Then in Chapter 6 I present various interface design patterns. These patterns are intimately related to the dynamic behaviors of their constituent objects. Such behaviors are documented with sequence diagrams. I also discuss interface patterns related to CORBA objects.

In Chapter 7 I elevate the discussion to the system level. I describe various object-oriented architectures, including procedural processing systems, client/server systems, layered systems, multi-tier systems, agents, and aggregations and federations. Note that the distinction between architecture and design is not absolute. In architecture we are more concerned with the coordination between components, overall system performance, and scaling properties. In design we focus on the details within a component, an interface, or a subsystem.

Chapter 8 gives summaries and notes for the preceding chapters, whereas Chapter 9 provides answers to all exercises.

The integrated case studies serve as real-life examples to illustrate the practical applications of the concepts. They appear at the ends of various chapters, culminating in Chapter 7 with a discussion of their system architectures. Readers are highly recommended to work through them in some detail. A concrete understanding of the basic concepts can only be built through hands-on design and implementation.

Sections with an asterisk after their titles may be skipped during the first reading. They are topics with somewhat narrower interests. Readers who are primarily interested in software system architecture may proceed directly to Chapter 7, which can be read as a survey of different architectural patterns.

Finally, the appendices provide various reference information. In particular, Appendix A summarizes UML notations, followed by a quick look-up table to all object designs appearing in the main text and exercises. Appendix B provides a list of code samples for each chapter. Appendix C lists the features of various object-oriented languages.

Online Resources

Fully functional code samples are available from http://www.awl.com/cseng/. The code samples have more than 40,000 source lines and are all written in Java. They cover nearly all examples described in the main text and most case studies. Appendix B lists the sample code for the chapters. Studying the code will help solidify the reader's understanding of the designs. Readers are encouraged to extend and enrich the sample code. Furthermore, students in courses on object-oriented programming languages may implement the designs appearing in the chapter exercises as additional exercises.

Acknowledgments

I thank my wife Monica for her patience and encouragement during this book project. I wish to thank Perry Cole, Dave Collins, Stevan Mrdalj, and Atma Sutjianto for their insightful comments and suggestions on the manuscript. Special thanks are due to Ross Venables, Paul Becker, and their colleagues at the editorial office for their efficient handling of the manuscript. The feedback from Amy Yuan and other students at the University of Maryland on an early version of the manuscript is gratefully acknowledged.

Basic Concepts

Traditional procedural programming implies a flow of steps. From step 1, step 2, to step N, the whole process can be represented by a flow chart, which may include decision points and branches. However, as computer programs are applied to more complex situations, such as interactive user interfaces and systems with interconnecting components, the keeping of all possible procedural branches in a number of programs becomes a formidable task. The situation is especially serious when a software development project involves a sizable team of people, who have to coordinate their subtasks such that the integrated system works seamlessly.

To overcome these difficulties, breaking a computer program into relatively self-contained pieces is critical. Often, such a decomposition reveals the intrinsic logical structure of the underlying problem. This leads to *object-oriented programming*.

This chapter discusses the basic concepts in object-oriented programming, which include object, class, association, aggregation, servant class, and inheritance.

1.1   THE NATURE OF OBJECTS

Objects are abstractions of physical entities or conceptual things. An object has states and an inherent identity. It attains certain behavior through a set of predefined operations, which may access or change its state.

An object encapsulates its properties (called *attributes*) and the operations that access or change those properties. The state of the object is determined by the values of its attributes. The object state is set by the object's operations. The inclusion of operations distinguishes objects from mere data structures. Operations are identified by their names and signatures (input, output, return arguments and their types). The implementations of operations are called *methods* in Java (or *member functions* in C++).

An object class is the abstract descriptor of a set of object instances. It describes a set of object instances that share the same attributes, operations, and relationship with other objects. For example, the Person class in Figure 1-1 contains attributes name and age, as well as operations for changing the name and incrementing the age. The Person class does not describe any specific person. The object instances of the Person class, on the other hand, have the information for actual persons.

For a physical entity, such as a person, the corresponding attributes are easily identified. Its operations, however, depend on how the object should behave in its environment and how it interacts with other objects. Determining the behavior of objects is a key to good object-oriented programming.

Objects corresponding to conceptual things also encapsulate attributes and operations. The only difference is that the attributes are properties or states that belong to a process, transaction, event, and so forth, rather than a physical object. A trade object example is shown in Figure 1-2.

Through abstraction, an object class generalizes a few specific object instances to a host of similar instances, thereby allowing efficient use of the implementation of its operations.

Although it is not our goal to map object designs to specific programming languages such as C++ or Java, it is beneficial to know how an object class is represented by such a language. Figure 1-3 shows the pseudocode for the Trade class. (The code is presented in Java style, but does not carry visibility modifiers like `public` or `private`. In other words, the default visibility is used.) The operation `calculatePrice()` retrieves the unit price (probably from a database), then calculates the total price, which is a property of the trade itself.

The term *object* is often used to indicate either an object class or an object instance. One simply needs to refer to the context to find out which meaning an "object" takes. Moreover, in performing object design, one often has to keep both meanings in mind to understand fully the relationships between objects.

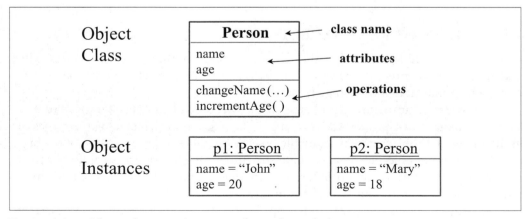

FIGURE 1-1. *Object classes and instances from physical objects.*

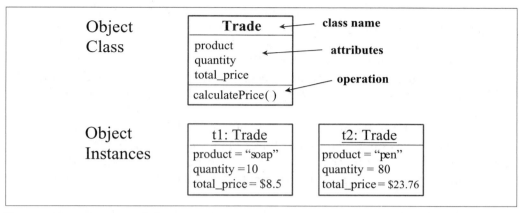

FIGURE 1-2. *Conceptual objects.*

```
class Trade {

  String product;
   int quantity;
  double total_price;

   // operations
    void calculatePrice( ) {
    // Retrievesunit_price, then
    // total_price = unit_price * quantity
    // Discount may apply for large quantities.
   }
  }
```

FIGURE 1-3. *Java-like pseudocode for the Trade class.*

1.2 UNIFIED MODELING LANGUAGE

When we discuss objects, it is natural to present them using certain structured notations, as we have done in Figures 1-1 and 1-2. This has proved to be an effective way of modeling objects and documenting object designs.

The Unified Modeling Language (UML) is a general-purpose modeling language designed to specify, visualize, and document the artifacts of a software system. The visual notations of UML are particularly suited for object-oriented software designs.

UML is a unification of previous modeling methods such as Booch [Booch 1994], OOSE (object-oriented software engineering) of Jacobson [Jacobson et al. 1992], and OMT (object modeling technique) of Rumbaugh [Rumbaugh 1991]. The development of UML began in October 1994, when Grady Booch and Jim Rumbaugh of Rational Software Corporation began their work on unifying the Booch and OMT methods. In the fall of 1995, Ivar Jacobson joined the unification effort and merged in the OOSE method.

In 1997, the UML Partners consortium was formed. The consortium produced UML 1.0, which was submitted to the Object Management Group (OMG). Further inputs from several other companies were later incorporated to produce UML 1.1 in September 1997. UML 1.1 has been submitted to the OMG for adoption [UML 1997].

Compared with previous modeling methods, UML has the following two advantages:

1. A unified standard of semantics and notations brings regularity and stability to the software industry. Companies can make greater reuse of previous object designs based on a mature modeling language. Tool developers can focus on enhancing features rather than catching up with several evolving standards.

2. The joint effort yielded improvements from previous methods. It also helped to strike a balance between expressiveness and simplicity. It allows the object modeling method to evolve as a single body rather than as separate efforts, eliminating the potential for confusing differences.

Today, many companies are incorporating UML as a standard in their development processes and products. UML can be used to model both object structures and behavior. Structural models (or static models) focus on object classes, attributes, and the relationship between objects. Behavioral models (or dynamic models) emphasize object interaction, collaboration, and states.

Next we briefly describe the basic features of UML, which are used to illustrate our discussion. Other more involved topics are covered in future sections when needed. We note that UML contains a rich set of semantics and notations, and we refer you to other reference books [Fowler et al. 1997, Page-Jones 2000].

1.3   UML NOTATION BASICS

We have already seen the notation for object classes in Figures 1-1 and 1-2. Here we specify it more precisely. As shown in Figure 1-4, a class (long form) is represented by a solid-outline rectangle with three horizontal compartments. The name of the class appears in the top compartment, which is followed by the attribute compartment and the operation compartment. In Figure 1-4 we have added some more operations like `getUnitPrice()` and `isDiscounted()`.

Note that by convention all attribute and operation names begin with lower-case characters, whereas class and type names are capitalized. Also, the type of an attribute or the return type of an operation is specified by a colon (:) followed by a type name, as shown in Figure 1-4. For an operation that returns nothing (`void`), the type is left empty. Also, we use verbs (possibly followed by the verb's object) for the names of operations. The most common operations are `get` and `set`, which retrieve and change certain attributes of an object. For operations that return a Boolean (true or false), the name typically starts with "is".

The short form of the class notation is simply a box with the class name. This form is used most often when analyzing object relationships and showing system object design. The short form can be combined with pseudocode for class definition to give a complete description of the design, thereby replacing the long form.

Before we leave this section, we list several other basic UML notations in Figure 1-5. A solid line connecting two classes indicates an association between them. The number on either end of the line gives the number of possibly associated objects on that end. More generally, a range can be specified in the form m..n, where m and n are the lower and upper bounds respectively. Examples are 0..*, 1..*, 0..1, and so forth. A single * indicates any integer, including zero. A diamond on one end of an association represents aggregation—in other words, one class is a component of another one. Finally, a triangle means inheritance. We discuss these concepts thoroughly in the coming sections.

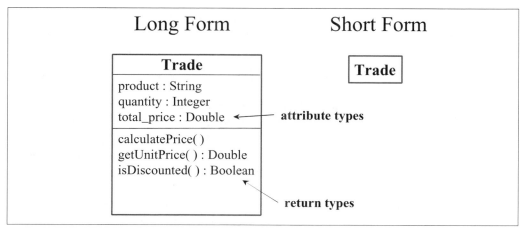

FIGURE 1-4. *Class notations in long and short forms.*

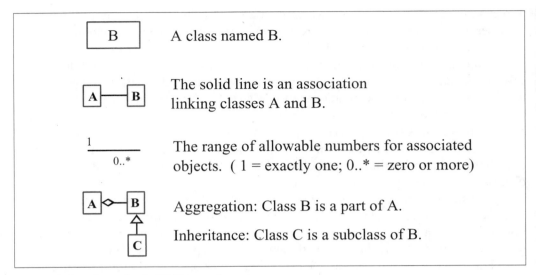

FIGURE 1-5. *Some basic UML notations.*

1.4 OBJECT CREATION AND DESTRUCTION

Because an object class is a template for its corresponding object instances, one must create the instances in order to use them. The creation of object instances, or *instantiation,* is a necessary process in any object-oriented program. At the time of instantiation, relevant attributes must be initialized and the object instance itself is assigned to a variable (an object reference). The operation for creating an object instance is called a *constructor.*

The UML notation for object instances was shown in Figures 1-1 and 1-2. The top compartment shows the name of the object (like p1), followed by a colon and the class name (all underlined; see Section 5.17 of [UML 1997]). In a specific programming language, the name of the object corresponds to a variable (object reference) name.

Once constructed, an object can be used until it is destroyed (explicitly or implicitly). Some languages (most notably C++) require explicit destruction operations of objects through *destructors* [Ellis & Stroustrup 1990]. In this case you can use a reference count to track the number of variables pointing to the object (Figure 1-6). When there are no variables pointing to the object, the reference count drops to zero and the object can be deleted. In UML design diagrams, destructors are usually omitted.

Other languages (such as Java and Lisp) rely on garbage collection and do not need explicit object destruction. Garbage collection greatly reduces the burden on the

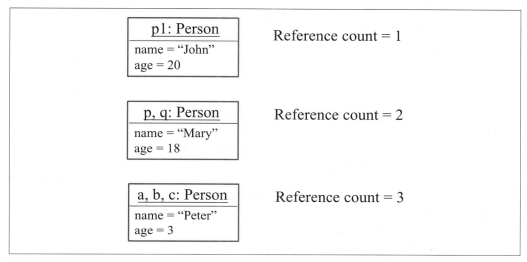

FIGURE 1-6. *Reference counts of object instances. Here the reference count is equal to the number of variables (or object names) that holds the object. (We have extended the UML notation slightly with a list of comma-delimited object names.)*

programmer to manage obsolete objects. It typically uses a "mark-and-sweep" process to reclaim memory used by obsolete objects. The process involves two steps. During the first step, the garbage collector scans all objects and marks those that are in use. During the second step, unmarked objects are swept away so that their memory space can be reused.

We consider memory management an implementation issue and omit it from our design discussion. However, to achieve good system performance, you should always create new objects judiciously. For example, you should reuse old objects whenever possible.

1.5   ASSOCIATIONS AND LINKS

The essence of object structure analysis or static modeling is to identify the precise relationships between classes. An association defines a relationship among two or more classes. A link, on the other hand, is the realization of such a relationship among two or more object instances. Thus, for example, a Person class may be associated with a Hobby class. A particular person may have several hobbies (object instances), each of which is related to the person by a link.

Relationships among classes come in many flavors, with various subtleties. Here we discuss some that are fundamental for the buildup of more complex relationships.

1.5.1 BINARY ASSOCIATIONS AND LINKS

Associations may be binary, ternary, or higher order. In practice, however, binary associations appear most often.

A binary association establishes a relationship between two classes. The corresponding binary links are the connections between the object instances of those two classes. As shown in Figure 1-5, a solid line connecting two classes indicates such an association.

A binary association is not part of either class, but depends on *both* of them [Rumbaugh 1991]. The same is true for higher order associations. Associations can also possess their own attributes and operations. They can therefore be modeled by classes. We discuss such association classes in Section 2.5.

An end of the association can be linked to any number of objects from the class associated with that end. In UML, you can explicitly specify the allowable range of numbers (Figure 1-5). This property of an association is called *multiplicity*.

The multiplicity symbol on one end of the line specifies the number of possible associated objects on that end for any given object on the other end. Note that a single * indicates any integer, including zero. In practice, 1, 0..1, 1..*, and * are the most frequent forms of multiplicity. For implementation, a multiplicity of 1 or 0..1 is distinctly different from that of 1..* or *. The former is related to a single variable, whereas the latter is related to an array or collection.

Figure 1-7 shows a Person-Hobby association, in which each person can have zero or more hobbies. In the Person class, a variable collection of Hobby objects (represented by Hobby[*]) is used to store the hobbies. In the Hobby class, on the other hand, a person variable holds the Person object interested in the hobby. Here for simplicity we have assumed that each Hobby object can be associated with only one person. The constructor `Hobby(name : String, person : Person)` sets up the link from the Hobby object to the Person object.

Associations are typically the embodiment of verbs in problem statements. In the example in Figure 1-7, a person *has* zero or more hobbies. Other examples are the following: A group *contains* many persons, a polygon is *made up of* multiple points and lines, and so forth. Because of this, one can use the verb as the *association name*. The association name in UML may also have an optional small black solid triangle next to it, which shows the direction of the action.

The role of a class in an association may be vague if the class name is too generic. In this case, you may specify the role of the class next to its association end. This is called a *rolename* in UML (compare with the Circle-Point example in Figure 1-11). In this book we generally choose class names that closely resemble their roles. However, we explicitly give the rolenames when there may be ambiguities.

It is rewarding to recognize the detailed design pattern for a specific association. This gives us a concrete understanding of the design with its implied implementation.

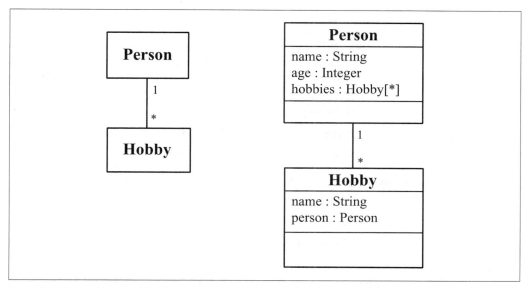

FIGURE 1-7. *A Person-Hobby association. Here Hobby[*] represents a variable collection of Hobby objects.*

Furthermore, a certain association type usually maps to a common pattern of attribute structure and operations. Such patterns often lead to effective reuse of previous designs, as seen in Exercises 1-1 and 1-2.

1.5.2 ORDERING AND SORTING

If the multiplicity at one end of an association is more than one, then the corresponding collection for the multiple objects can be ordered or sorted. This may be a design requirement, or it may be more related to implementation. The recognition of such association properties during design is often helpful. Some examples are shown in Figure 1-8.

In the Polygon-Point association, the points need to be ordered, say in the clockwise direction, so that the polygon can be formed by joining adjacent points with lines. Note that the order must be determined whenever a point is added to the collection. For implementation this requires a collection with ordering (for example, the Vector class in java.util or some other variable-length arrays).

In the Group-Person association, the persons need not be ordered when they are added to the group. However, it is often convenient to show the persons in alphabetical order. This requires that certain sorting functions be implemented either within the collection or during data retrieval.

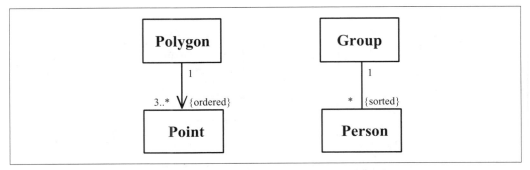

FIGURE 1-8.   *Ordered and sorted binary associations. Note also that the Polygon-Point association is unidirectional.*

1.5.3   NAVIGATION AND REFERENTIAL INTEGRITY

As shown in Figure 1-7, an association between two classes is implemented by variables that hold object references. Thus the hobbies variable in the Person class of Figure 1-7 allows us to navigate from a Person object to its hobbies, whereas the person variable leads us from a Hobby object to the associated person. Such navigation variables may appear in either one or both of the associated classes, depending on the need.

In our object design diagrams, we have implicitly assumed that bidirectional navigation is available. If one-way navigation is sufficient, we may use an arrow to indicate such associations. In this case an object reference gives a unidirectional link from the source object to the target object along the direction of the arrow (for example, the Polygon-Point unidirectional association in Figure 1-8).

Bidirectional navigation requires object references (or pointers) on both ends of an association when implemented with currently popular languages (such as C++ and Java). Hence it is the programmer's responsibility to ensure *referential integrity*. That is, both references should point to the right objects, and, when one reference is removed, the other one should be removed as well.

For unidirectional links, if obsolete objects are handled by garbage collection, then we do not have any problems with referential integrity. All we need to do is to delete the link when it is not needed. However, if explicit object destruction is used, then we need to ensure that the link is deleted together with the destruction of the target object. This can be achieved by embedding the link removal operation inside the destructor of the target object.

Thus, the essence of referential integrity is to ensure simultaneous creation and deletion of forward and backward link pairs. In general, we can encapsulate all such link manipulations in a small number of *core operations*, and we can use only these operations to handle the links.

Referential integrity is more closely related to implementation. However, in static object design we can alleviate this burden by using unidirectional links and resorting to bidirectional links only when necessary. In Chapter 2 we revisit the issue of referential integrity for each static design pattern.

1.5.4 TERNARY AND HIGHER ORDER ASSOCIATIONS

In real life, binary associations account for the majority of class associations. There are occasions, however, when ternary or higher order associations are needed.

An N-ary association establishes a relationship between N classes. The corresponding N-ary links (also known as N-tuples of values) are the connections between the object instances of those N classes. As shown in Figure 1-9, an N-ary association is shown in UML as a large diamond with a solid line connected to each of the associated classes. An optional association name can be placed next to the diamond. The association is not part of any of the N classes, but depends on *all* of them.

Multiplicity symbols can be used to specify or constrain the number of links between objects. The multiplicity symbol on an association end of a particular class specifies the potential number of links when the other N-1 object instances are fixed. Thus, in Figure 1-9, the multiplicity is interpreted as follows:

- A person can serve on as many as two committees only in any given year.

- Each committee can have three to five persons as members in any given year.

- A person can serve between one to four years on any specific committee.

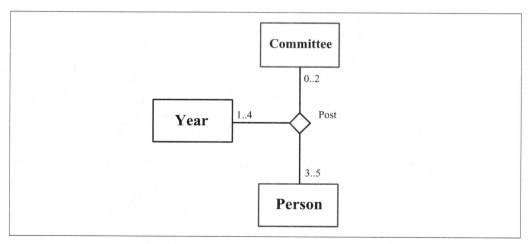

FIGURE 1-9. *A ternary association with multiplicity constraints. Each link in the association corresponds to a post in a committee.*

Because the range of any multiplicity symbol in Figure 1-9 is more than one, we need to use all three object references (committee: Committee, person: Person, year: Year) to specify a link uniquely. Such a set of object references (or other attributes that uniquely identify an object) is called a *candidate key*. In general, a candidate key is a minimal set of attributes that uniquely identifies a link [Rumbaugh 1991, p71]. We will see in Chapter 3 that candidate keys are used as primary keys in relationship tables.

The number of attributes in a candidate key depends on the multiplicity. For an N-ary association, this number can be between 1 and N. Therefore, at most N objects are allowed to specify an N-ary link uniquely. We call this the *candidate key requirement*.

For binary associations, this requirement implies that, at most, two objects are allowed to identify a link uniquely. Equivalently, both or one of the two associated objects must uniquely identify a binary link. Thus, if a relationship needs more than two object identifiers, the relationship is beyond a binary association.

To solidify these concepts, we present in Figure 1-10 a detailed design for the ternary association in Figure 1-9. The posts variable contains an array of object pairs. For Committee, the object pair is (Person, Year); for Year, the object pair is (Committee, Person); and for Person, it is (Committee, Year). These pairs constitute the links between the three classes of objects. The operation addPost adds a pair to the posts array.

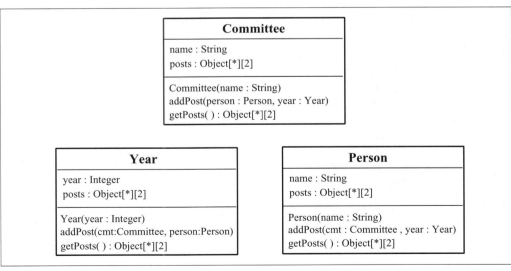

FIGURE 1-10.   *A detailed design for the ternary association in Figure 1-9. The posts variable contains an array of object pairs. For example, for Committee, the object pair is (Person, Year). Here, Object[*][2] represents a variable array of object pairs.*

The candidate key requirement is satisfied by forbidding duplicate object pairs in the posts arrays. The multiplicity constraints, on the other hand, may be enforced within the operation `addPost`. To ensure referential integrity, one may implement `addPost` in Committee as the core operation so that it also sets up backward links from the Year and Person objects (by invoking their `addPost` operations). Finally, to complete the design, one may add the operation `removePost`, which handles these requirements and constraints similarly.

1.6   AGGREGATION AND COMPOSITION

Aggregation is a special form of binary association and its indication is often suppressed during the initial phase of object design. Aggregation occurs when a class is a part of or a component of another one (the aggregate). As shown in Figure 1-11, a diamond on the aggregate end of an association signifies aggregation. Examples are Polygon-Point, Car-Part, and Circle-Point. In general, the multiplicity on the aggregate end of the association can be any integer. Thus, a part can be used in multiple cars (for car designs, not physical cars).

There is a strong form of aggregation, called *composition,* in which the component is an integral part of the whole aggregate. That is, there is a part-whole relationship. For example, in the Circle-Point association in Figure 1-11, the circle is created together with its central point. The circle cannot exist without its center. There exists a strong ownership of the components by their aggregate. The components and their aggregate may even have a lifetime relationship—they are created and destroyed together.

Both aggregation and composition have transitivity. That is, if A is a part of B and B is a part of C, then A is a part of C. Also, certain bulk or environmental

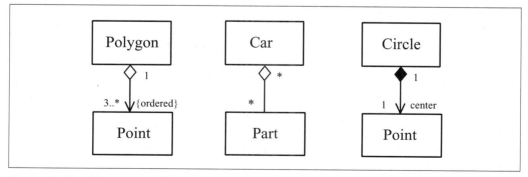

FIGURE 1-11.   *Examples of aggregation. The black diamond in the Circle-Point aggregation indicates composition, which is a strong form of aggregation. (Note that the rolename of the Point class is center.)*

TABLE 1-1. *A comparison of three types of binary association.*

CHARACTERISTIC	NORMAL ASSOCIATION	AGGREGATION	COMPOSITION
UML notations		◇━━━	◆━━━
Ownership	None	Weak	Strong
Multiplicity	Any	Any	One on aggregate side
Transitivity	No	Yes	Yes
Propagation of properties	Undefined	From whole to part	From whole to part

properties or operations of the whole may propagate to the part [Rumbaugh 1988]. In the Circle-Point example, moving the circle is equivalent to moving the center. In terms of implementation, transitivity implies that *recursive* functions may apply for certain operations on the entire aggregation tree.

The distinction between normal association, aggregation, and composition is often vague and subtle. They may differ only slightly in implementation. During the initial design phase we may simply use normal associations and then refine the design later. Table 1-1 compares these three relationships.

Because of the strong part-whole relationship (or ownership by the aggregate) in a composition, the multiplicity on the aggregate end must not exceed one. This will become more obvious when we discuss the servant class in the next section.

1.7   SERVANT CLASSES AND DELEGATION

The concept of servant classes appears most naturally when grouping attributes together. Consider the Circle class on the left of Figure 1-12. The coordinates (x0, y0) define the center of the circle. We can use a Point class to encapsulate (x0, y0) and its related operations (such as shifting the point). Hence the two attributes are replaced by a single one of type Point, which now becomes a servant class to Circle. In the Circle class on the right of Figure 1-12, the operation move(dx, dy) simply calls the one in Point to move the center by dx in the x direction and dy in the y direction.

From an implementation point of view, a servant class encapsulates data and operations needed by the master class and appears as an attribute in the latter. Consequently, a servant class is an integral part of its master. In other words, it can only serve one master class (having loyalty). Thus, the multiplicity on the aggregate end may not exceed one. From an object design point of view, the recognition of a servant class leads to higher level of abstraction and more reuse of designs.

The relationship between a master class and its servants is practically the same as composition. The term *composition* emphasizes the whole-part logical

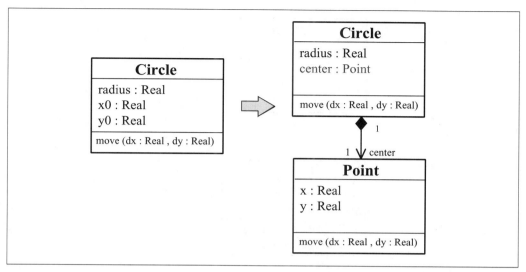

Figure 1-12. *Grouping attributes together to form a servant class. Note that the rolename of the Point class is center and that the association is unidirectional.*

relationship, whereas servant classes focus on providing services (operations) to the master. The master delegates some of its operations to the servant.

Compared with inheritance, delegation to a servant class is often the preferred way of reusing an existing class. We discuss this more after we study inheritance in the next section.

1.8   INHERITANCE

An object class describes a set of object instances that share the same attributes and behaviors. After a class is defined, we may extend it to a new class by adding new attributes and behaviors. The new class (the subclass) describes a set of object instances that inherit all attributes and behaviors from the previous class (the superclass). In addition, the subclass can override the inherited behaviors by providing new implementations for the inherited operations. This is often done to make the operations specific to the subclass or to enhance the efficiency of the operations.

For example, if we want to create a computer account for a person, we can extend the Person class in Figure 1-1 to a User class, as shown in Figure 1-13. Thus a user is a special type of person and has new attributes and operations related to the computer account of the person. Operations in the subclass can access the attributes and operations of the superclass (subject to visibility restriction, which is language dependent). Thus in the User class, you can still access the name and age of

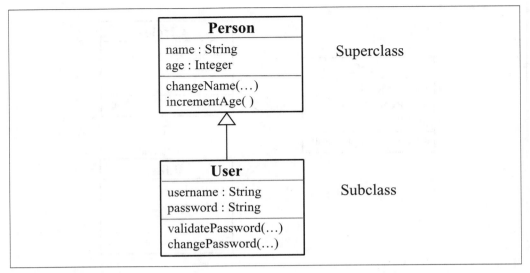

FIGURE 1-13. *A subclass inherits all attributes and behaviors from its superclass.*

Person. Furthermore, a User object can invoke both `changeName` and `incrementAge` operations.

In a specific programming language, visibility keywords (such as `private`, `protected`, and `public`) control whether an attribute or operation in a class is visible to its subclasses and other related classes. As a good practice, we should encapsulate all attributes and make them accessible only through predefined `get` and `set` operations (even to subclasses). Here, however, we focus on the object design and make the assumption that all attributes and operations are accessible to subclasses by default. The use of visibility keywords can be deferred to the implementation phase.

1.8.1 INHERITED VERSUS SERVANT CLASSES

Inheritance makes the attributes and operations of the superclass available to the subclass. However, the need to reuse the attributes and operations of a certain class is often not sufficient to warrant the use of inheritance. One must ensure that the subclass is indeed a special type of the superclass, or the class relationship may be inadvertently distorted.

To illustrate this point, consider the Circle and Point classes in Figure 1-12. In designing the Circle class, you may be tempted to generalize the Point class by adding a radius attribute, as shown in Figure 1-14. Operationally, the Circle class in Figure 1-14 will work as expected. That is, the inherited coordinates (x, y) represent the center of the circle, and the center can be shifted by calling `move(dx, dy)`. However,

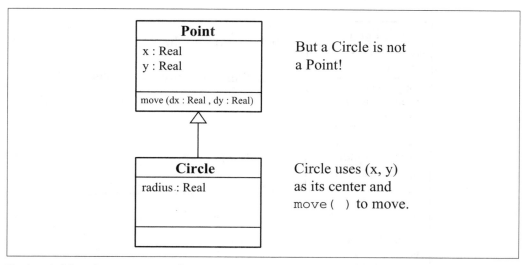

FIGURE 1-14. *An erroneous inheritance.*

when other class relationships are involved, we quickly realize that the inheritance in Figure 1-14 is ill-defined. For example, the Polygon in Figure 1-11 is composed of three or more points, which could now be circles!

The correct way to reuse the attributes and operations of the Point class is to treat it as a servant class to Circle, as was done in Figure 1-12. The key to a correct inheritance relationship is to verify that the subclass is a *special type* of the superclass (type-of relationship). Consequently, each instance of the subclass is also an instance of the superclass.

1.8.2 POLYMORPHISM AND OBJECT SUBSTITUTION

Polymorphism generally means that the same operation may behave differently on different classes. Putting this in the context of inheritance, we may issue the same command to different objects in an inheritance tree and expect to invoke the operation implementation specific to the object classes. Thus, if an operation op() is overridden by a subclass, calling op() through a subclass object invokes the implementation in the subclass. Otherwise, the call invokes the implementation in the superclass. Furthermore, if multiple subclasses all implement the operation op(), calling op() on a specific subclass object invokes the implementation in that subclass. (This is also called *dynamic binding*.)

Because each instance of a subclass is also an instance of the superclass, an object reference of the superclass should be able to hold a subclass object (Figure 1-15). The reverse, however, is not true.

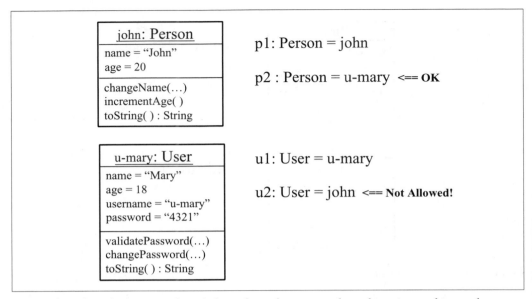

FIGURE 1-15. *Substitution of a subclass object for a superclass object in an object reference. Note that User is a subclass of Person and that the operation* toString() *of User supersedes that of Person.*

Substitution of subclass objects for superclass objects in object references works hand in hand with polymorphism. We can then invoke operations specific to a subclass object using an object reference belonging to its superclass.

For example, in Figure 1-15 the operation toString() of User supersedes that of Person. The call p2.toString() invokes the one in User because p2 actually holds a User object (u-mary). Moreover, with casting or narrowing to a subclass, we may use p2 to invoke operations defined only for the subclass. An example in Java is ((User)p2).validatePassword(…). Again, this works because p2 in reality holds a User object.

A more precise but abstract description of such object substitution is given by the *Liskov substitution principle,* which states that for each object instance s of a subclass S, there is an object instance g of its superclass G such that the behavior of any program in terms of G is unchanged if s is substituted for g [Liskov 1987].

The substitution principle together with polymorphism gives great simplicity and flexibility in implementing object-oriented programs. For example, we can build a heterogeneous container of objects. Each object in the container may belong to different subclasses that are derived from a common superclass. We can then invoke operations defined in the superclass but implemented differently in the subclasses. Each object then performs the operation specific to its own class. Another example is an *object factory*, which generates different types of objects (belonging to the same superclass) and returns an object reference of the superclass type to the caller.

1.9   EXERCISES

1-1.   Fill in the operations for the Person-Hobby design in Figure 1-7 and generate a detailed design diagram (with class notation in the long form such as that presented in Figure 1-4). Describe all operations and identify the design patterns related to the multiplicity items 1 and *.

1-2.   Add a Group class to the previous design such that each group can have zero or more persons, whereas each person can belong to only one group. Work out a detailed design diagram. Present the UML class notations in both long and short forms. Comment on how the design in Exercise 1-1 can be reused. Also, describe the changes needed during the reuse process.

1-3.   Design a family of Geometry objects by drawing the object diagram in short form. Call the superclass Geometry Item. Derive from it Line, Circle, Square, Ellipse, and Polygon appropriately. (Note: An ellipse has two focal points, which coincide in the case of a circle.) Describe how to use the Point class as a servant for these objects. For Ellipse and Circle, give two ways of using points.

1-4.   For the design in Exercise 1-3, what are some common operations for all the Geometry objects? Which operations are truly polymorphic? Describe how these polymorphic operations are implemented differently in different classes.

Common Patterns in Static Design

Although decomposing a problem into objects depends on the nature of the problem and the designer's subjective judgment, certain patterns involving a few interconnected classes often appear in object designs. These patterns are the building blocks or common patterns for more complex designs in larger systems. Common patterns provide reusable solutions for similar groups of problems [Gamma et al. 1995, Larman 1998]. These patterns are also known as *model frameworks* [D'Souza & Wills 1999].

In this chapter we discuss common patterns in static design, and we focus on the static relationships between classes and ignore their dynamic or time-dependent behavior. A concrete understanding of the object relationships behind these patterns is crucial for object-oriented designers and architects. It allows us to design with patterns (rather than with individual classes) and to reuse patterns as design components. For programmers, a pattern is often associated with a specific set of operations, which defines the behavior of that pattern. Thus, the use of design patterns will greatly expedite the design and implementation process.

The design patterns in this chapter are chosen because they appear often in real-life designs, and because as basic building blocks they fulfill specific functions in those designs. In the case studies and in the architecture chapter (Chapter 7), we will see how such building blocks form larger systems and contribute to the overall behaviors of the systems. Some of the patterns are the same as those presented in [Gamma et al. 1995]. Others are more fine-grained or fundamental from a structural point of view.

2.1   COLLECTION MANAGERS

This is one of the most common patterns in static object design. A manager class manages a collection of objects, including the creation and removal of those objects.

Figure 2-1 shows an example, which is similar to the Person-Hobby association presented in Section 1.5.1. We also use the following UML notations in Figure 2-1:

- The name or action of the association (manages) and its direction indicated by a solid triangle
- A note with textual information on the lower right corner
- The *stereotype* notation, which is shown in << ... >>. A stereotype is presented as a keyword string above the operations. It represents a group of operations or a usage intent for the operations. A stereotype may also be applied to a class name (or another UML element name), in which case the stereotype is presented as a keyword string above the class name. It represents a subtype or usage intent of the class.

The operations in UserManager are similar to those in the Person-Hobby association, except for addUser(user : User), which is not needed in UserManager because the manager is responsible for creating the user objects. In other words, the operation addUser(username : String) in Figure 2-1 is the only operation that creates a user.

A collection manager usually has an index to locate an object from a key (such as username). Creating objects through the manager ensures that all objects in the collection are indexed and can be retrieved from the key.

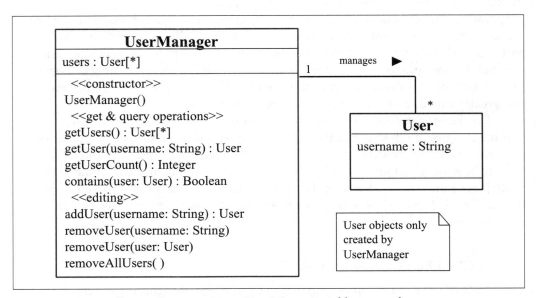

FIGURE 2-1. *A collection manager. Here, User[*] is a variable array of users.*

If the links between UserManager and User are bidirectional, we can maintain referential integrity by encapsulating all link manipulations in `addUser(username : String)` and `removeUser(user : User)`. All other operations should call them to add or to remove links. The same is true for a generic manager of an object collection.

2.2 CONTAINERS

Most operations in the collection manager can be abstracted into a container that contains generic objects. Figure 2-2 shows a container for generic objects. Note that the container only contains the objects and does not create them. Thus the `add` operation has an object as an input argument. This is the major different behavior between a container and a collection manager.

The name attribute of Object is used in `get(name : String)` as a key to locate the object. The `contains(object : Object)` operation returns whether the input object is in the container.

Obviously, one can reuse the Container class for the collection manager classes. There seems to be two apparently similar ways to achieve this:

1. Use Container as a servant class inside a collection manager class (delegation).

2. Derive a collection manager class from Container (inheritance).

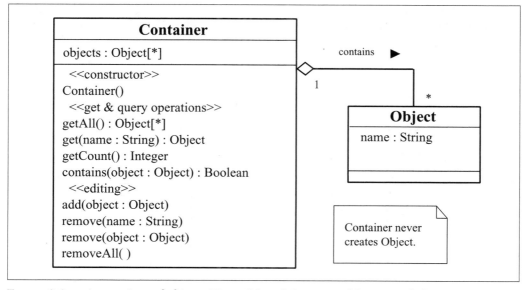

FIGURE 2-2. *A container of objects. Here, Object[*] is a variable array of objects.*

However, to enforce the behavior that the `add` operation (such as `addUser` in Figure 2-1) is the only way to create objects in a collection manager, we prefer the first approach—delegation. (The second approach allows objects to be created separately and then added to the collection.)

In more complex designs, Containers can be used in many places by collection managers or other classes. For example, suppose a Bank class manages multiple Account objects and Employee objects. You can have a Container for Account objects and another for Employee objects. Both Containers are used as servant classes in the Bank class.

In most cases the container holds unidirectional links to the objects. Thus, referential integrity is not a problem if obsolete objects are handled by garbage collection.

Finally, a container may contain a heterogeneous set of objects. Each object in the container may belong to different subclasses that are derived from a common superclass. We can then invoke polymorphic operations on the objects.

2.3 SELF-CONTAINING CLASSES, HIERARCHIES, AND NETWORKS

An object class may be associated with itself. In particular, a Container class may contain itself. This means that a Container object instance may contain other instances of the same class, leading to self-containing objects (Figure 2-3a). Such a recursive association yields a hierarchy or a tree. A vivid example is the directory hierarchy with folders and files shown in Figure 2-3b. In this case each folder can have zero or more subfolders, as well as zero or more files. Each file or folder can be contained by exactly one folder.

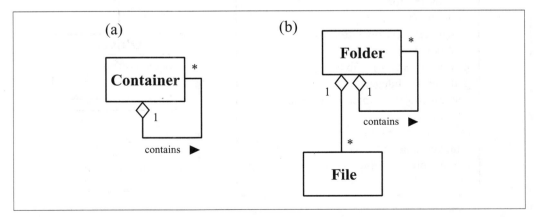

FIGURE 2-3. *(a) A self-containing Container. (b) A directory hierarchy with folders and files.*

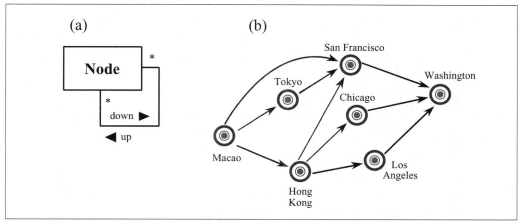

FIGURE 2-4. *(a) A self-association with arbitrary multiplicity on both ends forms a network of Node objects. The up and down notes indicate upstream and downstream directions. (b) A postal network in which each city has multiple connections in the incoming and outgoing directions.*

In a self-association such as Figure 2-3a, we will use the convention that the end of an association on the vertical side of a class box connects to lower level objects (downstream objects). The other end, which is at the bottom of a class box, connects to upper level objects (upstream objects).

If the multiplicity on the downstream side is 0..1, and the upstream side is also 0..1, then the self-association represents a linked list. Such a list is useful for holding objects with different versions (such as source code).

If, on the other hand, the multiplicity items are * on both ends of a self-association (see Figure 2-4a), then the objects form a network. An example is shown in Figure 2-4b, in which each node (city) has multiple connections in both the incoming (upstream) and outgoing (downstream) directions.

For the Node network in Figure 2-4a, we can create a sample detailed design (Figure 2-5).

Note that the operation isUpstreamTo(node : Node) may imply a recursive operation, meaning that the current node is an upstream node along some upstream path of the input argument node.

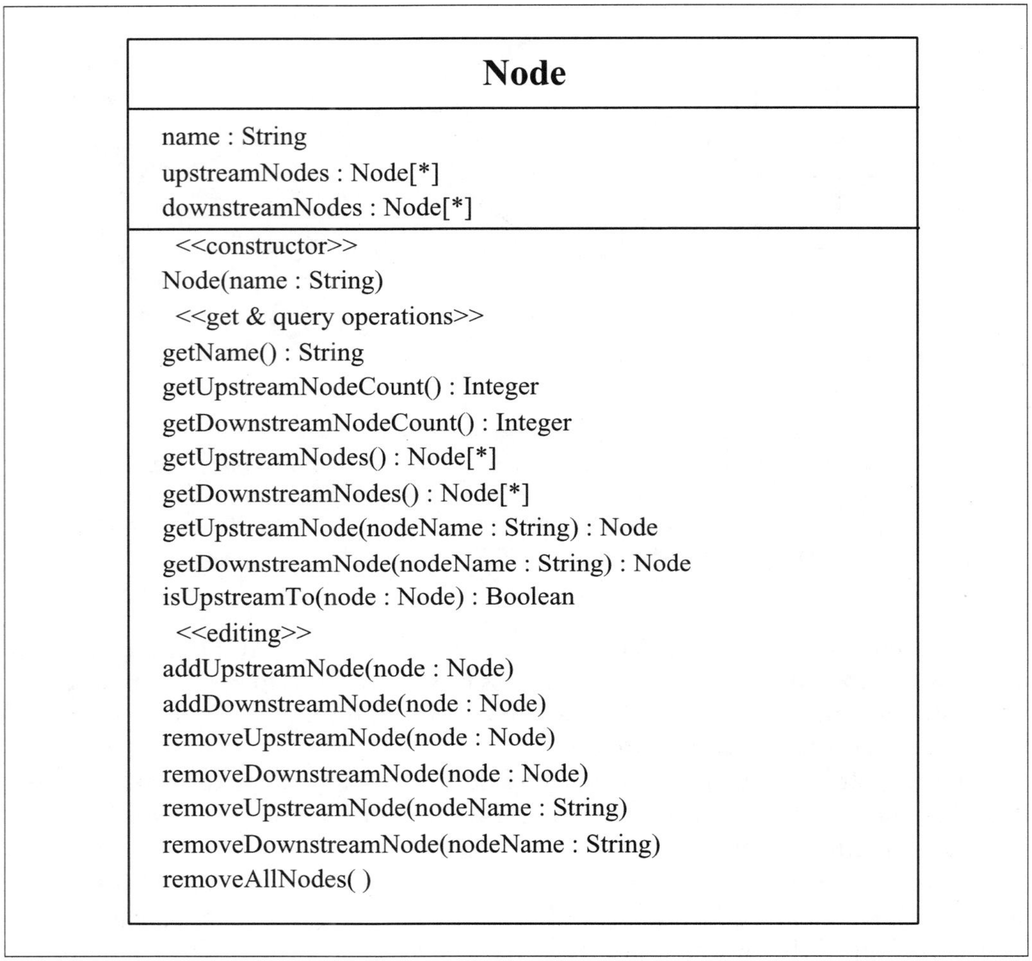

Node
name : String upstreamNodes : Node[*] downstreamNodes : Node[*]
<<constructor>> Node(name : String)   <<get & query operations>> getName() : String getUpstreamNodeCount() : Integer getDownstreamNodeCount() : Integer getUpstreamNodes() : Node[*] getDownstreamNodes() : Node[*] getUpstreamNode(nodeName : String) : Node getDownstreamNode(nodeName : String) : Node isUpstreamTo(node : Node) : Boolean   <<editing>> addUpstreamNode(node : Node) addDownstreamNode(node : Node) removeUpstreamNode(node : Node) removeDownstreamNode(node : Node) removeUpstreamNode(nodeName : String) removeDownstreamNode(nodeName : String) removeAllNodes( )

FIGURE 2-5. *Detailed design for the Node network.*

2.4   RELATIONSHIP LOOPS

Besides self-containment, recursive association may be the result of a complex relationship between two or more object classes. An obvious one is an aggregation loop. For example, A contains multiple Bs, which in turn contain multiple As. Such a loop is a simple extension of self-containment. A more interesting relationship loop forms when two classes are related by both aggregation and inheritance, as shown in Figure 2-6. Note that we use aggregation here as a representative association because it appears most often in such loops, and it is convenient for our discussion. Our analyses will apply to normal associations as well.

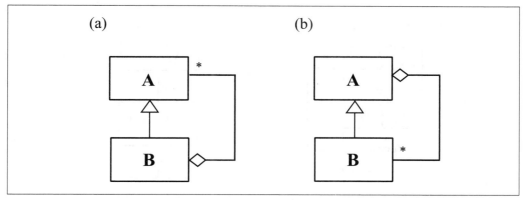

FIGURE 2-6. *Two-tier relationship loops, in which two classes are related by both aggregation and inheritance. (a) The subclass has backward containment of its superclass. (b) The superclass has forward containment of its subclass.*

In Figure 2-6a, B contains A, which is a superclass of B. This two-tier relationship loop is called *backward containment*. To see how this can occur in real life, let us extend our directory hierarchy example.

In Figure 2-3b, we first rename File to FolderItem because a file is an item in a folder. Now a folder is also an item in a folder, except that it can contain FolderItem objects, in addition to all the attributes of a file (for example, name, size, date). Thus in Figure 2-6a, we may identify A with FolderItem and B with Folder. In other words, Folder is a special type of FolderItem. It contains multiple FolderItem objects. The resulting FolderItem-Folder relationship loop is shown in the left part of Figure 2-7.

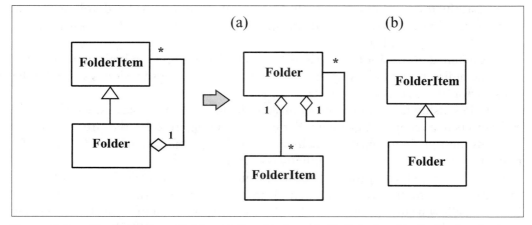

FIGURE 2-7. *The FolderItem-Folder relationship loop (left). Relationship fission breaks the loop into (a) aggregation and (b) inheritance relationships.*

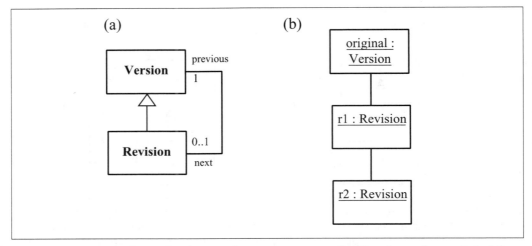

FIGURE 2-8. *(a) A relationship loop without containment. (b) The objects form a linked list.*

As in general aggregates, the operations inherited from FolderItem by Folder may be propagated to the components of Folder—in other words, FolderItem objects. Examples are remove(), setAccessPrivilege(), and so forth.

If the superclass contains its subclass, as in Figure 2-6b, the two-tier relationship loop is called *forward containment*. Such a loop also gives rise to recursive aggregation. In fact, any subclasses of A will inherit the aggregation. Because of this imposed relationship by the superclass, the forward containment loop appears less frequently in real life.

There are cases in which the relationship loop involves no containment. Figure 2-8 shows an example with the Version and Revision classes. The Version-Revision loop basically forms a linked list, with the original version as the head, followed by a chain of revisions. This design treats the original version distinctly from other revisions, which may be advantageous.

A detailed design for the Version-Revision relationship loop is given in Figure 2-9. The bidirectional link between a revision and its previous version is set up by the constructor of the revision object.

Relationship loops can be generalized to include leaf node classes, which are end objects in a recursive aggregate. For example, in Figure 2-10, the Group class contains multiple Item objects, which may be a Group object, or one of the two leaf node (Circle and Square) classes. Inherited operations such as draw(), move(), remove(), and so forth, propagate down the hierarchy recursively. In terms of implementation, this implies recursive functions that traverse down the hierarchy. These functions allow us to treat individual and composite objects uniformly. Figure 2-10 is the same as the composite pattern described in [Gamma et al. 1995].

Version	**Revision**
name : String author : String date : Date next : Revision	previous : Version

<< constructor >>
Version(name : String, author : String,
  date : Date)
 << get & set operations >>
getName() : String
getAuthor() : String
getDate() : Date
getNextRevision() : Revision
setName(name : String)
setAuthor(author : String)
setDate(date : Date)
setNextRevision(revision : Revision)
	<< constructor >>
	Version(name : String, author : String,
	  date : Date, previous : Version)
	 << get & set operations >>
	getPreviousVersion() : Version
	setPreviousVersion(revision : Version)

FIGURE **2-9.** *A detailed design for the Version-Revision relationship loop.*

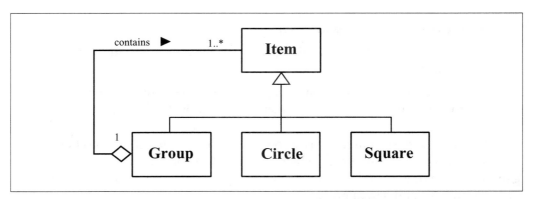

FIGURE **2-10.** *A relationship loop (backward containment) with leaf node classes (Circle and Square). Certain operations (such as* draw *and* move*) may propagate down the hierarchy recursively.*

To analyze and validate a relationship loop, we may use a procedure called *relationship fission.*

2.4.1 RELATIONSHIP FISSION

Relationship fission is the process of decomposing relationship loops into aggregation and inheritance relationships. That is, after fission, the aggregational and taxonomic relationships are represented by two separate diagrams.

In Figure 2-7, the relationship loop on the left can be decomposed as follows:

1. Starting from the Folder aggregate, we draw an aggregation between Folder and FolderItem.

2. Because Folder is a special type of FolderItem, we may substitute Folder with FolderItem. This implies that Folder may contain itself, which gives the self-containing association.

3. Finally, the taxonomic relationship is a simple copy of the inheritance tree.

Steps 1 and 2 yield Figure 2-7a, whereas step 3 yields Figure 2-7b.

Compared with the usual object design diagrams, which present both association and inheritance relationships together, the two separate diagrams offer

- A clear view of the classes in an aggregation tree
- An easy way to verify that the design satisfies the class association requirements
- A clear indication of a self-containing or recursive relationship, which leads to certain behavior (such as recursive functions)

We may use the technique of relationship fission to validate an object design against the original requirements, which can often be expressed in terms of aggregational and taxonomic relationships separately. Thus, the technique is part of an iterative analysis and design process.

Because relationship loops present more concise object patterns than the two separate diagrams (aggregation and inheritance), they are the preferred way to document a design. Moreover, relationship loops lead to cleaner implementation. For example, the Folder class in Figure 2-7 needs only one collection of FolderItems, rather than two collections (one for FolderItem and the other for Folder itself), as suggested by the aggregation diagram on the right of Figure 2-7.

The general procedure for relationship fission is as follows:

1. Starting from the top aggregate classes, draw the aggregation between classes.
2. Substitute superclasses with subclasses one by one. This can be achieved by simply moving the class along the inheritance symbol (the "fat arrowheads"). Draw the corresponding aggregation, which may lead to self-containment.
3. Finally, the taxonomic relationship is a simple copy of the inheritance tree.

The fission of the two-tier loop in Figure 2-6b is left as an exercise at the end of this chapter (Exercise 2-9).

2.4.2   INHERITANCE OF RELATIONSHIP LOOPS

When a class inherits from a relationship loop, the recursive relationship is also inherited. This usually leads to rather complex and sometimes unexpected (or undesired) relationships between the classes. For example, in Figure 2-11, the Secured classes offer additional security features and are subclasses of the Folder and FolderItem classes. In terms of the aggregation relationship, Folder and SecuredFolder are identical. That is, they can contain themselves and each other. FolderItem and SecuredFolderItem are also equivalent: They can be contained by either Folder or SecuredFolder.

Such a rich relationship between the subclasses may or may not be desired. To restrict certain relationships, one may either impose rules in the implementation (for example, regular Folder should not contain SecuredFolderItem). Alternatively, one simply does not inherit from the relationship loop, but builds a new relationship loop with appropriate association to the original one.

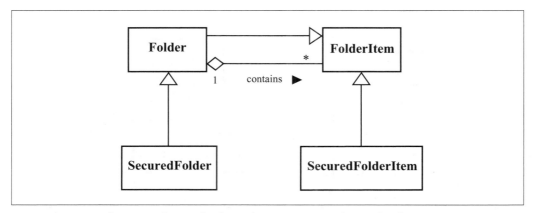

FIGURE 2-11. *Inheritance from a backward-containment relationship loop.*

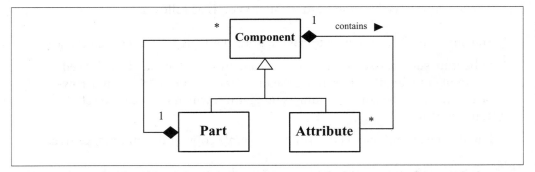

FIGURE 2-12. *A double relationship loop with both forward and backward containment.*

2.4.3 DOUBLE LOOPS*

An interesting combination of the forward and backward containment loops
in Figure 2-6 is the double relationship loop. As shown in Figure 2-12, the Attribute and Part classes are both subclasses of the class Component. Following the
procedure for relationship fission, we find that the Part class contains Part itself,
and the Attribute and Component classes. Attribute can have compound structures, containing other Attribute objects recursively. Part and Component can
contain Attribute, but not vice versa. When these relationships are desired, the
double loop is a compact design that generates very rich recursive structures.

2.4.4 THREE-TIER RELATIONSHIP LOOPS*

We can extend the two-tier relationship loops to three tiers. Figures 2-13
through 2-16 present a few nontrivial three-tier loops that have recursive

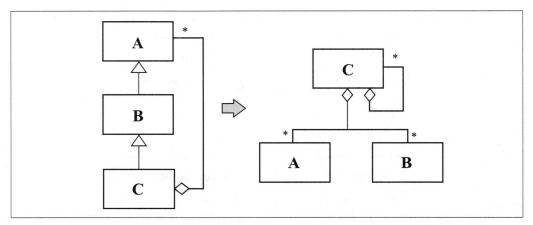

FIGURE 2-13. *A three-tier relationship loop with backward containment from subclass to
superclass. On the right we show the aggregation diagram after fission.*

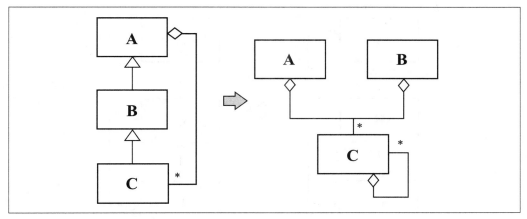

FIGURE 2-14. *A three-tier relationship loop with forward containment from superclass to subclasses. On the right we show the aggregation diagram after fission.*

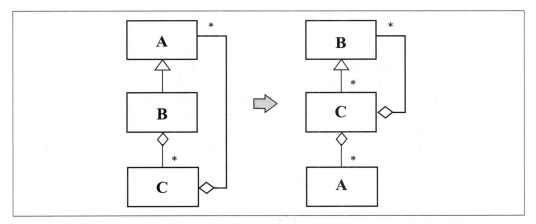

FIGURE 2-15. *A three-tier relationship loop with backward containment from subclass to superclass. Note that the loop has two aggregation associations.*

aggregation. One can carry on such analyses to N-tier relationship loops.

2.5 BINARY ASSOCIATION CLASSES

A link between two objects can possess its own properties. For example, a trade between a supplier and a buyer has properties such as the name of the product being traded, the quantity, and so forth. These properties belong to the trade, rather than to either the supplier or the buyer. Thus, link properties are the joint properties of two objects. (This aspect is similar to multiplicity.)

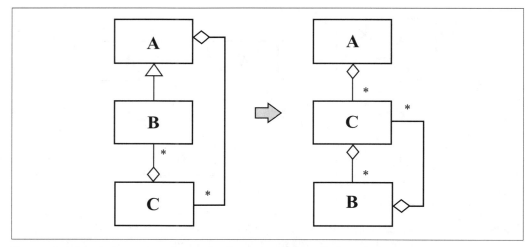

FIGURE 2-16. *A three-tier relationship loop. Note that the loop has two aggregation associations.*

Taking the link property concept one step further, one can introduce *association classes,* which encapsulate link properties and the operations on them. Figure 2-17 gives some examples. Each instance of the association class Trade in Figure 2-17a is connected to an instance of the association between Supplier and Buyer—a trade. Likewise, each job in Figure 2-17b is a link between a company and a person.

In UML, the association and its association class are connected by a dashed line, as shown in Figure 2-17. The one-to-one mapping between an instance of the association class and the corresponding link is implied. This suggests that properties valid for *all* links should be treated differently from other normal attributes of the association class.

For example, if in a company all job descriptions have 40 working hours per week (at least on paper), then we may associate working hours with a class-scope variable for the Job class (such as a static variable in Java or C++).

Binary association classes often appear along with other object patterns. In addition, there may be more than one association between two classes. Each one may have its own association class.

Figure 2-18 shows a partial view of a computer system that contains one or more users and file systems. The Folder and FolderItem classes form a backward relationship loop. Each FolderItem is related to a user by a Permission object (an association class), which encapsulates privileges such as read, write, and so forth. Each FolderItem is also owned by a certain user, which is the second association between the two classes. For each link between a pair of User and FolderItem objects, there is a unique Permission object.

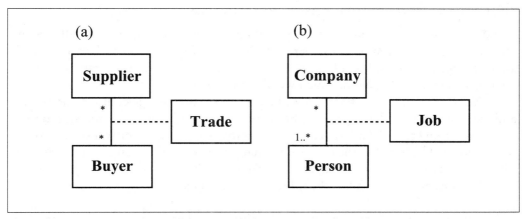

FIGURE 2-17. *Examples of association class shown in UML notation. Each instance of the association classes (Trade and Job) corresponds to one specific link of the associations.*

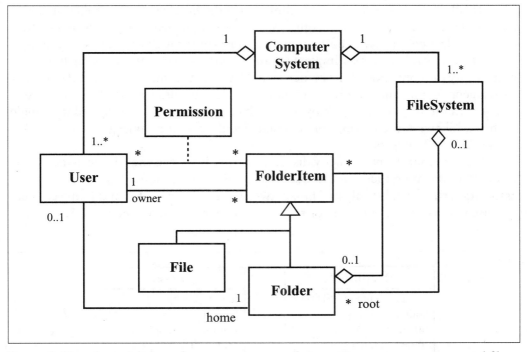

FIGURE 2-18. *A partial view of a computer system that contains one or more users and file systems. There are two associations between User and FolderItem. One of them has an association class (Permission).*

2.5.1 IMPLEMENTING BINARY ASSOCIATION CLASSES

The use of association classes is an important and useful technique, especially when the link properties are subject to operations, or when the links themselves are associated with other objects. For a binary association, its association class can be implemented in a standard fashion, which we illustrate next.

We start from the supplier side of Figure 2-17a. Besides the company name and address, we can have the buyer and the corresponding trade information stored in two arrays (buyers and trades). The indices in the two arrays identify a specific trade with a buyer. This satisfies the one-to-one mapping requirement on the supplier side. The same can be done for the Buyer class (Figure 2-19).

This design, however, has the following two deficiencies:

1. It relies on an index to match a trade with a supplier (or a buyer). Locating the index itself may affect the performance of the code.

2. The Supplier and Buyer objects for a particular trade should be kept with the Trade object because they are intrinsic parts of the trade.

To alleviate these problems, we simply include the Buyer and Supplier objects into Trade, as in Figure 2-20. In doing so, we have implemented a binary association class by a class connected to both Supplier and Buyer through normal associations.

More generally, we may implement any binary association classes, including multiplicity on both ends of the association, in a similar fashion. Figure 2-21 shows such a generic implementation for a binary association class L. Each A object is associated with mB (or a range given by mB) L objects, each of which is linked to a single B object. Likewise, each B object is associated with mA (or a range given by mA) A objects via the L objects.

We note that the multiplicity discussed earlier is for the ends of the association, rather than the multiplicity of the links. As discussed in Section 1.5.4, for a binary association there can be only one link between a specific pair of A and B objects (see the discussion of the candidate key requirement near the end of Section 1.5.4).

Supplier	**Buyer**
company_name : String address : String buyers : Buyer[*] trades : Trade[*]	name : String address : String suppliers : Supplier[*] trades : Trade[*]

FIGURE 2-19. *A design for the Supplier-Buyer association in Figure 2-17a.*

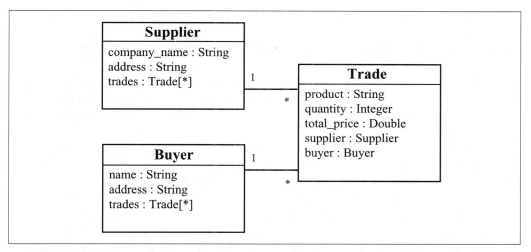

FIGURE 2-20. *A realization of a binary association class Trade. (The operations are omitted.)*

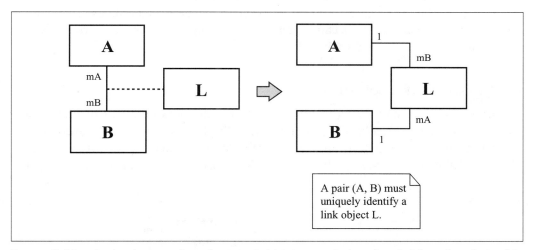

FIGURE 2-21 *An implementation of a generic binary association class L. Note that the multiplicity for class B (mB) becomes the multiplicity for class L on the A-L association. Likewise for mA. Also, the requirement in the note must be imposed on the right-hand side to make it equivalent to the left.*

The diagram on the right side of Figure 2-21, however, may actually relax this requirement. When both mA and mB are more than one in that diagram, a specific pair of A and B objects may be associated with more than one L objects. Thus, the candidate key requirement must be externally imposed on that implementation. This requirement ensures that a specific pair of A and B objects uniquely identifies an L object (as indicated on the right side of Figure 2-21). With this requirement, the class L on the right is truly a binary association class, as is the one on the left. (The candidate key requirement is not needed if either mA or mB equals one because then the candidate key for L contains only one object identification [ID].)

To enforce the candidate key requirement, you may, for example, add sanity checks to the program to ensure that a pair (A, B) is uniquely associated with one link object L. This is a good example of using dynamic object behavior to guarantee certain static relationships.

If, however, there can indeed be more than one link object for each pair of A and B objects, then an extra identifier (such as the object ID for L) is needed to pinpoint a specific link. This suggests that the relationship goes beyond binary and possibly leads to a ternary association.

To illustrate this point, we note that for each pair of Supplier and Buyer in Figure 2-20, there can indeed be more than one Trade object. To specify a Trade uniquely, we need an extra identifier. For example, we may use a Time class (which includes date). Now the trade association becomes ternary, with Trade being the ternary association class for Supplier, Buyer, and Time.

This approach of implementing the association class L as a linkage class between the associated classes can be generalized to higher order associations. We come back to this topic in Section 3.4.3.

2.5.2 RECURSIVE ASSOCIATION CLASS

Association classes may also be applied to links in self-containment or recursive association. In Figure 2-22, a Part object contains multiple Part objects recursively (such as parts of an automobile), forming a hierarchy of parts. Each link down the hierarchy is described by a Property object, which is an instance of a binary association

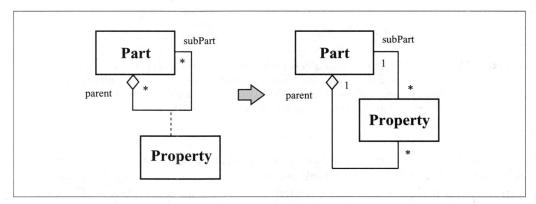

FIGURE 2-22. *A binary association class Property for the self-containing Part class.*

class. An example attribute in Property is count, which is the number of a specific parts contained in the parent part. Note that a part can be used in multiple parent parts. However, generally only one link is allowed between a specific pair of part and parent part. This candidate key requirement may again be enforced in the operation of the Part class.

For a higher order association, the meaning of an association class is similar. However, the constraints by multiplicity items on different arms of the association can become intriguing. We defer this discussion to Section 3.4.3.

2.6 THE HANDLE-BODY PATTERN

Sibling subclasses from a superclass are by definition mutually exclusive. That is, a subclass object can belong to *only one* subclass. This rigidity is sometimes inconvenient because an object may play different roles or attain different properties at different times. It may even have multiple properties at the same time. One way to loosen this rigid relationship is to use a role or property as the superclass and treat it as a servant class to the original superclass. The result is known as the *handle-body pattern* [Coplien 1992] or the *bridge pattern* [Gamma et al. 1995].

For example, in Figure 2-23 the standard inheritance leads to rigid subclasses. A subclass object can either be a User or a Buyer. However, in the real world, a user can also be a buyer, who has trade relationships with suppliers. To overcome this restriction we introduce a servant class Role. The Person class is now composed of multiple Role objects, as shown in the handle-body pattern of Figure 2-24. Consequently a person can simultaneously be a buyer and a user.

The essence of the handle-body pattern is the aggregation of multiple Property or Role objects. If we consider that the aggregate is in effect defined by its collection

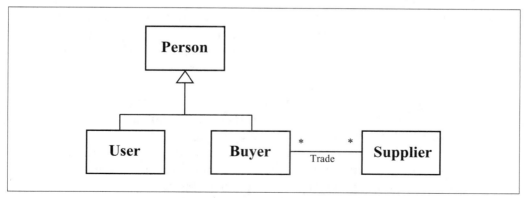

FIGURE 2-23. *Inheritance leads to rigid subclasses. A subclass object can only be either a User or a Buyer in this example.*

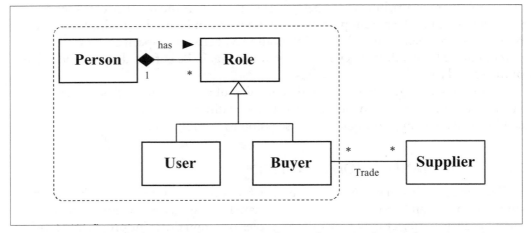

FIGURE 2-24. *A Role class is used as a servant class to the original superclass, giving rise to the handle-body pattern (inside the dashed frame). Now a person can be a Buyer and a User simultaneously.*

of Property or Role objects, then we can categorize different types of aggregate objects (for example, the Person objects in Figures 2-23 and 2-24) by their property or role collections. This leads to dynamic schema.

2.7   DYNAMIC SCHEMA

By *dynamic schema,* we mean an object design that can classify object instances on the fly, without modifying the design or recompiling the source code. Because objects have attributes, a simple approach is to classify objects by their attributes. In this way the attributes become metadata, which are data that describe other data or objects.

For example, a part is defined by its size, weight, part number, and so forth, which are the metadata of the part. An attribute may be an integer, a floating point number, or a string. These different types of attributes can be modeled as subclasses of an Attribute class, as shown in Figure 2-25. Thus, in this case we use a set of Attribute objects as metadata to describe another object (which belongs to the Part class).

Furthermore, we can group parts into categories. Parts within the same category share a common set of attributes (so that they can be compared or exchanged with one another). Each attribute is described by a property of the category. A Property object includes the name, type, and so forth, of the corresponding attribute. For implementation, the constructor of an Attribute includes a Property object as an argument, thereby setting up the link to the Property object.

The definition of a category through its properties constitutes a schema. The schema generated in Figure 2-25 is flexible. We can add, modify, and remove the

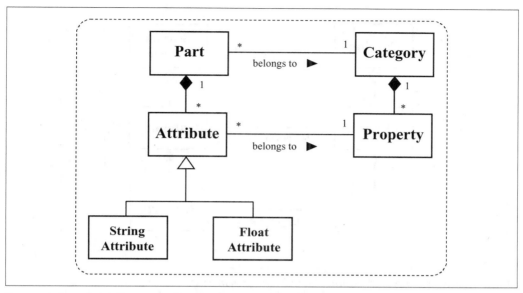

FIGURE 2-25.   *The dynamic schema pattern. The Category-Property aggregation serves as a blueprint for the Part-Attribute aggregation.*

properties in a category dynamically. The dynamic schema dictates the form of the Part-Attribute aggregation and therefore serves as a blueprint for a category of parts.

We note that the concept of dynamic schema is closely related to homomorphism, which is a mapping between associations [Rumbaugh 1991, p77]. In Figure 2-25, the Category-Property aggregation maps to the Part-Attribute aggregation. The mapping constitutes a homomorphism that ties the Category-Property schema to its instances (Part-Attribute pairs).

Based on the dynamic schema pattern of Figure 2-25, we can build larger systems that contain collections of parts and categories. We can even organize the parts and categories into a hierarchy or network format. An example of such a system is the Product Data Management System, which typically contains master parts (categories) and a catalog of parts (Figure 2-26). A part may have other parts as components, thereby forming a hierarchy. Similarly, the master parts may form a compositional hierarchy, as well as an inheritance tree. The latter actually defines a taxonomy for a group of categories.

2.8   SHARED OBJECT POOLS

A shared object pool has a collection manager that manages a limited number of objects. These objects are used simultaneously in multiple contexts. Such sharing

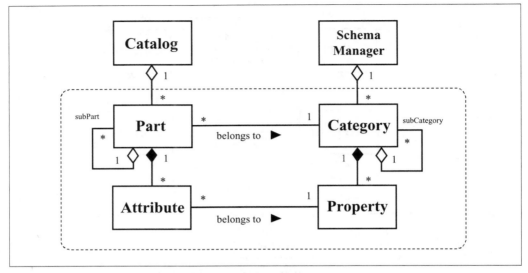

FIGURE 2-26. *A simplified Product Data Management System based on the dynamic schema pattern (within the dashed box). The subclasses under Attribute are omitted. Also, both the Part and Category classes contain their own compositional hierarchy.*

allows effective reuse of object information (namely, the attributes of the shared objects) in a large number of contexts. For example, a catalog contains a number of parts, which can be used to build different tools. Each part has its intrinsic attributes such as dimensions, weight, and so forth. When it is used in a tool, certain context information (for example, the type of mount and the number of identical parts) is needed. The parts are treated as shared objects and a Context class is used as an association class.

The object design for such a shared object pool is shown in Figure 2-27. To use a part, a Tool object invokes the getPart operation of the Catalog class, which either retrieves or creates the requested part. A link from Tool to Part is then set up, along with an associated context.

The key in the shared object pool pattern is that the multiplicity at the user object's end (such as the Tool object in Figure 2-27) can be more than one, and that each usage context is captured by a binary association class.

Some sample applications of the shared object pool pattern are

- **Text editors**—the basic set of characters are shared

- **Graphic editors**—certain labels or icons are used in multiple places

- **Product design**—parts are shared by multiple designs (as in Tool of Figure 2-27)

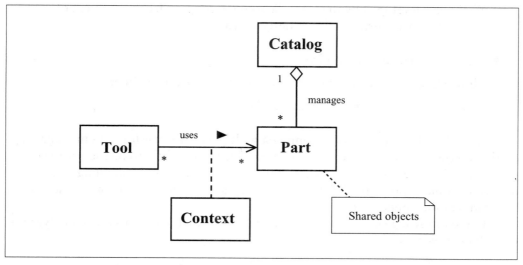

FIGURE 2-27.   *An object design using the shared object pool pattern. The multiplicity at the Tool end signifies sharing. Context contains extrinsic information for a part used in a specific tool.*

We note that this pattern is in essence the same as the "flyweight" pattern of [Gamma et al. 1995]. The shared objects are the flyweights and the collection manager (such as the Catalog class in Figure 2-27) is the flyweight factory, which creates the flyweights.

2.9   OBJECT MODEL FOR EXTENSIBLE MARKUP LANGUAGE

In Section 2.7 we discussed the dynamic schema pattern, which may be used to define the structure of a hierarchy of objects. For text documents or text-based data, on the other hand, the structures may be specified by annotations and markups. Because in both cases the underlying structures are hierarchical, we expect that they can be expressed in similar object models. This section gives an object-oriented perspective of such markups.

A markup language is a mechanism to identify structures in a text document or a text-based data stream. The Extensible Markup Language (XML) specifies a standard way to define annotations and markups for text documents or text-based data that may originate from a database or an object model [XML 1998]. XML is a restricted or simplified form of the Standard Generalized Markup Language [ISO 1986], which is a more general and rather complicated system for defining structured document types and markup languages. (The widely used Hyper Text Markup Language [HTML] is a realization or application of the Standard Generalized Markup Language.)

XML was developed by the XML Working Group under the auspices of the World Wide Web Consortium. It was designed to

- Make text markup easy and yet flexible
- Allow straightforward usage of XML documents over the Internet
- Make XML documents "human legible"

XML has the potential of becoming a widely used format for data interchange on the Internet. Because object-oriented applications are likely to be used at the end points for such interchanges, it is important to have a solid understanding of the underlying object model for XML. This allows us to use XML judiciously and optimally in real-life applications.

In the following subsections we describe some XML basics and then analyze the underlying object model.

2.9.1 XML BASICS

We begin with the text document in Figure 2-28 annotated with XML.

This "book" document contains most of the following XML specifics (they define a so-called well-formed XML document):

```
<?xml version="1.0" standalone="yes"?>
<book name="OO Design" category="software" >
  <chapter number="1"          name="Basic Concepts">          Attribute
    This chapter discusses the basic concepts of OO design.
    <section number="1.1" name="The Nature of Objects">
      This section defines what objects are.
    </section>
    <section number="1.2" name="Unified Modeling Language">
      This section introduces UML.                    Element
    </section>
  </chapter>          Start Tag
  <chapter number="2" name="Common Patterns in Static Designs">
    This chapter describes the common patterns in static designs.
  </chapter>          End Tag
</book>
```

FIGURE 2-28. *A simple text document annotated with XML. The XML elements, tags, and attributes are also indicated.*

1. The document starts with an XML declaration: `<?xml...?>`. This line also indicates the version of XML being used and whether the document is a stand-alone one. (We only consider stand-alone documents here.)

2. The document contains three types of "tags"—book, chapter, and section—each of which corresponds to an XML "element." The start tags (such as `<section>`) and end tags (such as `</section>`) mark the beginnings and ends of the elements. The tag names are defined by the user. All tags must be balanced—that is, all elements must have both start and end tags. (However, a special end tag may be used for empty elements.)

3. An element may contain zero or more elements or text areas. The order of these elements is significant (so that Chapter 1 appears first inside a book), and the containment should be properly nested (so that Chapters 1 and 2 do not overlap).

4. The start tag of an element may also have attributes (such as `name = "..."`). The order of the attributes is not important. All attribute values must be in quotes. The single-quote character (the apostrophe, `'`) may be used if the value contains a double-quote character, and vice versa. If both single and double quotes appear in a value, they should be replaced by `&apos;` and `&quot;`, as shown:

Quotation characters	'	"
XML special symbols	`&apos;`	`&quot;`

There is also a special end-tag rule. If an element contains nothing, then a special end tag (`/>`) may be used immediately after the last attribute of the element; for example, `<author last_name="Lau" first_name="Y-T"/>`. This kind of empty element is often used to pass data fields.

5. Finally, if there are any isolated markup characters appearing in the attribute values or text data, they must be replaced by the following XML special symbols:

Isolated markup characters	<	>	&
XML special symbols	`&lt;`	`&gt;`	`&amp;`

These rules define a "well-formed" XML document. However, documents may require that the tags be nested in a certain structure. For example, a chapter can contain sections, but not vice versa. This structural relationship can be defined by a *document type declaration*, which is optional in XML.

An XML processor or parser can read in the document type declaration and validate an XML document against the declaration. If the validation passes, the document is said to be a "valid" XML document. In this way XML provides a mechanism to impose constraints on the layout and logical structure of a document. Note that XML tags usually contain no information about the presentation format of a document.

In analyzing the object model of XML, we are primarily concerned with "well-formed" XML documents, as defined earlier.

2.9.2   XML OBJECT MODELS

Based on the "well-formed" rules of XML, an object model for XML documents can be readily constructed, as shown in Figure 2-29.

The model contains a backward containment loop. In other words, Element may contain its superclass Content, thereby allowing recursive aggregation. (Backward containment loops were discussed in Section 2.4. Also see Figure 2-10 for a similar example.) Thus, an Element may contain zero or more Attrs, Texts, and Elements. The collection of elements being contained is ordered. Each Element has a tag name, whereas each Attr has a name and a value. Note also that Content is an abstract class (as indicated by its italicized class name). This simply means that there is no instance of Content in an XML document.

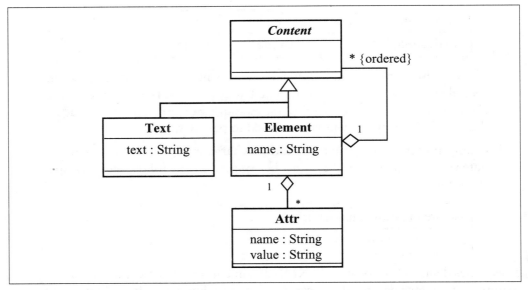

FIGURE 2-29.   *The object model of a well-formed XML document. Note that Content is an abstract class (as indicated by its italicized class name). The class Attr stands for an XML attribute. (We use the abbreviated name to distinguish it from class attributes.) The class Text contains a text block or area.*

As is obvious from Figure 2-29, the XML object model can describe nested text structures, tables, and so forth. Besides documents, it can also model hierarchical data structures. Thus, XML is often used as a format for structured data interchange.

A specific XML document can be viewed as an application of the presented object model. To convert an object model into an XML object model, one may employ the following procedure:

1. Decompose relationship loops into aggregation and inheritance relationships (see the discussion of the relationship fission technique in Section 2.4.1). Focus only on the aggregation parts.

2. Tag the classes with UML sterotypes <<Element>> and <<Attr>> as follows. For classes that may contain other objects or itself, use <<Element>>. For classes containing only (name, value) pairs, or attributes of <<Element>> classes, use <<Attr>>. (We generally prefer not to use <<Text>> for structured data because it requires an end tag for each attribute, which increases the tagging overhead.)

As an example, let's construct an XML object model for the Catalog hierarchy in Figure 2-26 (omitting the Schema Manager side). The Catalog class contains a hierarchy of Part objects, which in turn has multiple Attributes. Because both the Catalog and Part classes contain something, we tag them with the UML sterotype <<Element>>. Furthermore, we assume that each attribute is specified by a name and a string value. Thus, we simply treat the Attribute class as an <<Attr>> type. The object model is shown in Figure 2-30.

Based on this XML object model, it is straightforward to construct the corresponding XML document. Table 2-1 gives the explicit mapping rules.

Using these rules, we arrive at the following sample XML document, which corresponds to the object model in Figure 2-30:

```
<?xml version="1.0" standalone="yes"?>
<Catalog name="electronics">
 <Part name="resistorList">
  <Part name="resistor" partNumber="123" resistance="5.6
Ohm" power="0.1 W"/>
  <Part name="resistor" partNumber="323" resistance="1.2
Ohm" power="0.2 W"/>
 </Part>
 <Part name="capacitorList">
  <Part name="capacitor" partNumber="13" capacitance="1.6
```

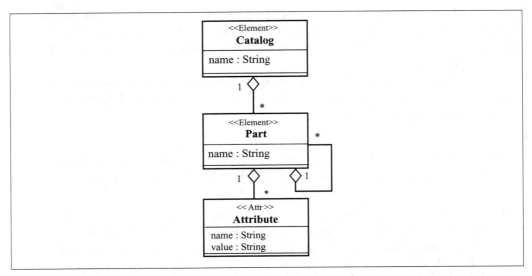

FIGURE 2-30.   *The XML object model for the Catalog hierarchy in Figure 2-26 (omitting the Schema Manager side). Note the UML stereotype notation in << ... >> (see Section 2.1).*

```
mF" voltage="20 V"/>
  <Part name="capacitor" partNumber="14" capacitance="0.1
F" voltage="5 V"/>
  <Part name="capacitor" partNumber="15" capacitance="200
mF" voltage="10 V"/>
 </Part>
</Catalog>
```

TABLE 2-1.   *Mapping from the class names and attributes of XML objects to XML elements and attributes.*

OBJECT STEREOTYPE	CLASS NAME	ATTRIBUTE
<<Element>>	Maps to an element name.	Each attribute maps to an XML attribute within this element.
<<Attr>>	Ignore.	The (name, value) pair becomes an attribute of the parent element.

2.9.3   THE STRENGTHS AND WEAKNESSES OF XML

When applying XML to markup text-based data that originate from databases or object models, certain issues should be kept in mind. First, although XML can handle many cases of structured data, it is by no means a full object-oriented language. In particular, XML

- Does not provide genuine links between objects. One can set up links by value (similar to the "hyperlinks" in HTML). However, they need to be interpreted by the object-oriented applications that use the links.

- Cannot handle multiple parent cases (multiplicity more than one on the aggregate side)

- Does not provide object-oriented features like inheritance and methods

Second, as a text-based tagging scheme, XML increases the overhead of data interchange because of nested tags and other separators.

Knowing these limits is important in selecting a data interchange format between object-oriented applications. However, XML does provide the following advantages:

- Human legibility and compatibility with text-based protocols such as the World Wide Web protocol (HTTP)

- Fast development and change cycle because it is extensible

- Widely available parsers, which translate XML documents into native object hierarchies

2.10 CASE STUDY: ATM SYSTEM SOFTWARE—PART 1

Now that we have learned the common patterns of static design, let's apply our knowledge to some real-life examples. Here we first give an overview of an automatic teller machine (ATM) system software project. Then we perform an object-oriented analysis and design. We start from a core pattern and then build up the model. Our focus here is on static design. Dynamic modeling for this case study is covered in Section 5.8.

2.10.1 Project Description

The purpose of this project is to build the ATM system software. The overall ATM system consists of multiple ATMs, a central server, the ATM system software, and related interface software. The following is an overview of the project and its concept of operation.

The ATM system software handles transactions among a network of ATMs and bank computers. Each bank has its own computer to maintain its own accounts and to process transactions. All ATMs communicate with a central server computer, which serves as a clearinghouse for all transactions at individual bank computers.

Transaction processing at bank computers is handled by individual banks and is out of the project scope. Software that runs inside each ATM is not part of this project either. However, the interfaces with the bank computers and the ATMs are included.

Bank customers with cash cards may access the ATM system via an ATM. When a cash card is inserted into an ATM, the ATM system will read the information on the card, prompt for the personal identification number, validate the identity of the customer, interact with the customer through the ATM, and communicate with the central server to process transactions. The ATM may also dispense cash and print records on request.

The requirements for the ATM system software include the following (see Section 2.10.2 for the meaning of the keywords *static* and *dynamic*):

1. It must keep adequate records of all ATM usage and transactions. It should have the capability to generate daily reports from these records. [*static*]

2. It must include security measures. [*dynamic*]

3. It must be able to handle concurrent access to the same account. [*dynamic*]

4. It should be open to allow future inclusion of cashier stations, Internet clients, and so forth. [*static*]

The constraints include the following:

1. The ATM system is owned by a consortium of banks.

2. The ATM system software runs on the central server.

3. Cash cards are issued and relation information is maintained by individual banks. All cards from the same bank share the same six-digit prefix numbers.

4. All ATMs have the same programming interface.

5. Each bank computer has its own programming interface, which may be different from the interfaces of other banks.

2.10.2 STATIC ANALYSIS AND DESIGN

There are two aspects of an object-oriented analysis and design: static and dynamic. The static part identifies the object classes and their static relationship. The dynamic part focuses on the interaction among objects and external interfaces. In the four requirements listed earlier, we have marked the first and last ones *static* because they directly impact the static design. The second and third requirements are more related to dynamic design. (Note that security is usually also related to static design. However, because the password information is stored in an individual bank's computer, we need only handle the dynamic interaction of such information.)

For the static part, the approach we take is first to find a core design pattern and then expand it by adding other objects. From the project description presented earlier, we find that potential objects within the ATM system software are transaction, cash card, bank, ATM, and so forth. To identify the core objects further, we can start with the requirements, especially those that involve data storage.

The first requirement—adequate records of all ATM usage and transactions—is the most important. Such records, or persistent data, are typically the core objects in a system. To simplify things, we may treat all ATM transactions within a card usage session as a single transaction log, which is a core object we should capture.

How is a transaction identified? It is an action taken by a customer (a cash card holder) at an ATM. In other words, it is associated with a link between a card and an ATM. This leads us to the binary association class (Section 2.5), which we adopt as our core design pattern in Figure 2-31.

Next, because the ATM system software needs to send card and transaction requests to the card holder's bank, it must know about the bank from its own database information. Because each bank issues its own cards, it is straightforward to use a bank information object BankInfo to manage a collection of cash cards (see the collection manager pattern of Section 2.1). Likewise, we add a top-level class ATM Manager to manage the collections of BankInfo and transactions. This gives us the partial design in Figure 2-32.

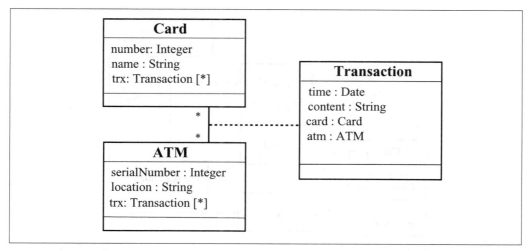

FIGURE 2-31. *The core design pattern (binary association class) for the ATM system software. The attributes are arranged similarly to those in Figure 2-20.*

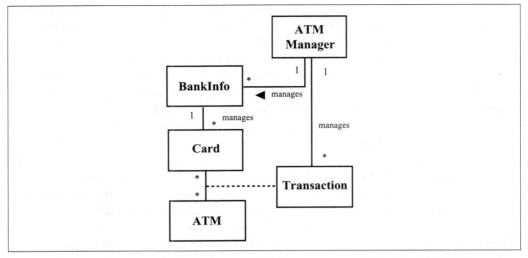

FIGURE 2-32. *A partial design built on top of the previous core design for the ATM system software.*

Finally, we may refine the design to accommodate other requirements, especially future needs to include cashier stations and Internet clients. This is easily achieved by replacing the class ATM with an abstract class Agent, which has three subclasses. Figure 2-33 shows the full ATM system software design. Note that we have also let ATM Manager manage the Agent class.

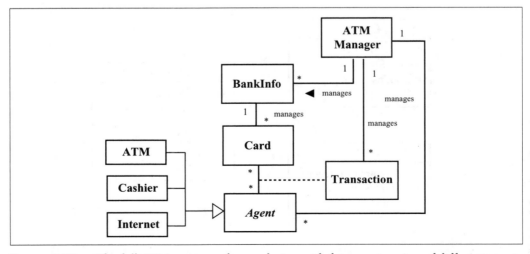

FIGURE 2-33. *The full ATM system software design with future expansion of different agents taken into account.*

In summary, we have built the static model with the association class and collection manager patterns. We will continue with part 2 (persistent object) of this case study in Section 3.6.

2.11   CASE STUDY: SHARED WHITEBOARD—PART 1

In this case study, our eventual goal is to develop a shared whiteboard that allows network users to conduct an interactive discussion using graphic markups and text annotations. Phase I of this project involves developing a stand-alone whiteboard. Then, during phase II, we will consider linking the separate whiteboards to form the shared whiteboard.

Here we list the requirements for the entire shared whiteboard (phases I and II) in a relatively formal format:

1. Introduction

    1.1. A whiteboard is a graphical tool that allows a user to overlay graphic markups and text annotations on a background image. It is not an image editor because the image is never changed. However, a user can use the whiteboard to edit and save the markups and annotations to a file, which is associated with the image.

    1.2. The shared whiteboard is an enhanced whiteboard capable of connecting multiple users over a network and allowing them to markup and annotate an image collaboratively in an orderly fashion. Thus, the shared whiteboard can be used as an ancillary tool to video conferencing tools or chat rooms.

2. Functional requirements

    2.1. The shared whiteboard shall display a noneditable background image, which is read in from a GIF or JPEG image file. (phase I)

    2.2. The shared whiteboard shall be able to support text annotation and the following graphic markups: straight line, circle, ellipse, and rectangle. (phase I)

    2.3. The shared whiteboard shall be able to create, select, move, and remove the previously stated annotations and markups, as well as be able to change their style (color, thickness of lines, font and size of text, and so on). (phase I)

    2.4. The shared whiteboard shall be able to save the annotations and markups to a file in CGM (computer graphics metafile) format, read them back, and display them. (phase I)

Note: CGM is an international standard for graphic display. The standard covers many geometric shapes and graphic elements. They are represented by a stream of byte data. In the byte stream, each graphic element is first declared (such as a line), followed by its coordinates or other information (such as the x- and y-coordinates of the two end points of a line). The resulting CGM file is a very compact representation of the graphic in a binary format. We do not need to know the details of CGM here except that it can be represented by an array of bytes.

2.5. Multiple shared whiteboards shall be able to form a collaboration group and view the same background image. Users may perform markup and annotation one at a time, with the updated display broadcast to all users in the group. (phase II)

2.6. Another user with a shared whiteboard may join an existing group by connecting to anyone in the group. Any user in a group may also disconnect without affecting the ongoing collaboration. (phase II)

2.7. For phase II, the types of markup may optionally be expanded to include polyline (for free-hand drawing), polygon, circular and elliptical arcs, and so forth. (phase II)

3. User interface

3.1. The user interfaces should follow the Windows standards. In particular, the following interface design paradigms should be followed:

- Ability to create, edit, and remove graphic markups through mouse manipulation
- Pull-down menus for all operations
- Buttons for frequently used operations

4. System attributes

4.1. The software should be platform neutral, allowing users to use it under various operating systems.

4.2. Security is not a concern because all shared whiteboards will be housed inside a secured local network. *(This assumption simplifies a lot of things.)*

In this part of the case study, we concentrate on the static object design of a stand-alone whiteboard.

The user interface is pretty standard. Under a main frame, there is a menu bar, which contains several menus. Next is the button panel, which has a set of buttons and other selection boxes. The main working area is below the button panel and we call it the DrawCanvas. It has a background image and allows graphic markups and text annotations.

A mockup of the user interface is shown in Figure 2-34. (We will need to add more menus for making connections and sending drawings to others during phase II.)

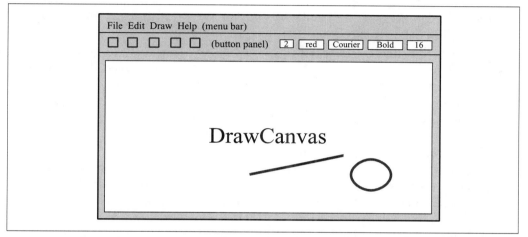

FIGURE 2-34. *A mockup for the user interface of the shared whiteboard (phase I), showing the menu bar, button bar, and DrawCanvas. Two graphic markups are also shown.*

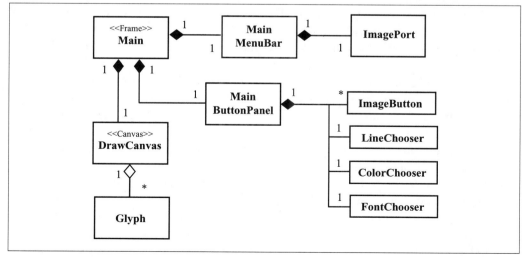

FIGURE 2-35. *The object model for the shared whiteboard (phase I).*

Based on the mockup, it is straightforward to construct the object model, which is presented in Figure 2-35. We have specified the following graphic components in the main button panel: several ImageButtons, a LineChooser, a ColorChooser, and a FontChooser. The buttons are shortcuts to frequent operations (such as cut, copy, and paste). The Choosers are selection boxes.

These graphic components form simple compositions. Their real power comes from their dynamic behavior. For example, when a user chooses a particular color with the ColorChooser, an event will be sent to the DrawCanvas class (described later) to set the color.

The ImagePort class is a servant class. It helps package the image and other graphic contents for sending to remote locations (needed during phase II) or for converting to other image file formats (not an official requirement). Because these operations can be invoked through the main menu bar, we put the ImagePort class under it for convenience. We will examine the details of the ImagePort class in part 5 of this case study (Section 7.10).

The DrawCanvas class represents the main drawing area. Because it supports most of the functional requirements, we expect it to include the most interesting operations for the whiteboard. DrawCanvas contains a set of *Glyphs*, by which we mean small graphic or textual elements, such as lines, ellipses, or text labels.

A detailed design for the DrawCanvas class appears in Figure 2-36. Note that some implied attributes (such as the mouse position) are not shown in the figure. Besides the background image and the glyphs, the attribute theGlyph is the selected glyph. The current selected type for glyph drawing is currentGlyphType. The constructor takes a background image as the argument. The display and editing operations are straightforward. They support the required editing functions. Mouse events (mouse down, up, drag, and so on) are processed by the two process operations, which handle the drawing, selection, moving, and so forth, of the glyphs.

The DrawCanvas class also defines a number of external connection calls. They include getting/sending glyphs and images from/to the image port or a file. We will examine the details of these calls in the dynamic modeling chapter (Section 5.9).

Continuing on to the Glyph class, we show a detailed design in Figure 2-37. The type attribute defines the glyph type (line, circle, ellipse, rectangle). The X, Y coordinates specify the end points or the bounding box for the glyph. For other future types, such as a polygon, attributes X and Y are arrays that represent the vertices of the polygon. Other attributes include line width, color, text, and so forth. The last attribute, key, is used for grouping and relating different glyphs. It is included as a placeholder for future use.

The constructor simply includes all basic attributes in its input arguments. Other operations are described in Table 2-2.

DrawCanvas
image : Image glyphs : Container theGlyph : Glyph currentGlyphType : Integer
<<constructor>> DrawCanvas(image : Image) <<display & editing>> paint(gr : Graphics) / refresh( ) / clear( ) copy( ) / cut( ) / paste( ) / erase( ) shift(dx : Short, dy : Short) processMouseEvent(e : MouseEvent) processMouseMotionEvent(e : MouseEvent) << external linkage >> getGlyphsFrom(imgPort : ImagePort) sendGlyphsTo(imgPort : ImagePort) getGlyphsFrom(file : String) sendGlyphsTo(file : String) getImageFrom(imgPort : ImagePort) sendImageTo(imgPort : ImagePort)

FIGURE 2-36. *Detailed design for the DrawCanvas class. Some* set *and* get *operations are omitted here. Graphics is a handle class of the graphic drawer for DrawCanvas.*

TABLE 2-2. *Operations in the Glyph class.*

OPERATION	PURPOSE	NOTES
clone	Creates a clone glyph of this glyph.	Same for all types of glyphs
draw	Draws the glyph on the canvas.	Different for different types
drawBound	Draws a bounding box around the glyph.	Same for all types of glyphs
intersect	Checks whether the input (x, y) intersects the glyph.	Different for different types
shift	Shifts the glyph's position by (dx, dy).	Same for all types
toCGM	Converts the glyph to CGM byte data using the CGM tool.	Different for different types

Glyph
type : Integer X, Y : Short [*] lineWidth : Integer color : Integer text : String key : Integer
<<constructor>> Glyph(type : Integer, X : Short, Y : Short, ...) clone( ) : Object <<display & editing>> draw(gr : Graphics) drawBound(gr : Graphics) intersect(x : Short, y : Short) : Boolean shift(dx : Short, dy : Short) << external linkage >> toCGM(cgmTool : CGMTool)

FIGURE 2-37. *Detailed design for the Glyph class. Some attributes,* set *operations, and* get *operations are omitted. A Short represents a 2-byte integer. Graphics is a handle class of the graphic drawer for DrawCanvas.*

As an example, the glyphs in DrawCanvas are created by the `process-MouseEvent()` operation, with the pseudocode that reads

```
void processMouseEvent(MouseEvent e) {
  for the case e being a mouse-pressed event,
      set X[0], Y[0] to the current position of the mouse;
  for the case e being a mouse-released event,
      first set X[1], Y[1] to the current position of the
      mouse; then,
      theGlyph = new Glyph(currentGlyphType, X, Y, . . .);
    add theGlyph to the "glyphs" collection;
    repaint the graphics;
}
```

Once created, the glyphs are displayed by the `paint()` operation in DrawCanvas. The following pseudocode shows the main content of this operation:

```
void paint(Graphics gr) {
  for each glyph in the "glyphs" collection,
```

```
        call draw(gr);
    if theGlyph contains a glyph, then
        theGlyph.drawBound(gr);
}
```

Note that the actual code for this operation is more involved because we need to handle other cases such as a new glyph being drawn, a selected glyph being moved, and so forth. Refer to the sample source code for details. (See Online Resources in the Preface.)

At this point a discussion about the design of the Glyph class is appropriate. There are, in general, two ways to model different types of glyph:

1. Flatten all glyph types into a single Glyph class and use a type attribute to delineate them. This may be termed a *parameterized class,* which is the strategy we have tacitly taken in Figure 2-37.

2. Classify different types into a hierarchy of subclasses under an abstract Glyph class. The Glyph class will define the operations common to all glyph types (such as `clone`, `drawBound`, and `shift` in Table 2-2).

Because the glyph type selection is determined by the attribute currentGlyphType in DrawCanvas, that attribute may be used directly in the constructor of the Glyph object in Figure 2-37. For the second approach, however, an additional object factory is needed. The factory takes the glyph type as part of the input and creates the appropriate subclass of Glyph. From this perspective, the first approach (*parameterized class*) is more straightforward when creating Glyph objects, although the second approach is more object oriented.

In terms of the amount of code, the first approach actually involves less coding. This is because you do not need to repeat the class skeleton code (such as constructors) for every subclass. In addition, in operations such as `toCGM()`, the handling of different glyph types appears in the same code block, making it easier to compare and track them. Thus, in practice, the choice between the two approaches becomes a matter of preference.

Finally, the conversion of glyphs into CGM is facilitated by a set of utilities shown in Figure 2-38. CGMTool contains a set of operations for generating CGM byte data. It knows nothing about glyphs and is used as a servant class by the class CGM.

The class CGM contains a set of glyphs and a byte array (buffer) for the corresponding CGM data. It handles the conversion of glyphs to CGM (using CGMTool) and CGM data into glyphs. A detailed design of the CGM class is presented in Figure 2-39.

The functionality of the CGM class is most conveniently illustrated by some pseudocode samples. To convert a set of glyphs into CGM, we do the following:

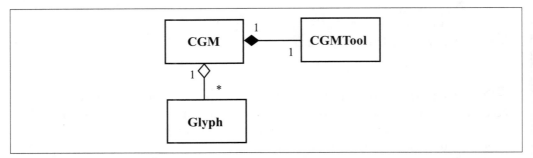

FIGURE 2-38. *CGM utilities for the shared whiteboard.*

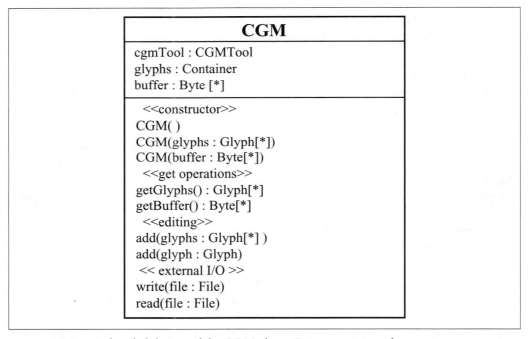

FIGURE 2-39. *A detailed design of the CGM class. (Private or internal operations are not shown.)*

```
set glyphs to an array of Glyph objects;
cgm = new CGM(glyphs);
cgm.add(glyph);  // add a single glyph
cgm.add(other_glyphs);  // add another array of glyphs
write the CGM data to a file using cgm.write(file);
  or
retrieve the cgm buffer using cgm.getBuffer();
```

The pseudocode for the backward conversion is

```
cgm = new CGM(buffer_with_CGM_data);
retrieve the array of glyphs using cgm.getGlyphs();
```

To read a CGM file and convert the data into glyphs, the pseudocode is

```
create a plain CGM object with cgm = new CGM(); then,
cgm.read(file);
retrieve the array of glyphs with cgm.getGlyphs();
```

With this we complete our phase I static design. In part 2 of this case study we will discuss the storage of the markups and annotations in files, and then in part 3 we will examine the dynamic behavior of the classes.

2.12 CASE STUDY: ACCESS CONTROL LISTS—PART 1

Access control lists (ACLs) appear often in enterprise software systems. They control users' access to digital resources, such as files, data, and so forth. Software systems contain users and groups of users. An ACL must therefore specify the access privileges of those users and groups.

In this case study we explore two designs of ACLs, which are based on different core design patterns. The first design, shown in Figure 2-40, uses the binary

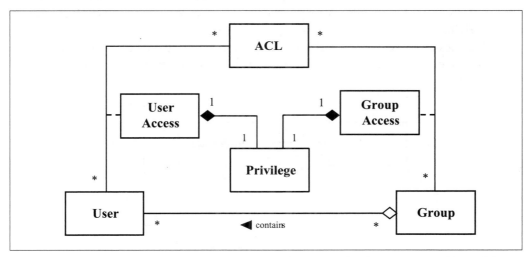

FIGURE 2-40. *A design for an ACL with users and groups. This design is typically used for fine-grained access control. (The User Manager class and Group Manager class are not shown here.)*

association class pattern. The class ACL is associated with multiple users and groups, which have association classes UserAccess and GroupAccess respectively. The Privilege class specifies the privilege for UserAccess or GroupAccess (such as read-only, read-write, and so on). Note that a user may appear in more than one group.

Thus, under an ACL object, there may be many users and groups. The ACL class will have the operation isPrivilegeGranted(user : User, requestedPrivilege : Privilege) : Boolean, which determines whether the user is granted the requested privilege. Certain policies may be embedded in this operation. For example,

- If a user appears in multiple groups, then pick the one with the highest privilege
- If a user appears as an individual in an ACL, then its privilege overwrites any settings in a group

One can see that this design allows very fine-grained access control. For instance, if we associate each FolderItem with an ACL, as in Figure 2-41, we may control how each user or group may access the item.

This design may become excessive in cases when we only need to control things by classes or categories. For example, a document management system may define the categories public, company proprietary, and trade secret. If we want to control access based on this classification scheme, we may use a different ACL design.

Figure 2-42 shows an ACL design using a relationship loop with forward containment. The Group class contains a number of users and ACLs. Each ACL is a special type of group associated with a privilege. It may also contain other ACLs as inner groups, which typically correspond to higher privileges or security levels. Note that a privilege is not associated with a user directly.

This design provides hierarchical group control and is typically used for category-based or coarse-grained access control. Again, appropriate policies may be

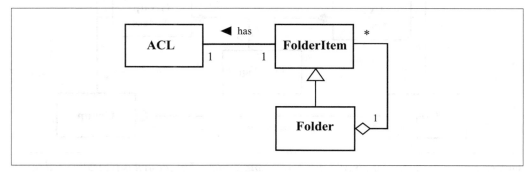

FIGURE 2-41. *Using an ACL to control the folder items.*

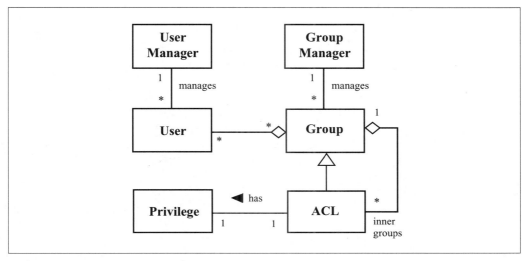

FIGURE 2-42.   *Another design for an ACL. This design is typically used for coarse-grained access control. Note that a privilege is not associated with a user directly. The User Manager and Group Manager classes are also shown.*

included in the operation `isPrivilegeGranted(user:User, requestedPrivilege: Privilege)` of the ACL class. For example,

- An inner group always has a higher privilege than its outer groups

- Sibling groups are unrelated as far as privileges are concerned

- If a user appears in multiple ACLs, then its privilege is determined by the innermost group to which it belongs

Using the coarse-grained ACL design, we may have nested levels of privileges or security. An example for two companies involved in a joint venture is given in Figure 2-43.

We continue with some applications of the ACL designs in Section 3.9.

2.13   EXERCISES

2-1.   One can use the Container class in Figure 2-2 as a servant class for the UserManager class. (a) Work out a detailed design diagram for User-Manager using this approach. Assume that User has two attributes: username and password. (b) If the links between UserManager and User are bidirectional, give a sample design for the User class. Describe

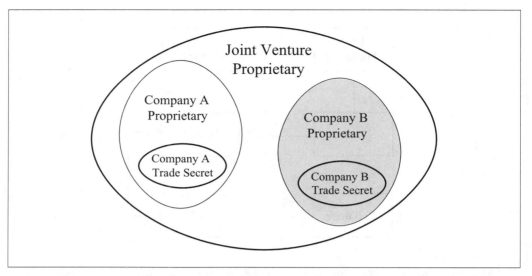

FIGURE 2-43. *An example of access control by categories using the coarse-grained ACL design.*

how to maintain referential integrity. Also, describe the details in the `addUser` and `removeUser` operations (for example, using a pseudo-code format). (We can assume that obsolete objects are handled by garbage collection.)

2-2. Give the reasons for using Container as a servant class inside a collection manager class (delegation), as opposed to deriving the collection manager from Container (inheritance).

2-3. Compare the Container class in Figure 2-2 with the one in the Java Abstract Windowing Toolkit package (java.awt.Container). Specifically, group the operations of java.awt.Container by their functions and point out the differences from those in our Container class. (You can find the document docs/api/java.awt.Container.html under the standard Java Development Kit directory. Also, ignore the fact that java.awt.Container is an abstract class.)

2-4. Draw a UML object diagram (in short form) for java.awt.Container and its superclass java.awt.Component. Describe the relationship between the two. (Note: The document for Component is in docs/api/java.awt.Component.html under the Java Development Kit directory.) If Frame is a subclass of Container, draw a sample picture with three levels of frames (shown as rectangular frames).

2-5.   Draw a UML object diagram (in short form) for the following classes in java.awt: MenuComponent MenuItem, MenuBar, Menu, and CheckboxMenuItem. Starting with MenuBar, draw a sample picture showing all four types of objects, excluding MenuComponent (which is an abstract class).

2-6.   Provide a detailed design for the directory hierarchy in Figure 2-3b. Include only basic attributes such as name, size, and date for the File and Folder objects. Use the Container class in Folder to holder subfolders and files.

2-7.   Provide a detailed design for the linked list for different versions of objects mentioned in Section 2.3. Use Version as the class name. Different versions are connected via object references to form a chain. Each Version object has a label and references to the previous and next versions.

2-8.   Discuss how to maintain referential integrity in the network of Figure 2-4a. In particular, identify a set of core operations from Figure 2-5 and describe the method invoked inside those operations to maintain referential integrity.

2-9.   Carry out relationship fission for the forward containment loop in Figure 2-6b. Can you give a practical example of such a relationship loop?

2-10.   Perform relationship fission and draw the aggregation diagram for the Menu class family in Exercise 2-5.

2-11.   Use a different approach from that in Figure 2-11 to associate the Secured classes to the original Folder and FolderItem classes. In particular, observe the requirement that a SecuredFolderItem cannot be contained by a regular Folder. Draw the object design in short form and carry out relationship fission to obtain the aggregation diagram.

2-12.   (a) An airplane has two pilots (Person objects) during each flight (Flight object). We can model a flight as an association class between Airplane and Person (see Figure 2-44a). Discuss whether this is a good way to model the three classes of objects. If not, propose a better design with a better way to use an association class.

        (b) Describe the relationship between the three classes of objects in Figure 2-44b.

2-13.   Provide a detailed design for the Part-Property classes in Figure 2-22. The attributes for Part are name and part number. For Property, the attribute is count. Include operations for cloning a Part object or its entire hierarchy. Note that all links are bidirectional. Describe in detail the core operations that ensure referential integrity.

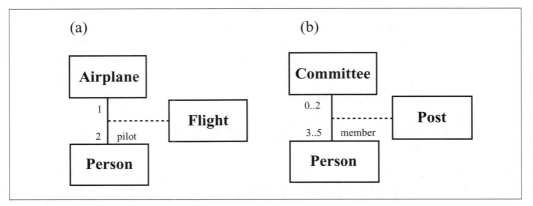

FIGURE 2-44. *Association classes for Exercise 2-12.*

2-14.   In a simple file directory system, such as that in Figure 2-7, each
        FolderItem object can belong to only one folder (a primary link). Gen-
        eralize this by introducing the sharing (symbolic link) concept. That is,
        a FolderItem object may be associated with more than one folder.
        However, there must be one and only one primary link between a
        FolderItem and its parent folder. The following policies should also be
        enforced:

   • The first time a FolderItem object is linked to its parent, the link is
     a primary one. All other links are symbolic.
   • If a primary link is removed, all other (symbolic) links should be
     removed as well.

   Use an association class to describe the type of link (primary or
   symbolic). Provide a detailed design and describe the behavior of
   the operations. In particular, describe in detail the core operations
   `addFolderItem` and `removeFolderItem` in the Folder class with
   regard to the stated policies. (These are the core operations that maintain referential integrity.)

2-15.   Consider the object model for the Folder-File hierarchy in Figure 2-3.
        Suppose we want to present or transfer the hierarchy data in an XML
        format. How should we tag the data? Construct an XML object dia-
        gram (in short form) for the Folder-File hierarchy. Also, write a sample
        XML file that uses the appropriate XML elements and attributes.

2-16.   Construct an XML object diagram (in short form) for the Menu family
        classes in java.awt (see Exercise 2-5). Give an example XML document
        for a typical menu containing File and Help.

2-17.   Modify the XML object model in Figure 2-30 to accommodate the case of having an additional "unit : String" attribute in the Attribute class. Give an example XML document for this case. Compare the new XML structure with the original one. Also, propose a way to optimize the XML document by shortening it. (Hint: You may change the element names.)

2-18.   Besides the binary association class, can you identify other patterns in Figure 2-18? (The binary association class may be a part of such patterns.)

Persistent
Objects

Our discussion so far has focused on objects and their structural relationships. Once we implement an object design with a specific programming language, the source code (or the compiled binary code) contains definitions of object classes along with their relationships. The code exists as a file in our computer system. However, the object instances generated when we execute the code are transient. That is, they cease to exist at the end of the code execution, unless we somehow make them persistent.

Thus, if we want to save the object instances as persistent data and be able to retrieve them later, we need to map them to a certain format and store it on a disk or other permanent medium (such as a database). This brings about *persistent objects,* which are representations of objects that exist independently of the processes that create them.

Persistent objects (or persistent data in general) are managed by database management systems (DBMSs). There are, in general, four types of database models: relational, extended relational, functional, and object-oriented [Cattell 1991]. They are distinguished by their allowable kinds of data and schema. The relational model is based on the simple concept of a table. The extended relational model adds to the relational model certain object-related capabilities. Functional models use a declarative functional query language to define and access the function values. The object-oriented model is built on the object paradigm.

Ideally, we should be able to perform a persistent object design without worrying about the underlying persistent mechanism or database model. After that, if the database model is not object oriented, we may follow a standard procedure or employ some semi-automatic tools to map the objects to the native database models. We may call this an object-oriented approach to database design.

In this chapter we first present some basic concepts on database management and persistent objects. We then discuss different strategies to make objects persistent, particularly those involving object-oriented databases and relational databases. We also examine object-relational mapping in detail, which is the main task of extended relational databases.

3.1 TRANSACTIONS AND DATABASE MANAGEMENT SYSTEMS

A logical unit of work done by a DBMS is called a *transaction*. For each transaction, there is a clear boundary of beginning and end. Besides organizing the stored data, the main task of a DBMS is to manage transactions. Transactions are

- **Atomic**—A transaction may be made up of many steps, all of which are considered one unit of work. They are either all executed (committed) or none is executed. If a transaction is aborted midway, all the steps that were performed from the beginning of the transaction to the point of failure are undone (rollback).

- **Consistent**—The system is said to be in a reliable state once a transaction is completed.

- **Isolated**—One unit of work cannot interfere with another unit of work.

- **Durable**—After a transaction is committed, the changes become permanent.

These are referred to as the ACID properties of transactions. They are the essential requirements of a DBMS.

The basic types of transaction are read and update. On committing an update transaction, the DBMS ensures that changes are saved in the database. For a read transaction, on the other hand, there is no change to the data.

The same principle should hold for persistent objects. Therefore, at the end of an update transaction, either the database is updated with all the transaction's changes to a persistent object, or the database is not updated at all. Thus, if a failure occurs in the middle of the transaction, or the transaction is aborted, the persistent object in the database remains unchanged.

When persistent objects are being accessed inside a transaction, the DBMS ensures that the retrieval is not compromised by other users sharing the data. Furthermore, initial access to a persistent object must always occur inside a transaction. Depending on how the transaction is committed, persistent objects may be accessible outside the transaction.

When objects are distributed, one may use a two-phase commit protocol to ensure that transactions across multiple databases are part of a single unit of work (a group transaction).

3.2 OBJECT-ORIENTED DATABASES

Object-oriented databases store persistent objects and provide complete support for objects and full DBMS functions (Figure 3-1) [Cattell 1991, Cattell & Barry 1997, Jackson 1991]. In particular, once retrieved into memory, an object is in the same state as when it was stored, and its operations can be invoked. For a group of objects, their inheritance and association relationships are also preserved.

Prototypes and early products of object-oriented databases first emerged in the mid 1980s. Among them were Iris DBMS [Fishman et al. 1989], ORION [Kim et al. 1989], GemStone [Bretl et al. 1989], OZ+ [Weiser & Lochovsky 1989], and ODDESSY (Object-Oriented Databases Design System) [Diederich & Milton 1989].

In addition to the basic DBMS functions mentioned earlier, object-oriented databases should provide the following tools [Jackson 1991]:

- **Object browser**—A tool to view the object data and object model (schema) in a database

- **Query facility**—A high-level, efficient, application-independent query facility that supports ad hoc queries. Ideally, certain query languages should be supported (for example, the Object Query Language [Cattell 1993]).

- **Database evolution utility**—A utility that provides support for changes to object models and consequently object data over time

The object database standard specifies an object model and a set of programming language bindings (including Java, C++, and SmallTalk) for object-oriented

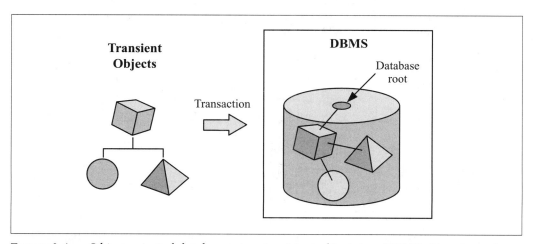

FIGURE 3-1. *Object-oriented databases store persistent objects in a DBMS. Also shown is a database root, which is the starting link to all persistent objects.*

databases [Cattell & Barry 1997]. Some basic concepts of object-oriented databases are discussed in the following subsections.

3.2.1 DATABASE ROOTS AND EXTENTS

A database root provides a way to locate an object in a database using a textual name. Applications can use database roots to locate persistent objects for performing queries or navigating to other persistent objects.

Database roots are the starting points of an object-oriented database. They are often top-level objects such as collection managers or containers. For example, in the Person-Hobby design of Figure 1-7, we can add a container to hold the Person objects and another one for the Hobby objects. These two containers (persons and hobbies) are then associated with database roots, as shown in Figure 3-2a.

A collection that contains all instances of a class is called the *extent* of the class. It is conceptually similar to a table in a relational database (see Section 3.4.1). An extent (such as persons in Figure 3-2a) contains all instances of the class (such as the Person objects in Figure 3-2).

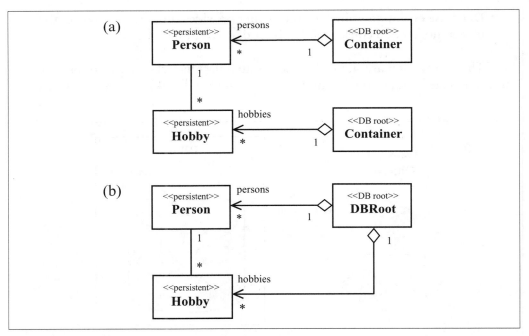

FIGURE 3-2. *Persistent objects for the Person-Hobby example. In (a), the Container class is used as the extent for the Person and Hobby classes. In (b), a single database root holds both extents. Note the unidirectional associations to the Person and Hobby objects, and the UML stereotype notation in << ... >>.*

Extents are often assigned as database roots so that they can be reached directly from a program. In Figure 3-2a, the two containers are used as database roots, as indicated by the UML stereotype <<DB root>>. Person and Hobby are used as persistent objects, which are indicated by <<persistent>>.

Alternatively, we may use a single database root to hold all the extents (using containers). Such is the case in Figure 3-2b and in other designs with a single top-level class (which is typically a collection manager). In this case we need to retrieve the top-level object before navigating to the extents and other objects. Figure 3-3 shows the detailed design for DBRoot in Figure 3-2b. (Only the attributes and operations related to persons are shown.)

In terms of implementation, an extent can be associated with a class-scope variable (such as a static variable in Java or C++), or it can be an attribute in a higher level manager class. With the first approach, the class manages its own instances through the embedded extent. With the latter approach, another manager class performs the management.

To access a Person object, change it, and then save it back, we do the following:

1. Initialize the DBMS by calling its application program interface functions.

2. Open the database.

3. Start a transaction.

DBRoot
persons : person[*]
<<constructor>> DBRoot() <<get & query operations>> getPersons() : Person[*] getPerson(name: String) : Person getPersonCount() : Integer contains(person: Person) : Boolean <<editing>> addPerson(person: Person) : Person removePerson(name: String) removePerson(Person: Person) removeAllPersons( )

FIGURE 3-3. *A detailed design of a sample database root. This figure includes only the attributes and operations related to persons. For hobbies, the details are similar.*

```
// pseudocode for updating persistent objects
initialize();
openDatabase("DB_filename");
beginUpdateTransaction();

  dbRoot = getDbRoot ("DB_root_name");
  person= dbRoot.getPerson ("name");
  person.changeName("newName");

commitTransaction();
closeDatabase();
```

FIGURE 3-4. *Pseudocode for updating persistent objects in an object-oriented DBMS.*

4. Call getDbRoot (or another equivalent operation) with a textual name such as DBRoot or PersonContainer. The operation returns the root object, from which we can call get(personName) to get a specific Person object.

5. We now have a Person object and can perform any operation encapsulated in it. In particular, we can change the attributes of the object. We can also navigate to any Hobby objects that the person has.

6. End the transaction.

7. Shut down the DBMS.

Figure 3-4 shows the pseudocode for updating persistent objects in an object-oriented DBMS.

3.2.2   PERSISTENCE-ENABLED OBJECTS

The stereotype <<persistent>> in Figure 3-2 indicates a persistent object or, more precisely, a *persistence-enabled* class. Persistence-enabled objects are the instances of such classes. They are objects that can be stored in a database. That is, they are initially transient objects that later become persistent objects. Persistent objects exist independently of the processes that create them.

The migration from transient to persistent objects is managed by a DBMS and is usually transparent to the application. To perform the migration, some DBMSs use a process called *transitive persistence,* which is described next.

When an application commits a transaction, the DBMS stores in the database any transient objects that are persistence-enabled and that can be reached transitively from any persistent objects. That is, when the transaction commits, persistence-enabled transient objects become persistent if they are referenced by other persistent objects. Because of this transparent process, persistent objects and regular objects behave the same and can be manipulated in the same way. This is one of the advantages of object-oriented databases.

To implement a persistence-enabled class, we first implement it as a normal class. Then, to make the class persistence-enabled, we adhere to one of the following approaches (depending on the specific DBMS):

- Mark the class with certain DBMS-specific keywords and then postprocess the code.

- Make a list of persistence-enabled classes and postprocess the code.

The post process usually scans through the entire set of persistence-enabled classes in an application and may also generate a *schema* for the object-oriented database. The schema is basically a blueprint of the database for the DBMS to store the object data.

3.2.3 DESTRUCTION OF PERSISTENT OBJECTS

Persistent objects can be destroyed in two ways:

1. Get the object reference and call the destruction function in the application program interface of the underlying DBMS.

2. Use the garbage collection utility from the DBMS to find and destroy unused objects.

The first approach puts all the burden on the programmers' shoulders. Because a persistent object may be associated with multiple persistent objects, one has to be careful not to destroy objects that are in use. The second approach offers a much easier way to manage unused persistent objects. We simply need to remove the links to those persistent objects that are no longer used. When a persistent object is not referenced by any other objects and is not a database root itself, it becomes an *orphan object*. The DBMS collects such orphan objects via a *mark-and-sweep* mechanism.

During the mark phase, the DBMS starts from all database roots and traverses down the object network to identify all reachable objects. After this, objects that are not marked are considered orphan objects. Then, during the sweep phase, the unmarked objects are destroyed. The DBMS may also free the storage used by the destroyed objects.

If we stick to the second approach, we can ensure referential integrity in the object database. That is, there are no references to destroyed objects inside the database.

3.2.4 SCHEMA EVOLUTION

Over time, the persistent object model or database schema will evolve. The object classes or their relationships may be changed. This process is known as *schema evolution*. The underlying DBMS needs to provide a mechanism or utility to facilitate the evolution, not only for the schema but also for the persistent object data.

The data in an object database are tightly coupled to its schema. Thus, a change in the database schema implies a necessary update to the persistent object data. This is especially important in a production environment, in which existing data must be converted to the new schema. One approach is to embed a unique class ID into each class of objects. A schema conversion utility may then use the IDs to convert the data to the new schema.

3.3 RELATIONAL DATABASES

The relational model was developed in the early 1970s based on a rigorous mathematical basis [Codd 1970, Codd 1990]. It provides a framework for assessing the quality of a database design. Before the formal development of the relational model, the database field was practically a collection of ad hoc methodologies. In the mid to late 1970s, some prototype relational databases were developed [Stonebraker 1976, Astrahan et al. 1976]. This was followed by more vigorous product development in the 1980s. The wide adoption of Structured Query Language (SQL) helped standardize different relational DBMSs [Date 1986, Date 1995]. Relational DBMSs represent a major improvement over previous databases, which were tightly integrated with database applications. Today, relational database products dominate the database industry. They are very mature and widely used in mission-critical enterprise applications.

A relational database consists of a collection of relations, or tables, and a specification of underlying domains for the entries in the table. The table is two-dimensional and its cell entries have atomic values. Each table may be viewed as having a fixed number of columns and a variable number of rows. The rows are the tuples, each of which is one record of data. The order of the rows is not important. The columns are fields of data. To identify a record uniquely, one field or a set of fields must have unique values within a table. These fields are collectively called the *primary key* of the table. In many cases an integer ID is used as the primary key.

In the relational model, rather than using links to relate data objects (as in object-oriented databases), data in different tables are related through matching field values (the so-called *foreign keys*, which are the primary keys of other tables). Thus the relational model forces us to take a value approach—to identify and relate records by value. This is a fundamental difference between the relational model and the object-oriented model.

The relational model also stipulates a set of normal forms, which are rules to prohibit redundancy in table organization [Date 1995]. There are many levels of normal forms. Each higher level form adds a constraint to the one below it and improves the consistency of the table. The first three normal forms are used most frequently and include the following:

1. **First normal form**—Each field value can only represent a single record (no multiple values).

2. **Second normal form**—In addition to the first normal form, each nonprimary key field must depend on the whole primary key. Thus, if the primary key is concatenated from two or more fields, a partial dependence exists when a field depends on only one of the fields in the primary key. Such partial dependence must be removed to satisfy the second normal form. On the other hand, if the primary key is a single field (as in most tables discussed here), this normal form is always satisfied.

3. **Third normal form**—In addition to the second normal form, all fields that are not part of the primary key should depend exclusively on the primary key. In other words, there should be no transitive dependence, in which a nonprimary key field depends on one or more other nonprimary key fields.

The first two forms are satisfied by virtually all tables, whereas the third one may be violated occasionally for the sake of performance. Going to normal forms higher than the second generally requires splitting a table into smaller ones. This, of course, introduces overhead in navigation and in query execution.

3.4 MAPPING PERSISTENT OBJECTS TO TABLES

Because of the predominant role of relational databases in businesses, many object-oriented applications need to map objects to tables. Data stored in these tables effectively become the persistent representation of the objects.

To store objects in a relational database, there are two approaches. With the first approach we build object-oriented applications around relational databases. Each object then needs to know how to store and retrieve its data. This requires extra programming in every class, and mapping from objects to tables, which can be complicated.

The second approach is to model the object structure in the relational database. This is difficult because relational databases have limited data types. Furthermore, many aspects of objects, such as inheritance, object references, and so forth, cannot be expressed directly in relational databases.

The first approach—building an object-oriented front end to a relational DBMS—is therefore the preferred one. To this end, commercial products are available. They help define the object-relational mapping and provide object-oriented interfaces to relational databases. Some even manage objects in an application server to optimize performance and to ensure data integrity. Such products, in effect, fall into the category of the extended relational model [Cattell 1991].

To achieve good performance in applying this approach, one needs to have a solid understanding of object-relational mapping. In a broader context, we may design a database using an object-oriented approach, followed by an object-relational mapping process [Heinckiens 1998]. In the next subsection we look at the mapping from objects to relational tables.

3.4.1 CLASSES AND BINARY ASSOCIATIONS

Generally, a class maps to one table. The columns (fields) correspond to the attributes of the class, and the rows (records) correspond to the instances of the class. One or more fields in the table constitute the primary key, with values that uniquely identify the records (the object instances). Conceptually, tables are like extents for persistent objects. Because they are visible directly from the DBMS, they are also the equivalent of database roots.

If a class attribute is a reference to another class, a separate table is generally needed to model the class associated with the attribute. The same is true for any complex data types (such as collections) not supported by the relational DBMS. This naturally brings about association between classes. Next we examine binary associations with association classes (see Figure 2-17). Binary associations without association classes can be considered special cases of them.

Figure 3-5 shows the tables corresponding to the object classes in Figure 2-17a, which is reproduced on the left of Figure 3-5. For the supplier objects the primary key is supplier_ID in the supplier table. For buyers, it is buyer_ID. However, for the Trade table, there is no trade_ID as the primary key. This is because Trade is an association class. Each row in the trade table is related to a specific link between Supplier and Buyer. Thus, the pair (supplier_ID, buyer_ID) constitutes the primary key for the Trade table. Note that a primary key is always a candidate key, which uniquely identifies a link (see Section 1.5.4).

In the Trade table, each supplier_ID or buyer_ID is also a foreign key for looking up the corresponding supplier or buyer. We call such a table that corresponds to an association class (or an association) a *link table*. A link table generally uses foreign keys to form its own primary key and does not have its own ID.

Note that a specific supplier_ID may have multiple associated buyer_IDs. The same is true in reverse. This multiplicity is exactly the same as that specified in the design on the left of Figure 3-5. Also, the same (supplier_ID, buyer_ID) pair may appear only once in the Trade table because each pair represents one link and therefore corresponds to one row in the Trade table. This is consistent with the candidate key requirement discussed near Figure 2-21.

For the Supplier-Buyer example, the link table is necessary because of the multiplicity on both ends of the association. This is also true for a generic binary association class, such as the one in Figure 2-21. Thus, for Figure 2-21, if both mA and mB are more than one, then both A_ID and B_ID are needed to identify a specific link between A and B. Here, A_ID and B_ID are the primary keys of Tables A and B respectively. Furthermore, the link table L has the pair (A_ID, B_ID) as the primary key. For binary associations without association classes, their link tables simply contain the pair (A_ID, B_ID) and no other fields.

For each A_ID, the number of values B_ID can take is given by the multiplicity mB. Similarly, for each B_ID, the number of values A_ID can take is given by mA. Again, the meaning of multiplicity is exactly the same as that in the UML notation.

If, in Figure 2-21, mA = 1 and mB > 1, then we can simply use B_ID to identify a link uniquely because there is only one link for each B_ID. In this case the link table L will have B_ID as the primary key. Now that tables L and B have the same primary key B_ID, we may even collapse them into one table. The process of absorbing the

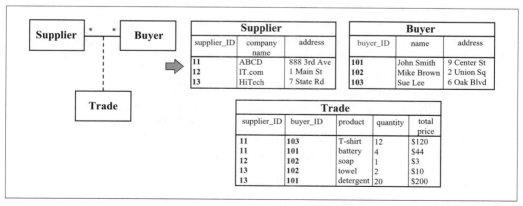

FIGURE 3-5.   *Mapping of a binary association to tables. The primary key values are shown in bold type. In the Trade table, supplier_ID and buyer_ID are foreign keys to the two tables on top. The pair (supplier_ID, buyer_ID) form the primary key for the Trade table.*

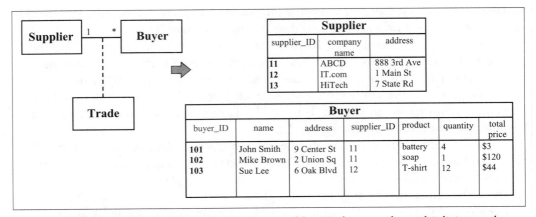

FIGURE 3-6. *Mapping of a binary association to tables. In this case the multiplicity on the Supplier side is one. The Trade table is collapsed into the Buyer table, which uses supplier_ID as a foreign key. This mapping also applies to the case without the Trade class. The Buyer table contains its own attributes plus supplier_ID.*

link table L into Table B is called *foreign key embedding* because the combined B table now contains the foreign key A_ID. An example using the Supplier-Buyer association is shown in Figure 3-6 (Buyer plays the role of Table B).

This procedure reduces the number of tables by one, resulting in better performance. However, it deviates from the standard class-table mapping pattern and reduces design rigor, making it difficult to generalize the multiplicity beyond one. (It does not, however, violate the third normal form of the relational model.) For the case mA > 1 and mB = 1, a similar argument can be made.

If, in Figure 2-21, both mA = 1 and mB = 1, then either A_ID or B_ID can be used to identify a link. That is, either can be the primary key for the link table L. The three tables can then be collapsed into one.

Finally, the Trade table in Figure 3-5 is somewhat idealistic because there can be only one trade between a specific (supplier, buyer) pair. This is because we have modeled the relationship with a binary association, which implies that each link is uniquely identified by a (supplier, buyer) pair (see Section 1.5.4). Exercise 3-6 extends this to trade relationships with multiple transactions.

3.4.2 AGGREGATION, COMPOSITION, AND SERVANT CLASSES

Now that we have established the mapping for binary associations, the mapping of aggregation and composition is just a special case. This is true because the relational model only captures relationships through value matching. The different behavior between normal association and aggregation or composition is lost.

In the case of having a servant class as an attribute, a separate table is generally needed to model the servant class associated with the attribute. The same is true for any complex data types (such as collections) not supported by the relational DBMS. The relationship between the master class and the servant class is again modeled by a link table, as in a binary association.

Finally, for one-to-one aggregation or composition, you may combine all three tables into the aggregate class table to gain performance. The same is true for a one-to-one master-servant relationship.

3.4.3 TERNARY AND HIGHER ORDER ASSOCIATIONS

The mapping of ternary and higher order associations to tables can be carried out as in binary associations. That is, each class maps to a table, which serves as the extent for the class objects. The N-ary association (or the association class) itself maps to a link table. The primary key of the link table is typically made up of foreign keys, which are primary keys of the tables in the association.

In Figure 3-7 we expand the ternary association in Figure 1-9 to include an association class called Post. Each of the three classes maps to a table, whereas the Post class maps to a link table, shown in Figure 3-8.

The multiplicity specified in Figure 3-7 can be translated to the following constraints in the link table:

- A person_ID can only be associated with as many as two committee_IDs in any given year.

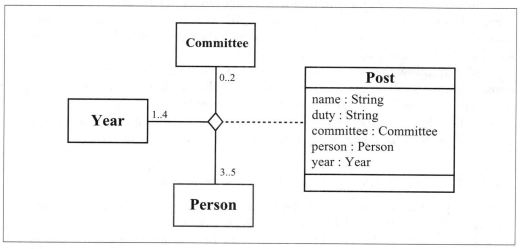

FIGURE 3-7. *A ternary association with an association class Post.*

Post				
committee_ID	person_ID	year	name	duty
1	103	2000	Chair	Chairs meetings
1	101	2000	Vice-chair	Supports the chair
1	102	2000	Secretary	Takes minutes
3	102	2002	Head	Calls meetings
3	101	2002	Member	Attends meetings
3	104	2002	Secretary	Takes minutes
3	105	2002	Treasurer	Handles money
2	105	2000	Chair	Chairs meetings
2	104	2000	Co-chair	Helps the chair
2	102	2000	Secretary	Takes minutes

FIGURE 3-8. *The link table corresponding to the association class Post in Figure 3-7. Note that year is the primary key of the Year class.*

- Each committee_ID must appear with three to five person_IDs in any given year (or, equivalently, the pair committee_ID and year must appear between three to five times in the link table).

- A person_ID can appear in one to four years for any specific committee_ID.

Because the range of any multiplicity symbol in Figure 3-7 is more than one, the primary key is the set (committee_ID, person_ID, year), which is the same as the candidate key discussed in Section 1.5.4. (Remember that a candidate key is a minimal set of attributes that uniquely identifies a link.)

We can follow the same procedure to build link tables for higher order associations. Thus, for an n-ary association, there are n tables plus one link table. Generally, the primary key of the link table is made up of the set (ID_1, ID_2, ... , ID_n), where ID_n is the primary key of the nth table. If any one of the multiplicity items of the classes is one, then the corresponding ID can be dropped from the set.

3.4.4 REDUCING TERNARY ASSOCIATIONS TO BINARY ONES*

Can we implement a ternary association class using binary associations? This is an intellectually interesting and yet practical question because binary associations are straightforward to implement. The answer is yes, provided we handle the multiplicity constraints properly.

Observe that in Figure 3-8, the foreign keys (such as person_ID) are indeed binary links to other class objects. Hence, we can set up binary associations from the link class to the other three classes. In Figure 3-9 we show such an implementation, in which we make the association class L a linkage class among all three associated classes. Note that this approach is similar to the one used in Figure 2-21 for binary association classes.

The specification of multiplicity is, however, rather subtle. Here we've encountered the concept of a *joint multiplicity constraint,* indicated by the dashed curves on the right of Figure 3-9. For example, each pair of A and B objects is associated with mC (or a range given by mC) L objects, each of which is associated with one C object. In other words, in the extent of L objects, each pair of A and B objects must appear mC times (or a range given by mC). Similar conclusions hold for mA and mB. This shows that we can indeed implement a ternary association class using binary associations if we enforce joint multiplicity.

There is, however, one more subtlety. As in Figure 2-21, the structure on the right side of Figure 3-9 is not equivalent to the one on the left. This is because it relaxes the candidate key requirement implied on the left. That is, an A, B, C triplet may be associated with more than one L object on the right of Figure 3-9. Again, we

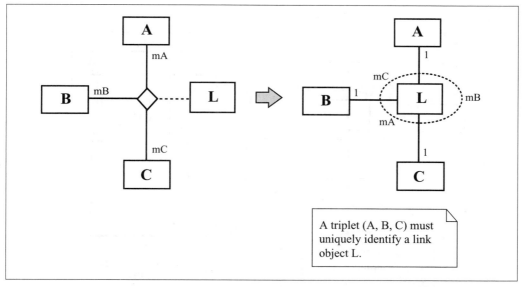

FIGURE 3-9.   *An implementation of the ternary association class L (left) using binary associations (right). The dashed curves on the right indicate joint multiplicity constraints. For example, each pair of A and B objects is associated with mC L objects, each of which is associated with one C object. The note on the right states the candidate key requirement implied on the left.*

must externally impose the requirement of ensuring that the A, B, C triplet is treated as a candidate key for the L objects.

To see these points more clearly, consider the example in Figure 3-10. On the left of the figure are multiple binary associations with joint multiplicity constraints. Notice that the joint multiplicity is equivalent to the multiplicity in Figure 3-7. Because the multiplicity on A, B, and C is all one, we may apply foreign key embedding, as we did in Figure 3-6. This leads to the link table L on the right of Figure 3-10 with the primary key (A_ID, B _ID, C _ID). The uniqueness of the primary key in the table automatically satisfies the candidate key requirement stated on the left.

The link table L is structurally the same as the Post table in Figure 3-8. In particular, the joint multiplicity can be translated to the following constraints in the L table:

- A specific pair (A_ID, B_ID) must appear between three to five times in the table.

- A specific pair (B_ID, C_ID) can appear only as many as two times in the table (in other words, be associated with as many as two A_IDs).

- A specific pair (A_ID, C_ID) must appear between one to four times in the table.

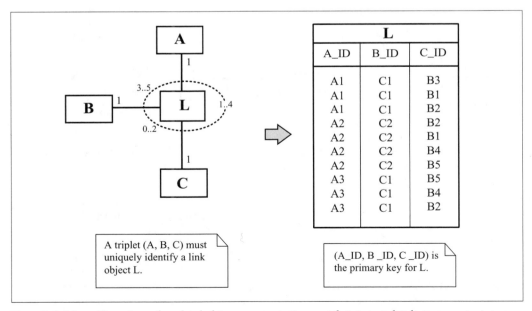

FIGURE 3-10. *Mapping of multiple binary associations with joint multiplicity constraints to a table. The joint multiplicity is equivalent to the multiplicity in Figure 3-7. Thus, for example, a specific pair (A_ID, B_ID) must appear between three to five times in the table.*

From these discussions we find that a ternary association class can indeed be implemented with binary associations, provided that its multiplicity is handled properly. Its mapping to tables is also consistent with the previous discussion in Section 3.4.3.

3.4.5   DEGENERATE TERNARY ASSOCIATIONS*

If one of the multiplicity constraints in a ternary association is exactly one and the others are not constrained (multiplicity being *), then the association degenerates into a normal binary one (without joint multiplicity). In this case the two representations are truly identical without externally imposed candidate key requirement.

For example, on the left of Figure 3-11, because mC = 1, the link table L has the pair (A_ID, B_ID) as the primary key. This means that the class L is indeed a binary association class between A and B. Each L object is associated with one C object. The reduced class diagram is shown on the right of Figure 3-11. The corresponding link table is shown in Figure 3-12.

The recognition of such degenerate ternary associations often helps simplify the object design. To illustrate these points more clearly, let us go through an example that deals with the central aspect of university life—teaching.

A university has a number of departments, each of which has a number of instructors. Each department offers many courses. Because there is a limit to class size, a course may be offered in more than one session. For example, one session may be offered on Mondays and Wednesdays, whereas another may be taught on Tuesdays and Thursdays. Multiple sessions may also be offered at the same time but in different classrooms.

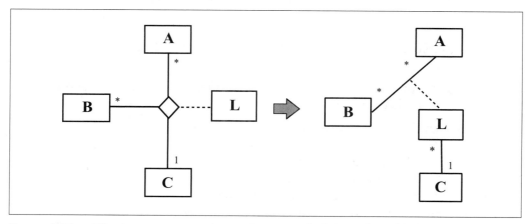

FIGURE 3-11.   *The degenerate ternary association on the left can be reduced to the normal binary associations on the right.*

L		
A_ID	**B_ID**	**C_ID**
A1	C1	B3
A1	C2	B1
A1	C3	B2
A2	C1	B2
A2	C2	B1
A2	C3	B4
A2	C4	B5
A3	C1	B5
A3	C2	B4
A3	C3	B2

(A_ID, B _ID) is the primary key for L.

FIGURE 3-12. *The link table for a degenerate ternary association. The pair (A_ID, B_ID) constitutes the primary key.*

Each session is conducted in a classroom on one of the university campuses and is taught by one or two instructors. The same instructor may teach multiple sessions of the same course (different schedules though). Each instructor may also teach multiple courses.

Let's build a database that captures all course session information. To do this, we first identify the core object design pattern for the problem. Noting that a session is associated with a schedule, a course, and a classroom, we first try to model a session as a ternary association class of the latter three, as shown in Figure 3-13.

The multiplicity constraints in Figure 3-13 for the ternary association imply the following:

1. For a given course, multiple sessions may be offered at the same schedule but different classrooms.

2. For a given course, multiple sessions may be offered at the same classroom but different schedules.

3. For a given classroom and schedule, there can be only one session.

Note that a schedule may represent multiple time slots, such as 10 A.M. to 11 A.M. on Mondays and 1 P.M. to 2 P.M. on Wednesdays.

The third statement means that the pair (Schedule, Classroom) uniquely identifies a session because the teaching must occur in one classroom at a certain time. Thus, we may reduce the ternary association into a binary one according to Figure 3-11. The result is shown in Figure 3-14.

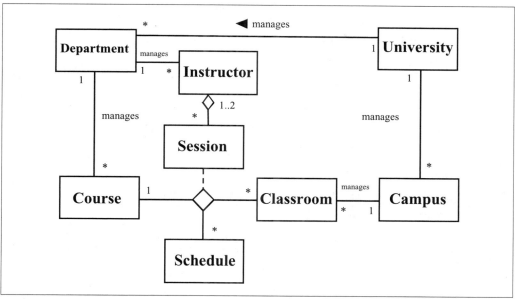

FIGURE 3-13. *The object model simulating university teaching. Session is modeled as a ternary association class here. The association name "manages" indicates an action from left to right or top to bottom, unless otherwise specified by a solid triangle.*

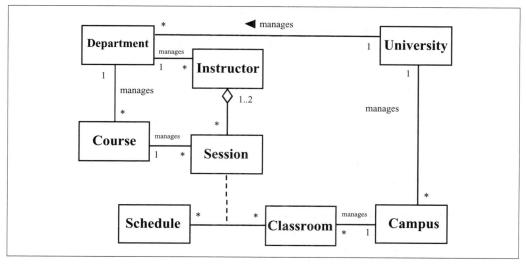

FIGURE 3-14. *The object model simulating university teaching. Session is now modeled as a binary association class between Schedule and Classroom. The association name "manages" indicates an action from left to right or top to bottom, unless otherwise specified by a solid triangle.*

TABLE 3-1. *Sample data for Session objects. Each row corresponds to a Session object.*

SESSION NUMBER	COURSE NAME	SCHEDULE	CLASSROOM	INSTRUCTOR 1	INSTRUCTOR 2
1081	Physics-101	M1-2 and Th2-3	C-A31	John	Jack
2081	Physics-201	W1-2 and F2-3	C-A31	John	Jack
3081	Physics-301	T1-3	C-P03	Jack	—
7031	Math-102	T10-12	D-102	Mary	—
7032	Math-102	Th10-12	D-102	Mary	—
2231	Drama-201	W9-11	S-904	Jane	—
4231	Drama-401	F9-11	S-904	Jane	—
3031	English-101	W3-5	T-234	Tom	—
4031	English-201	W3-5	T-236	Tony	—

Session is now modeled as a binary association class between Schedule and Classroom. We can verify that the three previous statements are indeed fulfilled by the new design. In particular, the third statement is simply the candidate key requirement implied in a binary association.

Some sample data related to the Session objects are presented in Table 3-1. From the data we can see that before constructing a Session object, we should have the Course, Schedule, Classroom and Instructor objects created already. The Session object ties these objects together to give the essential information on teaching. (In a relational database, the session number is the primary key for the Session table.)

Hence we see that degenerate ternary associations, such as the one on the left of Figure 3-11, can be reduced to normal binary associations, which are easier to implement. Note, however, that when the multiplicity is more restricted, the reduction may impose unintended restrictions. See Exercise 3-9 for an example.

3.4.6 INHERITANCE

The relationship model has no equivalent concept of inheritance. It is then the responsibility of the database application to capture and handle such relationships. For the inheritance tree in Figure 3-15, we use the "one class/one table" mapping approach to form the tables in Figure 3-16. The subclass tables are straightforward, except that the primary key is the same as that of the superclass table. This is because each instance of the subclass is also a special instance of the superclass. By using the same primary key, we can retrieve the inherited fields (name and age) from the superclass (Person) table.

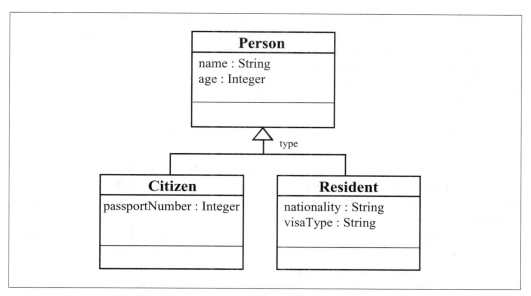

FIGURE 3-15. *One superclass and two subclasses in an inheritance tree.*

Person			
person_ID	type	name	age
1	citizen	John Smith	19
2	resident	Mike Brown	73
3	citizen	Sue Lee	55
4	resident	Jaimi White	24
5	resident	Tom Chan	66
6	person	Julie Lyon	20

Citizen	
person_ID	passportNumber
1	123-456
3	987-654

Resident		
person_ID	nationality	visaType
2	UK	F-1
4	Brazil	H-1
5	China	H-1

FIGURE 3-16. *The tables corresponding to the inheritance tree in Figure 3-15, under the "one class/one table" mapping approach. Each table contains its own class attributes. Note the "type" field in the superclass table.*

For the superclass table, an additional field "type" is needed to identify the type of class to which a record belongs. During a query, we would first go to the Person table, find the person_ID and type. If the type is "resident," then we would jump to the Resident table to retrieve additional data. Note that the database application should ensure that person_ID appears only once among all subclass tables.

If either the Resident class or the Citizen class has subclasses, then an additional "type" field is needed in the corresponding Resident or Citizen table. Such a "type" field helps navigate down the inheritance tree.

The current "one class/one table" mapping approach is simple. It satisfies all three normal forms described earlier and can be easily generalized to more complicated situations. However, any operation is likely to involve multiple tables, which often leads to performance problems.

Noting that the primary key is the same for all tables in an inheritance tree, we can combine them into a single table. The large table will contain the union of all fields from all classes in the tree, including the "type" fields from different levels. Undoubtedly, some cells will be empty (null) in the combined table. Which fields are meant for a particular row depends on the "type" field. This dependence on a non-primary key field violates the third normal form. Once again, we gain performance with a combined large table by sacrificing the consistency of the table organization. We return to this example in Section 3.5.1.

3.4.7 Mapping Rules Summary

Listed in Table 3-2 are the rules for standard object-relational mapping.

The rules lead to tables that are compliant with the first three normalization forms but may be poor in performance because of the large number of tables generated. Performance can be improved by combining tables.

TABLE 3-2. *Object-relational "one class/one table" mapping rules.*

OBJECT-ORIENTED STRUCTURES	RELATIONAL TABLES
Class A (with simple attributes)	Table A with primary key A_ID
Binary association between classes A and B, with an association class L, and multiplicity mA and mB	Table A with primary key A_ID and table B with primary key B_ID If mA > 1 and mB > 1, the link table L has primary key (A_ID, B_ID). If mA = 1 and mB > 1, the link table L has primary key B_ID. Table L may be absorbed into table B, which contains A_ID as a foreign key.

OBJECT-ORIENTED STRUCTURES	RELATIONAL TABLES
	If mA > 1 and mB = 1, the link table L has primary key A_ID. Table L may be absorbed into table A, which contains B_ID as a foreign key.
	If mA = 1 and mB = 1, the link table L can use either A_ID or B_ID as the primary key. Table L may be absorbed into table A or B.
Aggregation, composition, and servant classes	Can be treated the same way as binary associations
N-ary association between N classes, with an association class L	N tables with primary keys ID_n, where n lies between 1 and N
	The primary key of the link table L is made up of the set (ID_1, ID_2, ... , ID_N). If any one of the multiplicity items of the classes is one, then the corresponding ID can be dropped from the set.
Inheritance tree	One table for each class in the tree. All tables in the tree share the same primary key. Inherited fields of subclasses are stored in superclass tables. Superclass tables at all levels need additional "type" fields to distinguish the type of subclass for each record.

Two or more tables that share the *same* primary key can be combined into one table. This is often done to improve performance by avoiding expensive joint operations or navigation between tables. The trade-off is degraded table flexibility and extensibility, making it harder to add or remove a relationship. In the case of inheritance, the combined table may also violate the third normal form of the relational model (some field values may be dependent on nonprimary key fields).

3.5 A CRITICAL COMPARISON BETWEEN RELATIONAL AND OBJECT-ORIENTED DATABASES

The relational model is simple and elegant. Effective techniques have been developed to optimize operations within a single table. For example, binary tree and indexed sequential access methods allow efficient query operations. However, object relationships that are fully captured by the object model are missing in the relational model. They have to be coded into the relational database applications as extra logic. The entity-relationship used in the design of relational tables does not include object behavior. There is also a mismatch between the data types in tables and those in objects.

Moreover, one needs to handle operations such as storing, reading, searching, and deleting a network of objects. The transient objects need to be managed as well, because, for example, an object identity in a database is lost as soon as the object is loaded into memory. Because of these issues, programming an interface for storing objects in relational tables is not trivial.

On the other hand, relational databases have dominated the market for years. They are more mature than object-oriented database products. Consequently, neither model can claim a total victory. It may be in the best interest of an organization to leverage existing investments in relational technology while augmenting it with object-oriented techniques.

In this regard we advocate an object-oriented approach to database design, followed by a standard mapping process to relational models. In Table 3-3 we first compare the characteristics of the two types of databases and then examine a working example in detail.

TABLE 3-3. *Comparison of object-oriented and relational databases.*

OBJECT-ORIENTED DATABASES	RELATIONAL DATABASES
There is efficient navigation between objects via object references.	Navigation between related objects may require expensive joint table operations.
Objects of the same class may scatter to different physical locations in a database, slowing down query and other operations.	High-performance searching and querying within a single table is supported.
Persistent objects appear as familiar and normal objects. They enjoy full object-oriented relationships.	Tuples (rows in a table) are used to represent records (the counterparts of objects). Relationships between records are modeled by relationships between values, thereby forcing a value approach.
Requires a solid understanding of object-oriented design. Data are intimately tied to the object design.	The relational model is supported by a sound mathematics foundation. The tables are very simple and easy to understand. They allow a high level of data independence.
There are no widely adopted standard data manipulation languages.	There exists a standard data manipulation language (SQL).
Highly extensible and flexible. New classes of objects can be incorporated by extending the existing classes. Data types are not limited by predefined types. It is easy to incorporate complex types. There is no mismatch of data types.	Insufficient mechanism for extension. In particular, it does not have a mechanism to model inheritance. These databases are appropriate for simple data types and records that do not have many relationships. Complex data need to be flattened into tables.

3.5.1 OPTIMIZATION OF RELATIONAL TABLES

A primary task of a DBMS is to provide query services. Let's examine the process of optimizing the table design in Figure 3-16. In doing so, we will use the following query as our example:

Query: Find all persons age 65 or older who are also residents with an H-1 visa.

For the tables in Figure 3-16, the steps to carry out the query include the following:

1. Select all rows from the Person table with age greater than or equal to 65 and type equal to resident. Put the rows into a temporary collection.

2. For each row in the collection, use its person_ID to find the corresponding visaType in the Resident table. If the visaType does not equal H-1, remove the row from the collection.

3. The temporary collection now contains the rows that satisfy the query requirements. (Only one row, "Tom Chan," is returned in our example.)

We can build indices to improve the operation within a table. However, the bottleneck in this process is the operations involving two tables. When more tables are involved through association or inheritance, the performance scales poorly with an increasing number of tables.

For the previous query, a simple remedy is to include the inherited attributes in subclass tables. This results in the larger Citizen and Resident tables (Figure 3-17). The Person table now has only one row.

With the modified tables, the query process involves only one step:

1. Select all rows from the Resident table with age greater than or equal to 65 and visaType equal to H-1.

This readily gives the row "Tom Chan" as the result. Now suppose we also need to find all persons younger than 25. With the partially optimized tables in Figure 3-17, this again requires operations across tables. To optimize the tables fully, we notice that all three tables in Figure 3-16 actually share the same primary key. Thus, we may simply combine them into one. The combined Person table is shown in Figure 3-18.

With the combined table, the original query also involves only one step:

1. Select all rows from the combined Person table with age greater than or equal to 65, type equal to resident, and visaType equal to H-1.

Person		
person_ID	name	age
6	Julie Lyon	20

Citizen			
person_ID	name	age	passportNumber
1	John Smith	19	123-456
3	Sue Lee	55	987-654

Resident				
person_ID	name	age	nationality	visaType
2	Mike Brown	73	UK	F-1
4	Jaimi White	24	Brazil	H-1
5	Tom Chan	66	China	H-1

FIGURE 3-17. *Partial optimization of the tables in Figure 3-16 by including the inherited attributes (name and age) in the subclass tables. We retain person_ID as the primary key to show the relationship with the tables in Figure 3-16.*

Person						
person_ID	type	name	age	passportNumber	nationality	visaType
1	citizen	John Smith	19	123-456		
2	resident	Mike Brown	23		UK	F-1
3	citizen	Sue Lee	55	987-654		
4	resident	Jeff White	24		Brazil	J-1
5	resident	Tom Chan	66		China	H-1
6	person	Julie Lyon	20			

Empty Values

FIGURE 3-18. *The combined Person table fully optimizes the three tables in Figure 3-16. Note that the third normal form is violated because some fields (such as visaType) may or may not be meaningful, depending on the value of the "type" field, which is not part of the primary key.*

TABLE 3-4. *Optimization strategies.*

OPTIMIZATION	CHARACTERISTICS	COMMENTS
Not optimized	One table for each class. Each table contains its own class attributes.	Observes table normalization.
Partially optimized	Subclass tables include inherited attributes.	Tables are normalized but the inheritance relationship is lost.
Fully optimized	Superclass table contains all attributes from subclasses.	Violates the third normal form.

This can be made very efficient with appropriate indexing of the fields. To sum up, the basic strategy to improve relational table performance is to combine tables that share the same primary key. Table 3-4 lists the optimization strategies.

Next we turn to an analysis of the same query in an object-oriented database.

3.5.2 OPTIMIZATION OF PERSISTENT OBJECTS

First we make the classes in the inheritance tree of Figure 3-15 persistent. Then we add a persons extent to the superclass Person, as shown in Figure 3-19. Because both Citizen and Resident objects are a special kind of Person object, they can be contained in the extent. The persons extent is thus analogous to the combined Person table in Figure 3-18.

The query involves only one step:

1. Select all Person objects from the persons extent (via the database root) with age greater than or equal to 65, with the object itself being an instance of class Resident, and visaType equal to H-1.

Although this process is similar to the operation for the combined table, it may not be as efficient as in the table case. This is because the table elements may be organized in a more compact way in a relational DBMS.

To improve performance, we can take advantage of the navigational efficiency of objects. Specifically, we can partition an extent into multiple subextents according to a certain key. Each subextent contains a subset of the objects in the class. We can also build multiple partitions using multiple keys, or layered partitions using structured keys. Because these subextents contain direct references to objects, searching by keys becomes highly efficient.

As an example, let's modify the design in Figure 3-19 by adding containers (subextents) that contain visa holders (who are residents). Each subextent corresponds to one visa type, which is the key for the subextent. A container in the database root (called visaTypes) holds all visaHolders subextents (Figure 3-20). This simple approach works because there exists only a small number of visa types.

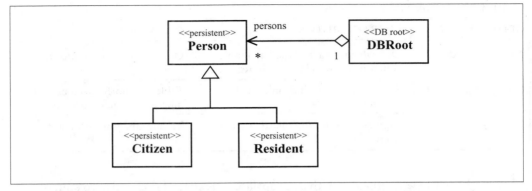

FIGURE 3-19. *Persistent object design for the inheritance tree in Figure 3-15. Note the unidirectional association with the Person objects.*

The query steps are now the following:

1. From database root visaTypes, go to the subextent for H-1 visas.
2. Select all resident objects from the H-1 subextent with age greater than or equal to 65.

Although there are two steps, the first step may dramatically cut down the number of objects that need to be searched in the second step. When there is a huge number of persistent objects, such extent partitioning is often very effective, provided that the keys take only a small number of values.

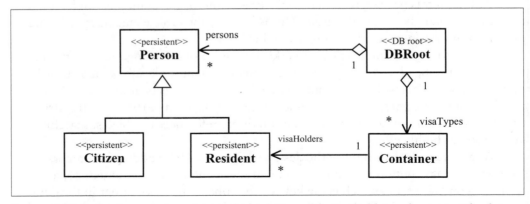

FIGURE 3-20. *An improved persistent object design with visaHolders subextents. The database root contains the persons extent and the visaTypes container.*

3.6 CASE STUDY: ATM SYSTEM SOFTWARE—PART 2

Here we revisit the ATM system software case, focusing on persistence. Based on the requirements in Section 2.10, all classes in Figure 2-33 need to be made persistent. We select the class ATM Manager to be the database root. From this root we can reach the collection of transaction records, bank information, and agents. An updated design is shown in Figure 3-21.

In Figure 3-21, an optimization feature has also been added using the subextent technique described earlier. By adding the DailyLog class, which groups the transactions by date, we can expedite the report generation of daily transactions.

3.7 CASE STUDY: SHARED WHITEBOARD—PART 2

According to the requirements in Section 2.11, the markups and annotations of the whiteboard are to be stored in CGM files. To associate a CGM file with the image that it annotates, we may set its filename to be image_name.cgm, where image_name is the filename of the image (excluding the file extension).

Thus, the CGM data are persistent representations of the glyphs and we do not need to make the glyph objects themselves persistent. Nonetheless, if we prefer to put the image and its glyphs together, we can encapsulate the image pixels and the CGM

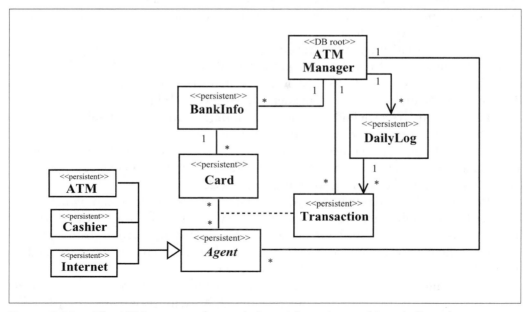

FIGURE 3-21. *The ATM system software design with persistent objects indicated.*

data in an object (for example, the ImagePort class). We may then make that object persistent. The resulting data file thus contains the complete information for the image.

3.8 CASE STUDY: A RENTAL BUSINESS—PART 1

In this case study we will design a database for SuperRent, which is a chain of entertainment rental stores owned by a friend of ours. We will find out how the stores operate and what information needs to be kept. We then use the object-oriented approach to obtain a persistent object design, which may be mapped to relational tables or may be implemented in an object-oriented database.

We will develop this case in two steps. First, during the initial analysis and design phase, we focus on a single rental store. We then extend the design to accommodate multiple stores in the chain. We will progress in an iterative way. That is, we will gather some requirements, analyze them, do some design. Then we will examine more requirements, and do more analysis and design.

3.8.1 INITIAL ANALYSIS AND DESIGN

By talking to our friend, we know that a rental store in the SuperRent chain rents videotapes to its members. Each rental item has a unique serial number and belongs to a title, which may have multiple copies for rent. A member may rent multiple items at a time. The rental rate and duration for an item depends on whether it is a new release, a promotional title, or a normal one. The store manager needs to get a daily report of all items rented each day.

We first try to identify the objects based on this information. An easy way is to pick out the nouns or physical objects in the preceding paragraph. Hence, some potential objects are Store, Videotape, Member, Item, Title, Copy, Manager, and Report. We then analyze each in some detail, as shown in Table 3-5.

From this analysis we find that the relevant objects are Store, Member, Item, and Title. They are mainly related by the collection manager pattern. Hence, Store manages a collection of Members, and Title manages a collection of Items. We may also add a Catalog to manage a collection of Titles so that Titles may be grouped into categories. The initial design is shown in Figure 3-22.

In Figure 3-22, a Member is associated with multiple Items, each of which may be rented by a member. This relationship is, however, not satisfactory because we learn from our friend that the store needs to keep a record of all rentals by member (for accounting and other purposes). This implies that each item may be associated with more than one member (through different rentals).

To accommodate this requirement, we remove the association between Member and Item and then introduce a new object—Rental. A Member or a Store may have multiple Rental objects. Furthermore, each Rental may have multiple Items, each of

TABLE 3-5.   *Analysis of potential objects.*

POTENTIAL OBJECTS	ANALYSIS
Store	Has a group of members; rents tapes to them.
Videotape	Can be rented by members. For now, it is the same as Item. If the store offers other types of rental items (such as games), then we should treat videotape as a type of item. We will leave this to the full design later.
Member	May rent items (videotapes for now).
Item	Rented by members; has a unique serial number and belongs to a title.
Title	May have multiple copies, which are the same as Item.
Copy	Is the same as Item.
Manager	Is a user of the database application, and thus is not part of the persistent object design.
Report	Is a formatted presentation derived from the persistent objects, and thus is not part of the persistent object design.

which may be rented multiple times. Each Rental originates from a store and has one renter. This gives rise to the modified design in Figure 3-23.

In Figure 3-23 we let the store manage the rentals. Thus, the store is responsible for creating the Rental objects. Each Member, on the other hand, may contain a number of Rental objects. Because of these links, Rental becomes the central object in our design.

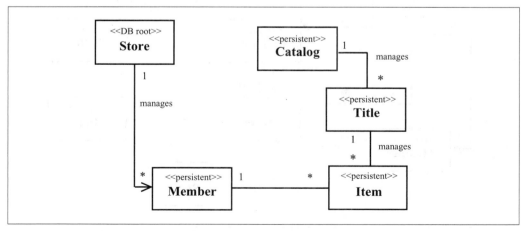

FIGURE 3-22.   *The initial design for a rental store. The association name "manages" indicates actions from left to right or top to bottom.*

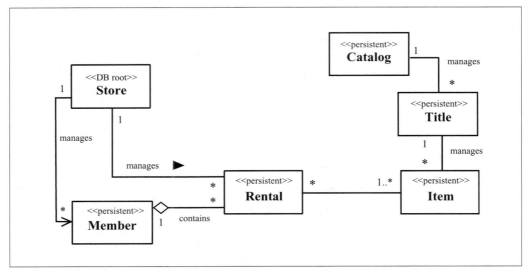

FIGURE 3-23. *A modified design for a rental store. Here a Rental object is introduced to handle multiple rentals for each item. The association names "manages" and "contains" indicate actions from left to right or top to bottom.*

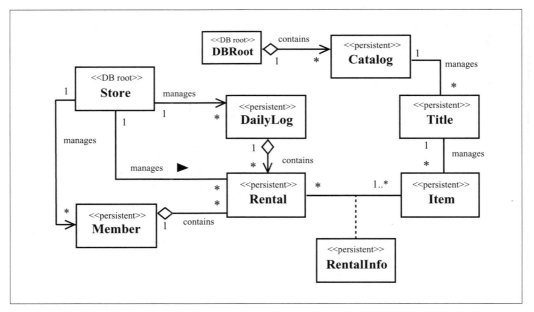

FIGURE 3-24. *The design for a single rental store. The association class RentalInfo is a core pattern of the design.*

Note that Rental is not an association class between Store and Member. This is because a specific pair (Store, Member) may be related to multiple rental objects (see the discussion of the candidate key requirement in Section 1.5.4 and near Figure 2-21).

For a specific rental, detailed information such as rate, due date, and so forth, may vary from item to item. Such rental information is therefore best modeled as an association class between Rental and Item. This association class is added as a core pattern to the design, which is shown in Figure 3-24.

In Figure 3-24 we have added a database root (DBRoot) to hold a number of catalogs. Also, the DailyLog class allows us to find rentals by date quickly. Next we continue the analysis for multiple stores.

3.8.2 FULL OBJECT DESIGN FOR MULTIPLE STORES

Being an entrepreneur, our friend plans to build an information system such that all SuperRent stores work as a whole. In particular, SuperRent will allow members to rent items from any store and return them to any store. This requires changes in the previous object design.

Rentals and members should now be managed by SuperRent, rather than a particular store. We therefore replace Store with SuperRent as the database root. However, we still need to track at which store each item is located when it is returned. For this we can let SuperRent contain a set of Store, each of which has a collection of in-store items. Also, we add a link from Rental to Store to identify where the rental originates.

Furthermore, SuperRent needs to check each rented item daily to find out whether it is returned or overdue. For marketing and planning purposes, the rental statistics of each title are needed. For example, what are the top ten video titles this month? Finally, besides videos, SuperRent also rents games, DVDs, and so forth.

To fulfill these additional requirements, we add the following features to our design. First, we use a DueDate object to hold RentalInfos of the same due date. This helps the daily check on overdue items. Second, we add subclasses like Video, Game, and so forth, under the Title class. These give rise to the final design in Figure 3-25. Because the entire rental history of any item is kept, the rental statistics can be readily generated.

Besides the core association class pattern, both the collection manager and container patterns are used. The DBRoot (database root) now also holds all the Item objects. This is useful for quickly locating an item by its serial number.

3.8.3 DETAILED OBJECT DESIGNS

Next we find out from SuperRent the information needed for each object in the design. This leads to the attributes for the classes and the detailed object designs. The operations are mostly straightforward adaptations from the corresponding patterns.

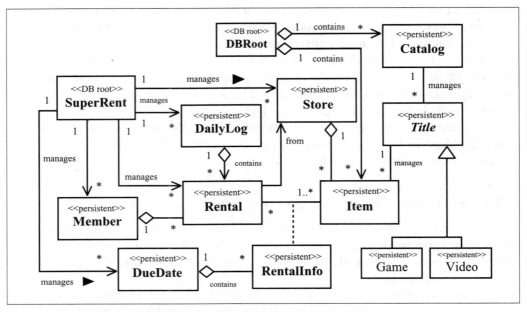

FIGURE 3-25. *The complete object design for SuperRent.*

The database root SuperRent (Figure 3-26) manages the objects Store, Member, Rental, DailyLog, and DueDate. The five `add` operations also create the corresponding objects.

The Store class is a container for the Item objects, which can be identified by their serial numbers (Figure 3-27).

SuperRent
adminPassword : String stores: Container members : Container rentals: Container dailyLogs: Container dueDates: Container
<<constructor>> SuperRent( ) SuperRent(adminPassword)   <<get & query operations>> getStores() : Store [*] getStoreCount() : Integer getStore(name : String) : Store contains(store : Store) : Boolean

```
getMembers() : Member [*]
getMemberCount() : Integer
getMember(id : Integer) : Member
getMember(name : String) : Member
contains(member : Member) : Boolean

getRentals() : Rental [*]
getRentalCount() : Integer
getRentalsBetween(dateA : Date, dateB : Date) : Rental [*]
contains(rental : Rental) : Boolean

getDailyLogs() : DailyLog [*]
getDailyLogCount() : Integer
getDailyLog(date : Date) : DailyLog
contains(dailyLog : DailyLog) : Boolean

getDueDates() : DueDate [*]
getDueDateCount() : Integer
getDueDate(date : Date) : DueDate
getDueDatesBefore(date : Date) : DueDate [*]
getDueDatesBetween(dateA : Date, dateB : Date) : DueDate [*]
contains(dueDate : DueDate) : Boolean

  <<editing>>
addStore(name : String, location : String, phone : String) :
        Store
removeStore(name : String)
removeStore(store : Store)
removeAllStores( )

addMember(id : String, name : String, address : String, phone :
          String) : Member
removeMember(id : String)
removeMember(member : Member)
removeAllMembers( )

addRental(date : Date, renter : Member, store : Store) : Rental
removeRental(rental : Rental)
removeAllRentals( )

addDailyLog(date : Date) : DailyLog
removeDailyLog(date : Date)
removeDailyLog(dailyLog : DailyLog)
removeAllDailyLogs( )

addDueDate(date : Date)
removeDueDate(date : Date)
removeDueDate(dueDate : DueDate)
removeAllDueDates( )
```

FIGURE 3-26. *SuperRent detailed object design.*

```
┌─────────────────────────────────────────────────────────────────────────┐
│                                  Store                                    │
├─────────────────────────────────────────────────────────────────────────┤
│ name : String                                                             │
│ location : String                                                         │
│ phone : String                                                            │
│ manager : String                                                          │
│ items : Container                                                         │
├─────────────────────────────────────────────────────────────────────────┤
│   <<constructor>>                                                         │
│ Store(name : String, location : String, phone : String, manager :        │
│     String)                                                               │
│   <<get & query operations>>                                             │
│ getName() : String                                                        │
│ getLocation() : String                                                    │
│ getPhone() : String                                                       │
│ getManager() : String                                                     │
│ getItems() : Item[*]                                                       │
│ getItemCount() : Integer                                                  │
│ getItem(serialNumber : Integer) : Item                                    │
│ contains(item : Item) : Boolean                                           │
│   <<editing>>                                                             │
│ addItem(item : Item) : Item                                               │
│ removeItem(serialNumber: Integer)                                         │
│ removeItem(item : Item)                                                    │
│ removeAllItems( )                                                         │
└─────────────────────────────────────────────────────────────────────────┘
```

FIGURE 3-27. *Store detailed object design.*

The Member class (Figure 3-28) contains Rental objects, which carry all the rental data for the member. There is no removeRental operation because rental items should not be removed once added. They remain in the collection as part of the member's rental history.

```
┌─────────────────────────────────────────────────────────────────────────┐
│                                 Member                                    │
├─────────────────────────────────────────────────────────────────────────┤
│ id : String                                                               │
│ name : String                                                             │
│ address : String                                                          │
│ phone : String                                                            │
│ rentals : Container                                                       │
├─────────────────────────────────────────────────────────────────────────┤
│   <<constructor>>                                                         │
│ Member(id : String, name : String, address : String, phone : String)     │
│   <<get & query operations>>                                             │
│ getId() : String                                                          │
│ getName() : String                                                        │
│ getAddress() : String                                                     │
│ getPhone() : String                                                       │
```

```
getRentals() : Rental[*]
getRentalCount() : Integer
getRental(date : Date) : Rental
contains(rental : Rental) : Boolean
  <<editing>>
addRental(rental : Rental) : Rental
```

FIGURE 3-28. *Member detailed object design.*

The Rental class (Figure 3-29) manages a set of RentalInfo objects. The store attribute records the store from which this rental is procured. The operation `addRentalInfo` will ensure there is no duplicate Item object associated with this Rental object before creating a new RentalInfo object. The operation `calculateTotalFee` calculates the total fees for the rental. Note that this fee may increase if some items become overdue. The `feePaid` attribute is updated by the operation `makePayment`.

The operation `isOverdue` will flag if there are any overdue items. The operation `isClosed` returns true if all items are returned and the full payment has been

```
                              Rental

date : Date
renter : Member
store : Store
feePaid : Float
rentalInfos : RentalInfo [*]

  <<constructor>>
Rental(date : Date, renter : Member, store : Store)
  <<get & query operations>>
getDate() : Date
getRenter() : Member
getFeePaid() : Float
getRentalInfos() : RentalInfo[*]
getRentalInfoCount() : Integer
getRentalInfo(serialNumber : Integer) : RentalInfo
getRentalInfo(item : Item) : RentalInfo
contains(rentalInfo : RentalInfo) : Boolean
isOverdue() : Boolean
isClosed() : Boolean
calculateTotalFee() : Float
  <<editing>>
addRentalInfo(item : Item) : RentalInfo
makePayment(payment : Float)
```

FIGURE 3-29. *Rental detailed object design.*

made. Again, there is no `removeRentalInfo` operation because all RentalInfo objects remain in the collection as part of the rental history.

The association class RentalInfo (Figure 3-30) encapsulates detailed rental information, including the due date and the rental rate. It also tracks the return date of each item and flags overdue status with the operation `isOverdue` (if the item has not been returned).

RentalInfo
dueDate : Date dailyRate : Float rental : Rental item : Item dateReturned : Date
<<constructor>> RentalInfo(dueDate : Date, dailyRate : Float, rental : Rental, item : Item)   <<get & query operations>> getDueDate() : Date getDailyRate() : Float getRental() : Rental getItem() : Item getDateReturned() : Date isReturned() : Boolean isOverdue() : Boolean   <<editing>> setDateReturned(date : Date)

FIGURE 3-30. *Rental Info detailed object design.*

DailyLog
date : Date rentals : Container
<<constructor>> DailyLog(date : Date)   <<get & query operations>> getDate() : Date getRentals() : Rental[*] getRentalCount() : Integer getRentalsBetween(timeA : Time, timeB : Time) : Rentals [*] contains(rental : Rental) : Boolean   <<editing>> addRental(rental : Rental)

FIGURE 3-31. *Daily Log detailed object design.*

The class DailyLog (Figure 3-31) contains a set of Rental objects. Note that there is no `removeRental` operation because a Rental should not be removed once added.

The class DueDate (Figure 3-32) contains a set of RentalInfo objects.

For Item, if the store attribute is null, then the item has been rented. Otherwise, a non-null store attribute indicates to which location the item is returned. Item contains a set of RentalInfo objects (Figure 3-33). The last one has the last rental

DueDate
date : Date rentalInfos : Container
<<constructor>> DueDate(date : Date)   <<get & query operations>> getDate() : Date getRentalInfos() : RentalInfo[*] getRentalInfoCount() : Integer contains(rentalInfo : RentalInfo) : Boolean   <<editing>> addRentalInfo(rentalInfo : RentalInfo) removeRentalInfo(rentalInfo : RentalInfo)

FIGURE 3-32. *DueDate detailed object design.*

Item
serialNumber : Integer title : Title store : Store rentalInfos : RentalInfo [*]
<<constructor>> Item(serialNumber : Integer, title : Title)   <<get & query operations>> getSerialNumber() : Integer getTitle() : Title getStore() : Store getRentalInfos() : RentalInfo[*] getRentalInfoCount() : Integer getLastRentalInfo() : RentalInfo contains(rentalInfo : RentalInfo) : Boolean   <<editing>> setStore(store : Store) addRentalInfo(rentalInfo : RentalInfo)

FIGURE 3-33. *Item detailed object design.*

information. Its `isReturned` operation should return true if the item is in a store. The store location of an item may change from one rental to another. Also, each item belongs to a title and has a unique serial number.

The class Title is an abstract one. It carries some basic data for all videos, games, and other rental titles. It manages (Figure 3-34) Items, which are copies of the same title. There is no `removeItem` operation because items should not be removed once added. The class also includes the rental code, which identifies whether the title is a new release, a promotional one, and so forth. A title belongs to a catalog.

Title
name : String description : String rentalCode : Integer catalog : Catalog items : Container
<<constructor—none since it is abstract class >>   <<get & query operations>> getName() : String getDescription() : String getRentalCode() : Integer getCatalog(): Catalog getItems() : Item[*] getItemCount() : Integer contains(item : Item) : Boolean   <<editing>> addItem(serialNumber : Integer) setRentalCode(code : Integer)

FIGURE 3-34. *Title detailed object design.*

Video
director : String cast : String duration : Integer year : Integer
<<constructor>> Video(name : String, description : String, director : String,   cast : String, duration : Integer, year : Integer)

```
    <<get & query operations>>
getDirector() : String
getCast() : String
getDuration() : Integer
getYear() : Integer
    <<editing—none except those inherited >>
```

FIGURE 3-35. *Video detailed object design.*

The classes Video (Figure 3-35) and Game (Figure 3-36) are subclasses of Title. They carry different data specific to their own class.

Finally, a Catalog (Figure 3-37) is simply a container of multiple titles.

Game
producer : String year : Integer

`<<constructor>>`
Game(name : String, description : String, producer: String, year : Integer)
   `<<get & query operations>>`
getProducer() : String
getYear() : Integer
   `<<editing—none except those inherited >>`

FIGURE 3-36. *Game detailed object design.*

Catalog
name : String titles : Container

`<<constructor >>`
Catalog(name : String)
   `<<get & query operations>>`
getName() : String
getTitles() : Title[*]
getTitleCount() : Integer
contains(title : Title) : Boolean
   `<<editing>>`
addTitle(title : Title)

FIGURE 3-37. *Catalog detailed object design.*

3.9   CASE STUDY: ACCESS CONTROL LISTS—PART 2

In part 1 of this case study we described two different designs for ACLs. Here we apply the designs to a sample case.

One of our colleagues maintains a document control system that uses a very simple form of access control. The data are stored in relational tables. There is a need to migrate the current control scheme to a more fine-grained one that can handle multiple user groups. The new scheme must also accommodate the existing scheme with minimal changes in the table structures.

Let's first examine the existing tables, then map them to an object design and investigate its migration to a fine-grained ACL. Finally, we map the resulting object design to tables.

The tables relevant to the document control system are presented as follows. The Type table (Table 3-6) lists four types of documents. The User table (Table 3-7) contains all users, each belonging to a type. The File table (Table 3-8) gives a list of documents with their paths and types. (The shaded columns represent primary keys.)

TABLE 3-6.   *Type Table.*

TYPE_ID	DESCRIPTION
1	Public
2	Internal
3	Managerial
4	Administrative

TABLE 3-7.   *User table.*

USER_ID	NAME	TYPE_ID
u_john	John	4
u_mary	Mary	3
u_jane	Jane	2
u_jack	Jack	1

TABLE 3-8.   *File table.*

FILE_ID	PATH	TYPE_ID
1	C:\data\fileA	1
2	C:\data\fileB	4
3	D:\data\fileC	2
4	F:\data\fileD	3

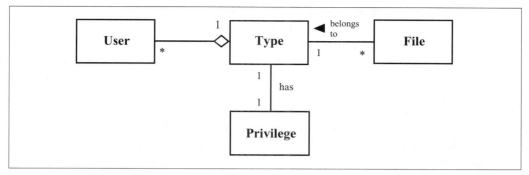

FIGURE 3-38. *The object model for the simple access control scheme. The Type object plays the role of both Group and ACL objects here. Each type of users has exactly one privilege (read-only).*

The user types effectively divide the users into groups, with an implied order. That is, a user of type 4 has all the privileges of type 3 users, and so forth. This leads to the following rule for access authorization. (Access means read-only in this case.) If user.type ≥ file.type, then access is allowed. Otherwise access is denied. For example, a user trying to access fileD must be of type ≥ 3 (managers or above).

An object model for this simple scheme can be readily constructed and is shown in Figure 3-38. This object model is a simplified form of the coarse-grained ACL in Figure 2-42. In the simple scheme, an ACL object is not used and the Type object plays the role of both Group and ACL objects. Also, each Type has exactly one privilege (read-only), which is suppressed in the tables.

For the new requirements, a user may belong to multiple groups and may have different privileges under different ACLs. Hence, the fine-grained ACL in Figure 2-40

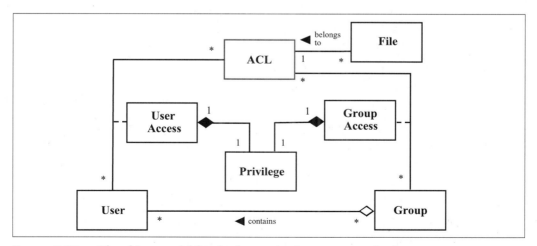

FIGURE 3-39. *The object model for the fine-grained access control scheme.*

is directly applicable. Figure 3-39 shows the new ACL design. Our challenge now is to find a migration path from the old scheme to the new one.

As we described earlier, in the old scheme the users are divided into four ordered groups. Also, the Type object plays the role of both Group and ACL objects. Thus, we may add the four types to the new Group (Table 3-9) and ACL (Table 3-10) tables.

Note that in Tables 3-9 and 3-10 we have also added four new groups and three ACLs for the project series. The User table (Table 3-11) is the same as before, except that we have renamed the foreign key type_ID to group_ID.

The group_ID in Table 3-11 indicates the original group to which a user belongs. In the new scheme, however, a user may belong to multiple groups. This information is given by the User-Group link table (Table 3-12).

The Privilege table (Table 3-13) has four rows, of which read-only is the implied access privilege in the old scheme. Note that the privileges are ordered. That is, a user having a higher privilege will be granted access to operations that require lower privileges.

TABLE 3-9. *Group table.*

GROUP_ID	NAME
1	Public
2	Internal
3	Managerial
4	Administrative
1001	Project managers
1002	Project engineers
1003	Contract controllers
1004	Company B

TABLE 3-10. *ACL table.*

ACL_ID	DESCRIPTION
1	Public
2	Internal
3	Managerial
4	Administrative
100	Project series 100/all
200	Project series 200/managers
201	Project series 200/engineers

TABLE 3-11.   *Modified User table.*

USER_ID	NAME	GROUP_ID
u_john	John	4
u_mary	Mary	3
u_jane	Jane	2
u_jack	Jack	1

TABLE 3-12.   *User-Group link table.*

USER_ID	GROUP_ID
u_john	1003
u_mary	1001
u_jack	1004

TABLE 3-13.   *Privilege table.*

PRIVILEGE_ID	DESCRIPTION
1	No access
2	Read-only
3	Read-write
4	Full control

Now the access privileges for each group are given by the GroupAccess table (Table 3-14), which corresponds to the association class GroupAccess in Figure 3-39. The setup of this table is the key to reusing the old tables, because in the old scheme a user of higher type has all the privileges of the users in lower types. For the new scheme, this translates into the following: Group 4 appears four times in the GroupAccess table and is associated with acl_ID 1 to 4. Similarly, group 3 appears three times, and so on and so forth. All ten rows for the four groups have the same read-only privilege.

The GroupAccess table also contains other new access settings for the new groups. The table UserAccess (Table 3-15) contains settings for individual users, which overwrite those from the groups (if the latter settings exist).

The File table (Table 3-16) is the same as before, except that we rename the foreign key type_ID to acl_ID.

To see how the new scheme works, let us examine fileE. Any user trying to read a file must have a privilege of at least 2. Because fileE belongs to acl_ID = 200, we

TABLE 3-14. *GroupAccess table.*

GROUP_ID	ACL_ID	PRIVILEGE_ID
1	1	2
2	1	2
2	2	2
3	1	2
3	2	2
3	3	2
4	1	2
4	2	2
4	3	2
4	4	2
1001	100	4
1001	200	4
1002	100	3
1002	201	4
1003	100	3
1003	200	3
1004	100	1
1004	200	2

TABLE 3-15. *UserAccess table.*

USER_ID	ACL_ID	PRIVILEGE_ID
u_john	100	4
u_john	200	2
u_mary	100	4
u_mary	200	4
u_jane	200	1
u_jack	100	2

TABLE 3-16.   *Modified File table.*

FILE_ID	PATH	ACL_ID
1	C:\data\fileA	1
2	C:\data\fileB	4
3	D:\data\fileC	2
4	F:\data\fileD	3
5	F:\data\fileE	200
6	F:\data\fileF	201
7	F:\data\fileG	100

begin by checking whether a user belongs to that group. The results for all four users are listed here:

- From the UserAccess table, we find that User u_john is in access list 200 and has privilege 2. Thus, he can read fileE but cannot write to it. (Note: Although according to the User-Group and AccessGroup tables, u_john is has privilege 3, it is overwritten by the individual setting in UserAccess.)

- From the UserAccess table, user u_mary is also in access list 200 and has privilege 4. Thus, she has full control of fileE.

- In contrast, u_jane is in access list 200, but has privilege 1. Thus, she cannot access fileE.

- User u_jack is not in access list 200 in the UserAccess table. So we go to the User-Group table. He belongs to group 1004, which is linked to access list 200 with a privilege level 2 in the GroupAccess table. Thus, he can read fileE but cannot write to it. (If a user has more than one privilege through different groups, the highest privilege is used.)

Next let's try to apply the new scheme to an old file, such as fileC. For fileC, which belongs to acl_ID = 2, the results for all four users are the following:

- From the User table, u_john belongs to group 4, which is linked to access list 2 with a privilege 2 in the GroupAccess table. Thus, he can read fileC (but cannot write to it).

- Similarly, u_mary and u_jane can both read fileC.

- In contrast, u_jack belongs to group 1, which is not linked to access list 2. Thus, u_jack cannot read fileC.

From this we have verified that the new scheme, in fact, covers the old one. All the original tables are reused with very minor changes. The new scheme requires five additional tables.

To sum up, the procedure for retrieving a user's privilege under a particular ACL is as follows:

1. If the user appears as an individual in the ACL, then the corresponding privilege is returned.

2. Otherwise, go through each group containing the user and collect the group privileges under the specific ACL. If multiple privileges are found, the highest one is returned.

3. Finally, if no privilege is found, then the default privilege (for example, no access) is returned.

We continue with the use cases of this case study in Section 5.11.

3.10   EXERCISES

3-1.   Map the Polygon-Point design in Figure 1-11 to relational tables. Give one or more nontrivial examples of Polygon and identify the primary key for each table. Discuss the constraints on the values in the link tables according to the multiplicity given in the figure. Which tables can be combined? Discuss the reason to combine or not to combine the tables.

3-2.   Design the relational tables for the network of Node objects in Figure 2-4a. In particular, use the postal network in Figure 2-4b to populate the tables. Include the city and country names in the nodes and the distance between the nodes in the tables.

3-3.   Does the link table in Figure 3-8 satisfy the third normal form? If not, what needs to be done to make it compliant? What kind of changes are implied in the object model? (The third normal form requires that, in addition to the second normal form, all fields that are not part of the primary key should depend exclusively on the primary key [Date 1995]. See Section 3.3 for details. Also see Figure 3-18 for an example.)

3-4.   Design a set of relational tables for the inheritance tree in Figure 3-40. Give some example records for each table. (Ignore all attributes that may appear in the object model.) Describe the steps to navigate to a D object instance (a row in the D table) starting from the A table.

3-5.   Map the FolderItem-Folder relationship loop in the left part of Figure 2-7 to tables. Treat all folder items that are not folders as files.

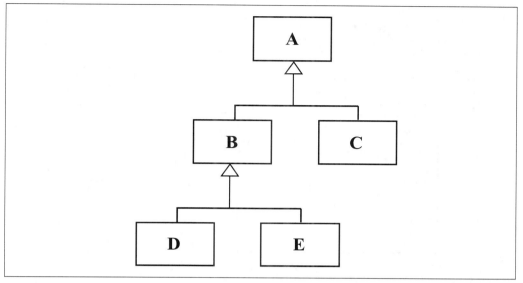

FIGURE 3-40. *Inheritance tree for Exercise 3-4.*

Include some typical attributes for the classes and give some nontrivial examples. Discuss the restrictions that apply to the values of the foreign keys in the link table. Describe the steps for the query: Find all files under the Reports folder with names that match the pattern J*.doc, assuming that there is only one folder of that name.

3-6. Extend the Trade table in Figure 3-5 by adding a transaction_ID column and renaming the table to Transaction. The transaction_ID is a primary key in the new table (Figure 3-41). It uniquely identifies a transaction between a supplier and a buyer. Thus, in this case a trade relationship is associated with multiple transactions. Give one or more object designs in the short form for the new Transaction table along with the Supplier and Buyer tables. Verify that the design maps to the tables in Figure 3-41 by using the rules in Table 3-2.

3-7. In real life, designs are often derived from data. Table 3-17 is from a software consulting firm, and it lists the current assignments of their consultants. The table obviously violates the normal form requirements. Examine the data and come up with an object-oriented design, then map the objects to normalized relational tables using the standard approach. (This can be called an *object-oriented approach to table normalization.*)

Supplier		
supplier_ID	company name	address
11	ABCD	888 3rd Ave
12	IT.com	1 Main St
13	HiTech	7 State Rd

Buyer		
buyer_ID	name	address
101	John Smith	9 Center St
102	Mike Brown	2 Union Sq
103	Sue Lee	6 Oak Blvd

Transaction					
transaction_ID	supplier_ID	buyer_ID	product	quantity	total price
1	11	103	towel	12	$60
2	11	103	battery	4	$44
3	12	102	soap	1	$3
4	13	102	towel	2	$10
5	13	101	detergent	20	$200

FIGURE 3-41. *Transaction tables for Exercise 3-6.*

3-8. Discuss the similarities and differences between the designs in Figures 3-42a and 3-42b. Assume that both mA and mB > 1. What is the root of the differences?

3-9. Are the two designs in Figures 3-43a and 3-43b equivalent? Discuss the reasons.

3-10. A cosmetics vendor has a sample invoice shown in Figure 3-44. The invoice can be used for institutional and individual customers. For institutional customers, a purchase order number (PO #) may be used, in addition to the credit card number.

TABLE 3-17. *Table for Exercise 3-7.*

NAME	SOCIAL SECURITY NUMBER	ASSIGNMENT	PERCENTAGE	HOURLY RATE	COMPANY	ADDRESS
John Smith	123-45-6789	Database work	60	$55	ABCD	888 3rd Ave
Tom Chan	582-54-5528	Network setup	40	$70	ABCD	888 3rd Ave
Mike Brown	473-55-8721	Web design	100	$80	IT.com	1 Main St
John Smith	123-45-6789	Database work	40	$60	IT.com	1 Main St
Sue Lee	743-31-3782	Database work	100	$65	IT.com	1 Main St
Tom Chan	582-54-5528	Network setup	60	$75	HiTech	7 State Rd

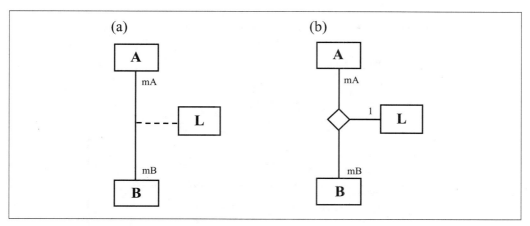

FIGURE 3-42. *Designs for Exercise 3-8.*

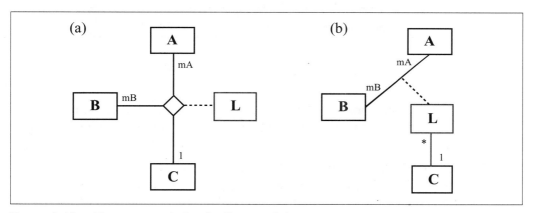

FIGURE 3-43. *Ternary association for Exercise 3-9.*

Notice that the shipment accompanying an invoice may not have everything that was ordered. Separate shipments carry the unshipped items. All such separate shipments belong to the same order and have their own total amounts.

(a) Provide a design in short form for a set of persistent objects representing all the information for such invoices. Ignore, for now, the possibility of having multiple shipments. Identify the core design pattern. Also, list the essential attributes for each class in the design. The design should support periodic queries by customer name, and sales reports by week and by item.

(b) Next, incrementally change the previous design to allow multiple shipments within an order. Also, the cosmetics vendor decided to

	Invoice				
Ship To: Jane Smith 9 Center St Cape Town, MD 20900			Date: Sep. 22, 1999		
Order #: 68822 Credit Card #: 123456789			Customer #: 1023 Customer Department #: n/a Customer PO #: n/a		
Item #	Name	Unit Price	Quantity ordered	Quantity shipped	Sub-Total
08311	Eye Cream	$20	1	1	$20
08401	Face Cream	$15	1	1	$15
08706	Toner	$18	1	1	$18
14749	Hair Gel	$15	2	2	$30
14748	Shampoo V	$20	3	0	$0
Note: Unshipped items will be billed with future shipment.				Shipment Total : $83	

FIGURE 3-44. *An invoice for Exercise 3-10.*

implement a bonus system based on sales made by their sales representatives. How would you capture this information? Provide a modified design to include these new requirements.

3-11. Map the binary associations in Figure 3-45 to tables. Can foreign key embedding be used between Session and Instructor? If it can, discuss the advantage and disadvantages. (Note: This object design is part of Figure 3-14.)

3-12. A general contracting office has a small database with the fields and tables presented in Table 3-18. Of them, the Contract table contains

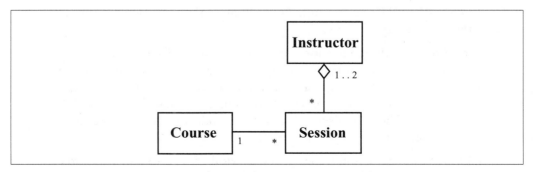

FIGURE 3-45. *Binary associations for Exercise 3-11.*

three foreign key fields (client, manager, and controller), each containing a person_ID.

Draw an object design diagram in short form for these tables. Make the objects persistent and add an appropriate database root to hold the objects.

It appears that the status of a person may change over time. For example, a manager may switch companies and may even become a client in a future contract. However, the database needs to keep historical data for all contracts. Provide a simple solution that can cover such a situation but with minimal or no changes to the current data tables.

TABLE 3-18. *Tables for Exercise 3-12.*

TABLES	FIELDS (primary key in bold)
Contract	**contract_ID**
	title
	start_date
	end_date
	amount
	client (=> person_ID)
	manager (=> person_ID)
	controller (=> person_ID)
	status
Person	**person_ID**
	lastname
	firstname
	company_ID
	phone
	fax
	email
Company	**company_ID**
	name
Note	**note_ID**
	contract_ID
	contents
	author
	date

3-13.   An object designer is designing a database to capture the work environment in her company. On the static side, the company has a job description for each employee (Person). Each employee has one supervisor. However, the work environment in the company is actually quite dynamic. A person may be involved in more than one project simultaneously. He or she may play the same role in different projects (for example, a developer working on different software components). The person may also play different roles when working on tasks for the same or different projects. For example, a person may be a project manager on one project (task being management) and a quality controller on another (task being quality assurance). Each role may involve more than one person (for example, one developer working on component A and the other working on component B).

The initial design for the persistent objects is shown in Figure 3-46. Treat the previous statements as requirements and comment on the validity of the design. Discuss any deficiencies you find and propose an improved design.

3-14.   An international dance competition is held each year. Each team in the competition consists of one man and one woman. A person can be on only one team in any year. Table 3-19 lists the scores of some teams.

Based on this information, three students proposed three different object designs for the Team table (Figures 3-47a–3-47c). Which one is correct and why?

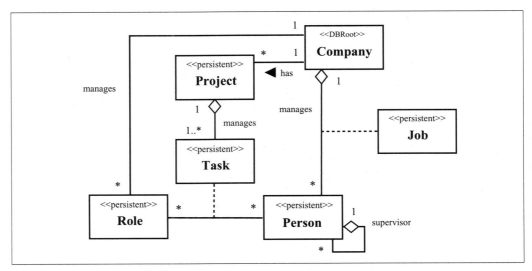

FIGURE 3-46.   *Company projects initial design.*

TABLE **3-19.** *Team table for Exercise 3-14.*

MAN	WOMAN	YEAR	SCORE
John	Sue	2000	95
Mike	Jane	2000	90
John	Mary	2001	85
Tom	Jane	2001	88
John	Sue	2002	95
Tom	Jane	2002	92

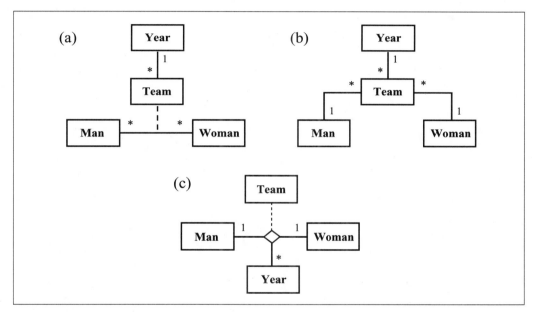

FIGURE **3-47.** *Dance team object designs for Exercise 3-14.*

Advanced Topics in Object Modeling

This chapter introduces some advanced topics in object modeling. They include abstract classes, multiple inheritance, interfaces, inner classes, collections, packages, components, and nodes. These are extensions to the basic object concepts. As a precursor to the next chapter, we describe the basic UML notations for dynamic modeling. We also discuss the reverse engineering of object designs and the identification of irreducible patterns.

4.1   ABSTRACT CLASSES

An abstract class is a superclass of at least one other class, but it may not instantiate any objects itself. This is because it only partially defines the data structure and behavior of a class of objects. The structure and behavior must then be completed in its subclasses.

Abstract classes can be used to hide different implementations of the same concept. They define the behavior of this concept, but the actual implementation is done in the subclasses. In particular, abstract classes may contain *abstract operations,* with a form or signature that is defined in the abstract classes but with an implementation that must be implemented by concrete subclasses.

Abstract classes are thus most useful for organizing class hierarchies. They enable overall object management across subclasses. The base class of an inheritance tree is often an abstract class. For example, the XML Content class in Figure 2-29 is an abstract class. Because of object substitution (see Section 1.8.2), an object reference of the base class can represent any one of its subclasses.

Template methods may also be defined in an abstract class [Gamma et al. 1995]. A template method defines the skeletal implementation of an operation by referring to abstract operations that are further defined in the subclasses. Different subclasses may therefore provide different implementations of those abstract

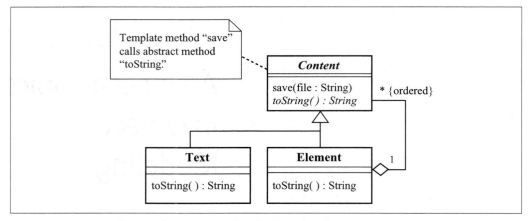

FIGURE 4-1. *Template method* `save` *in the abstract class Content. The operation* `toString()` *is abstract in the Content class. The Attr class under Element has been omitted.*

operations to attain different behaviors. For example, the XML Content class in Figure 2-29 may have a template method `save(file : String)` that does the following:

1. Opens the file and handles any errors during the process

2. Invokes `toString()` and writes the returning string to the file

3. Closes the file and returns

Figure 4-1 shows the class design with the template method `save(file : String)`, which invokes the abstract operation `toString()`. For the Text subclass, `toString()` simply returns its text data. For the Element subclass, `toString()` will first append to the returning string its tag name and its attributes list—for example, `<chapter number="1" name="Basic Concepts">`. Then it will go through its list of Content objects and invoke their `toString()`. The results from these calls are appended to the returning string. At the end of the list, a closing tag such as `</chapter>` is added.

Using the template method, the common behavior (such as opening and closing a file) is factored out, whereas the specific behavior of the subclasses is determined by an implementation of the abstract operations (such as `toString()`, which converts an XML tag to a string).

4.2 MULTIPLE INHERITANCE

In principle, a class may inherit attributes and operations from more than one class. Such multiple inheritance will work if the attributes and operational behaviors of the superclasses complement each other. However, in real life different people are likely to maintain the source code of different superclasses, and the source code itself may evolve over time. Thus, unless a strict and stable software development environment is maintained, multiple inheritance is prone to conflicts between the superclasses.

In today's fast-changing software environment, avoiding such conflicts may become a hassle. In view of this, avoiding multiple inheritance appears to be a good strategy. In fact, some languages such as Java do not allow multiple inheritance at all.

On the other hand, we may modify an object design to prune away multiple inheritance. Such workarounds often involve servant classes (delegation) or duplication of implementation [Rumbaugh 1991, p67]. For example, in Figure 4-2a, the class User-Buyer inherits from both User and Buyer. We may use Buyer as a servant class to avoid the multiple inheritance, as shown in Figure 4-2b. The behaviors of the Buyer class can then be used selectively. Alternatively, we may restructure the inheritance tree and use the handle-body pattern described in Figure 2-24.

This practice is also in line with the *separation-of-concerns philosophy* implied in object-oriented development. Developers of the superclasses need not worry much about potential conflicts with each other, whereas the subclass designers can flexibly include or exclude behaviors from the servant class.

Often, when we intend to use a class, we are primarily concerned with its interface, rather than its internal data structure or operation implementation details. For example, when we need to provide a caller with multiple sets of operations from more than one class, we need only adopt the operational signatures from those

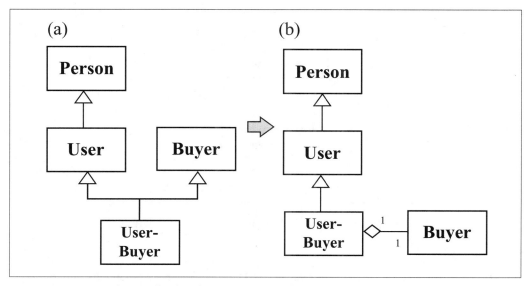

FIGURE 4-2. *Avoiding multiple inheritance using a servant class.*

classes. That is, only operational signatures need to be inherited. Such special inheritance is fulfilled by implementing *interfaces,* which we describe next.

4.3 INTERFACES

An interface specifies only the operations of a class visible to the external world without revealing its internal structure or implementation. Formally, an interface is similar to an abstract class with only abstract operations and no attributes.

To use an interface, a concrete class must implement or realize an interface. For example, the class Geometry Item in Figure 4-3 implements the operation `move()` defined in Movable. Note that the UML notation for implementing an interface is similar to that for inheritance, except that the solid line is replaced by a dashed line.

There is also a shorthand notation for interfaces implemented by a class. An interface may be displayed as a small circle with the name of the interface placed near the symbol (Figure 4-4). The circle may be attached by a solid line to the class that supports or implements it. This indicates that the class provides all operations in the interface.

Another common way of indicating interface implementation is shown in Figure 4-5. Interface A is implemented by the class A_Impl, which is a normal class that can have instances. We call such a class an interface implementation (IF Impl) class. Often, we simply draw the class notation for A_Impl, which implies that it is the implementation for interface A. Such notations appear frequently in dynamic object modeling.

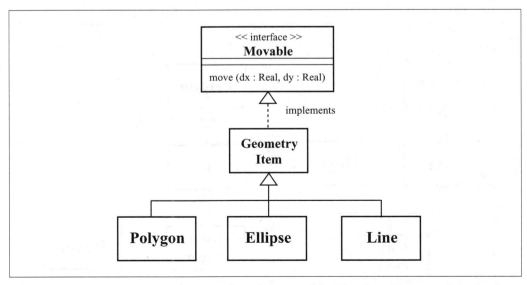

FIGURE 4-3. *UML notation of an interface class Movable. The class Geometry Item implements the operation defined in Movable.*

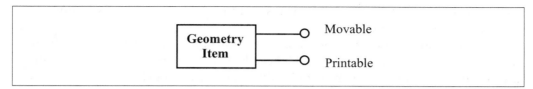

FIGURE **4-4.** *Shorthand UML notation of interfaces Movable and Printable implemented or supported by the Geometry Item class.*

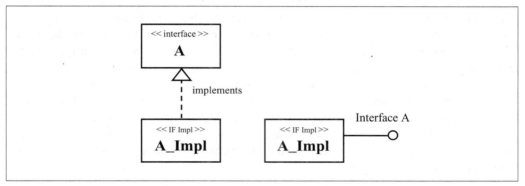

FIGURE **4-5.** *Interface A and its implementation class A_Impl. Here, IF Impl stands for interface implementation. The notation on the right has a shorthand interface notation (a circle connected to the box by a line), which may be omitted.*

As in regular classes, interfaces can have inheritance relationships. The subclass interfaces inherit all the operations of the superclass interfaces. Consequently, an inheritance tree of interfaces can be built, in which the subclass interfaces have richer or more restricted behavior than their superclasses.

In a broader context, interfaces are typically used to specify or to restrict externally visible operations of software components, such as those for a server in a client/server architecture. We discuss this in Section 5.3.

4.4   INNER CLASSES

Inner classes are used in certain languages (most notably Java) to promote object encapsulation and to make some aspects of coding more convenient. An inner class is local and contained within an outer class. The life span of an inner class object is completely subordinate to its outer class object. Because an inner class is local to its outer class, it can access private data of the outer class. An inner class object is usually dependent on the private data of its outer class. This is the main feature that makes inner classes convenient. (The same functionality can be achieved by passing arguments to an external class. This means that inner classes are simply a convenience, rather than a necessity.)

Because inner classes are not visible to the outside world, they do not participate in any static object relationship. Hence, they do not appear in static object diagrams. They may, however, play a role in dynamic object modeling.

4.5   COLLECTIONS

The notion of collection certainly goes beyond object-oriented programming. However, in object-oriented designs, especially those involving persistent objects, the choice and organization of persistent collections are crucial to the performance of the object manipulations. Here we describe some general concepts and a relatively standard set of collections.

A collection is a group of objects. A generic collection does not specify the order of the elements, or whether duplicate or null elements are allowed. In the following discussion we consider the subclasses of the generic collection. These subclasses define certain behaviors that are important to the detailed design and implementation of the objects. Table 4-1 shows different collections that can be classified by the following three behaviors:

1. **Indexing**—If a collection is indexed, its elements can be accessed efficiently via their keys. Thus an index is implemented by a keyed data structure. Each key can map to at most one element. In this regard a key is similar to the primary key in a relational table. Among the collections, Set and Bag do not use any key, and therefore they are not indexed. The rest of the collections all have indices, which can be ordered or unordered:

   • An unordered index is best for exact-match queries and can be implemented by a hash table. Examples in Table 4-1 are Dictionary and Map,

TABLE 4-1.   *The behaviors of different collections. Also shown are some examples of each type of collection.*

| COLLECTION | INDEXING | | DUPLICATES | NULLS | EXAMPLES |
	KEY	ORDERING			
Set	No	—	No	No	Set
Bag	No	—	Yes	No	Bag
Dictionary/Map	Yes	No	Yes	Yes	Hash table, tree map
List/Sequence	Yes	Yes	Yes	No	Linked list
Array	Yes	Yes	Yes	Yes	Array, vector

which use the hash codes of the keys to build the hash table. The keys can be any objects that have hash functions to generate hash codes.

- An ordered index optimizes range queries, such as a price between $12 and $20. It can be implemented with linked lists, expandable arrays, or binary trees.

2. **Duplicates**—A Set does not allow duplicate elements, whereas a Bag does. The rest of the collections generally allow duplicates because each element is indexed.

3. **Nulls**—Some collections do not allow null elements. Set and Bag have no keys, and therefore do not store any null elements. List contains only non-null elements by definition.

Note that the names of the collections in Table 4-1 may differ from those used in specific languages or library packages.

The key to high performance in persistent object manipulation is to optimize object access for critical operations. Remember that an index is a keyed data structure for accessing objects in a collection. We may build layered keys or multiple indices on different keys for a single collection of objects.

4.6 PACKAGES

Packages are containers to organize and mange object model elements, such as classes. A package contains a group of model elements. For a group of classes, they together perform a self-consistent set of functions. For example, the Java Windowing Toolkit java.awt contains classes for graphical user interfaces (GUIs) in a Windows environment. Likewise, java.awt.image has classes for creating and modifying images.

Because a package itself is considered a kind of model element, it may be part of another package. However, each element can be owned by only a single package. Hence, the package hierarchy forms a strict tree, and the packages can be used as the bases for configuration management and access control. Also, packages can cross-reference each other, thereby creating dependency between them.

Based on this description of packages, we arrive at the object diagram in Figure 4-6. It has a typical backward containment with a leaf node (Class). We note that in the UML model there are more intermediate classes between Model Element and Package. Examples include Name Space, Generalizable Element, and Classifier. These details are omitted in Figure 4-6.

Dependency is treated as an association class in Figure 4-6. It describes the relationship between Model Elements (such as between packages). Note also that Model Element is an abstract class.

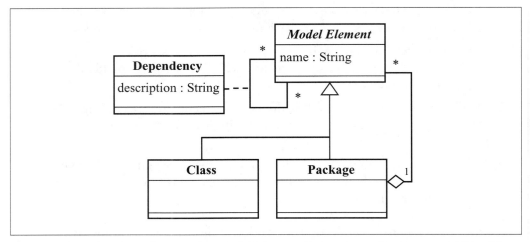

FIGURE 4-6. *The object diagram for Model Element, Dependency, Package, and Class. Note that Model Element is an abstract class.*

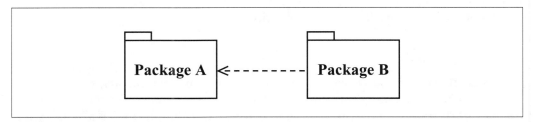

FIGURE 4-7. *Package B depends on or uses certain features of Package A.*

In UML, a package is shown as a large rectangle with a small rectangular "tab" on the upper left corner (like a manila folder). If the contents of the package are not shown, then the name of the package is placed within the large rectangle. If they are shown, then the name of the package may be placed within the tab. Dependency is represented by a dashed arrow, as shown in Figure 4-7.

4.7   COMPONENTS

A software system is typically implemented in a number of components. Put another way, a component represents a piece of an implementation that can be deployed and used in a system. It interacts with other system components and provides a set of functions to the system. Example components include source code and binary code (dynamic link libraries, executables, and so on).

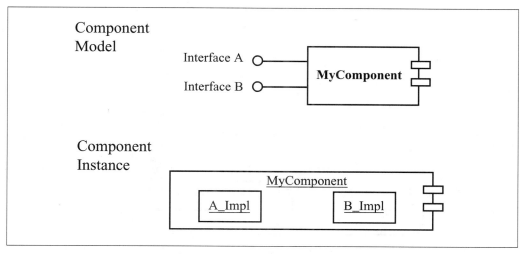

FIGURE 4-8. *Notations for a component with two interfaces. Here, A_Impl stands for the implementation of interface A (similarly for B_Impl).*

Components are more related to implementation and runtime behavior of objects than to object design. Like classes, components can have instances when they are deployed in a real system. A component instance represents a runtime unit, which may contain multiple object instances. The same component may be deployed multiple times, corresponding to multiple component instances.

In UML, a component model is shown as a rectangle with two small rectangles protruding from its left side (Figure 4-8). A component may support certain interfaces, which are usually shown as small circles connected to the side of a component. For component instances, one may put the interface implementation objects inside the component box. These implementation objects are, however, hidden from the external world except via the operations defined by the interfaces.

4.8 NODES

A node is a runtime physical object that has processing capability, such as a workstation or a server. A node may contain component instances and other physical things such as databases. These components live or run on the node. Node is part of the UML deployment diagram, which is a graph of nodes connected by communication channels (connectors). In UML, nodes are denoted by cubical blocks, as shown in Figure 4-9.

Although it is possible to have node types and node instances, as in object classes and instances, we will not make this distinction for nodes, and generally we

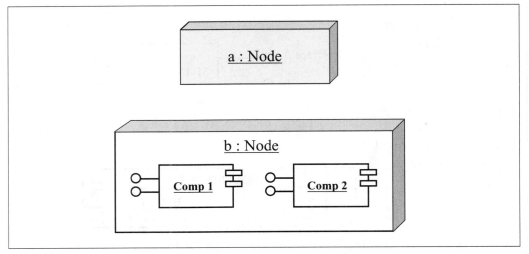

FIGURE 4-9. *UML notations for nodes. Here, node b contains two components, Comp 1 and Comp 2.*

treat nodes as instances. We feel that this makes nodes more akin to runtime physical objects.

In Chapter 7 we use nodes extensively in our architecture diagrams. A description of architecture diagrams is given in Section 7.1.

4.9 UML NOTATION BASICS FOR DYNAMIC MODELING

As a precursor to Chapter 5, we describe briefly the basic UML notations for dynamic object modeling. The notations are summarized in Figure 4-10.

A use case documents a sequence of events between a system and a user (an actor). A system may have one or more use cases, which describe how the system is typically used. These use cases can be organized and displayed with use case diagrams, as in Figure 4-10a.

For a use case, its sequence of message exchanges between the actor and the system may be documented in a table with two columns (one for the actor, the other for the system). As we further analyze the activities within the system, we may depict the interaction between different system components or objects by sequence diagrams.

A sequence diagram depicts a set of message exchanges among object instances and an actor (for example, a user). In Figure 4-10b, time progresses vertically downward. The solid arrows denote operation invocations, including the creation of objects. A dashed arrow indicates the return of control to the caller. The thick vertical

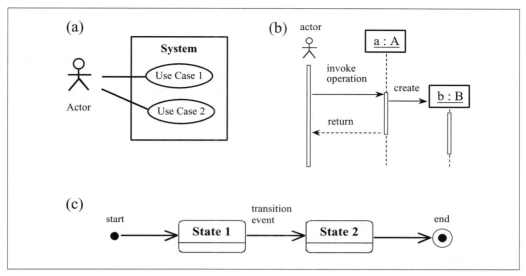

FIGURE 4-10. *Basic UML notations for dynamic modeling. (a) A use case diagram. (b) A sequence diagram. (c) A statechart diagram.*

bars (or tall thin rectangles) represent the activation span of objects. During activation, an object is performing an action either directly or through a subordinate procedure.

Finally, a system or an object may exist in a number of discrete states. In this case we may use a statechart diagram to record the entire life cycle of the system or the object. As in Figure 4-10c, the statechart diagram summarizes the states of a system or an object, along with the transition events between states. The transition events typically correspond to certain use cases for the system. We discuss more details of these notations and their usage in Chapter 5.

4.10 REVERSE ENGINEERING AND IRREDUCIBLE PATTERNS

As in any design work, object design is an iterative process. We go back and forth between requirement analysis and design to consolidate and refine our ideas. In this regard, reverse engineering of object designs is a useful approach.

Suppose we arrive at a draft design. We can analyze its object relationships and identify its functions, pretending that we do not know what it was for. We can then compare the findings with the original requirements. This reverse-engineering process often reveals unforeseen features in the draft design that are in conflict with the requirements, or even vague areas in the requirements that may need clarification.

In analyzing object designs, an effective technique is first to identify the *irreducible patterns*. Irreducible patterns are the minimal building blocks in an object design that carry a meaningful or self-contained set of functions. Most of the static design patterns in Chapter 2 (and the interface patterns in Chapter 6) are such irreducible patterns commonly found in real-life designs. Decomposing a complex design into irreducible patterns helps us isolate the structures and functions of the design.

As an example, we show in Figure 4-11 a draft object design for a hierarchical network. The classes Network and Node are subclasses of the abstract class Module. They uniquely identify a Link object. The irreducible patterns contained in this design are

- **Backward relationship loop**—between the classes Module and Network

- **Object managers**—Network and Node managing Link objects

- **Binary association class**—Link as the association class for the pairs (Node, Module) and (Network, Module). (Note: Using the rule in Figure 2-21, we can identify Link as the association class.)

Using these patterns, we can infer the structure and possible functions of the design. Furthermore, the recognition of these patterns allows us to tighten the design by pruning redundant features. For example, Link is also the association class between Node and Network. Exercise 4-3 deals with these issues.

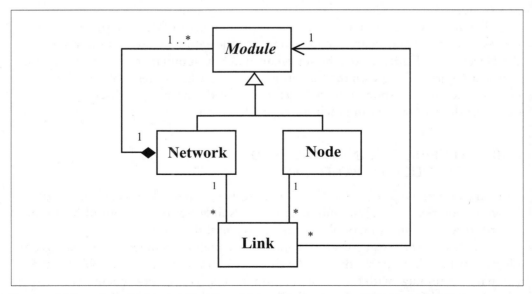

FIGURE 4-11.   *A draft object design for a hierarchical network. Note that Module is an abstract class.*

4.11 EXERCISES

4-1. Identify the abstract classes in the Java Abstract Windowing Toolkit package (java.awt).

4-2. The following is a representative list of classes in the java.awt package. Note that all classes are a subclass of java.lang.Object. Draw a diagram showing the dependencies between the related packages (java.lang, java.io, java.awt, java.awt.event, java.awt.image).

- Class java.awt.AWTEventMulticaster (implements java.awt.event.ActionListener, ...)
- Class java.awt.Component (implements java.awt.image.ImageObserver, java.awt.MenuContainer, java.io.Serializable)
  - Class java.awt.Button
  - Class java.awt.Canvas
  - Class java.awt.Checkbox (implements java.awt.ItemSelectable)
  - Class java.awt.Choice (implements java.awt.ItemSelectable)
- Class java.awt.Event (implements java.io.Serializable)
- Class java.awt.MenuComponent (implements java.io.Serializable)

4-3. Using the irreducible patterns found for the draft object design in Figure 4-11, infer the structure and possible functions of the design. Provide an example of the hierarchical network structure. Present a possible simplification of the design.

4-4. Two students come up with two different object designs (Figures 4-12a and 4-12b) for libraries that lend books to borrowers. Explain the reason behind each design. Which one is better? Give a design (in short form) that combines the strength of both. Identify the irreducible patterns in your design. Note that a library can loan books to other libraries, besides individuals.

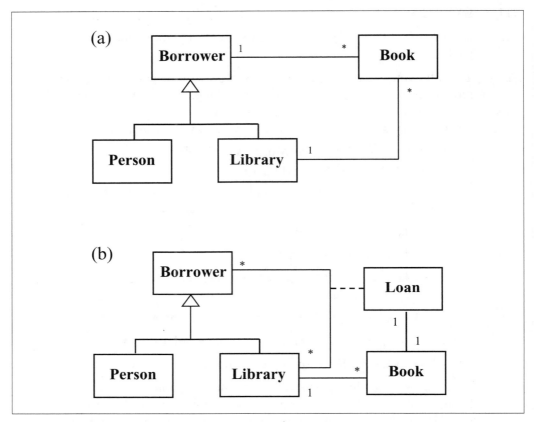

FIGURE **4-12.**   *Borrowing books object designs for Exercise 4-4.*

Dynamic Object Modeling Basics

Our focus so far has been on static design and modeling, in which we identify the object classes and their static relationships. The topic in this chapter is modeling the dynamic behavior of objects. Dynamic modeling describes the pattern of communication between objects that are linked together in static designs. Such dynamic behavior can be derived from use case analyses and documented with object sequence diagrams. In this chapter we also introduce the important concepts of client/server and distributed objects.

5.1   USE CASE ANALYSES

A use case describes how a software system is typically used. Thus, anyone building the system must have at least one use case in mind. More formally, a use case documents a sequence of events for an end-to-end process between a system and its user (called an *actor*). Use case-driven object modeling and analysis is a useful approach to software development [Jacobson et al. 1992, Rosenberg & Scott 1999].

Use cases are *not* requirements, but they illustrate and imply requirements. They are therefore very useful in understanding the desired behavior of a system and in deriving detailed requirements. A complex system often has many use cases, which may be organized into a hierarchy. When analyzing the system requirements, you should identify a handful of critical or high-priority use cases—those that the system must support. The design should initially be driven by these use cases, and then later should be refined with other use cases.

The UML use case diagram is mainly for organizational purposes. As shown in Figure 5-1, a phone user (the actor) interacts with the telephone system to make a calling card call or a collect call. There may be more actors in the system who use these two use cases or other additional use cases. One use case may also use or extend another use case. The use case diagram allows us to display multiple use cases

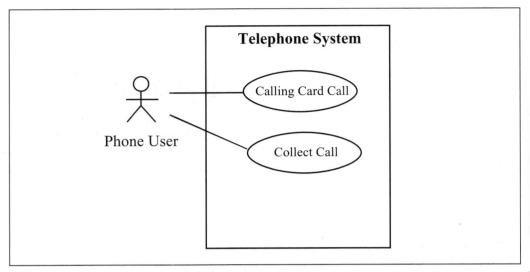

FIGURE 5-1. *A UML use case diagram with two use cases. The actor (the stick figure) is a phone user who interacts with the telephone system to make a calling card call or a collect call.*

with such "use" or "extend" relationships. Here, instead of drilling into these details, we concentrate on the more important aspect—use case analysis.

In a use case analysis, the first thing is to identify the system and the actor. The system can be the whole software system being designed, or it can be a component or package within the whole system. The actor is external to the system. It interacts with the system by sending and receiving messages. Note that the actor can be a human being or a different software component.

As an example, let us examine the use case of making a phone call with a calling card. The system is the telephone company's switching and billing system (we do not distinguish the two for now). The actor is the card holder. The use case is presented as a list of actions taken by the actor and the system (Figure 5-2).

As shown in Figure 5-2, each action generates a signal or a message, which in turn triggers the next action. Thus, a use case can be viewed as a sequence of message exchanges between the actor and the system. This naturally leads to the UML sequence diagram, which we discuss in Section 5.2.

The keys to use case analyses are summarized as follows:

- Define a clear boundary for the system with which the actor interacts.

- Organize and name use cases from the actor's usage perspective, rather than from the compositional or object-oriented breakdown of the system.

Use Case: Making a phone call with a calling card
Actor: A phone user with a calling card
Description: This use case describes the scenario of a calling card holder
making a telephone call.
Typical course of events:

ACTOR	SYSTEM
Picks up the phone.	Gives a dial tone.
Dials access phone number.	Plays a greeting message.
Enters card number, access code, and phone number.	Authenticates the number and code. Connects the call on success. Returns a message on failure.
Proceeds with the call . . .	
Ends the call by hanging up the phone.	Logs the call information to the card holder's account.

FIGURE 5-2. *Sample use case.*

- Focus on the critical use cases first.

- Write the sequence of events from the actor's point of view. Present *what* the actor sees from the system, rather than how the system does things.

- Discuss the use cases with the customer or other potential users.

5.2   SEQUENCE DIAGRAMS

In general, objects interact with each other by sending messages. The receiving object performs work by invoking certain operations and returns the results to the sending object. This process is similar to function calls in procedural programming. (Most messages go to object instances. Some, notably static methods, may go to object classes.)

A sequence diagram depicts a set of message exchanges among object instances in a use case (or a collaboration within a use case). This is in contrast to a use case table, which does not specify the messages between objects. As an example, we show in Figure 5-3 the sequence diagram for adding a user in the collection manager of Section 2.1. (The UserManager class uses the Container class as in Exercise 2-1.)

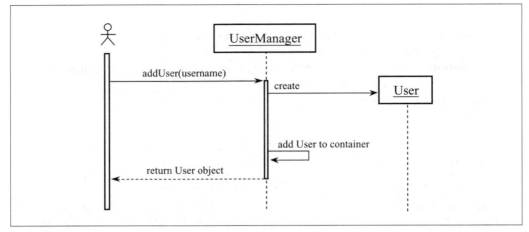

FIGURE 5-3. *The sequence diagram for adding a user in the collection manager of Section 2.1. The actor (the stick figure) initiates the sequence, which ends when a User object is returned to the actor. Note that all objects are object instances. The object names are suppressed and the class names are underlined.*

Time flows vertically downward in Figure 5-3. The solid arrows denote method calls such as addUser. A dashed arrow indicates the return of control to the caller. Such return arrows are optional and are often omitted. Note that an object may invoke its own methods, in which case the arrows point back to the object itself. Method calls that create objects have arrows pointing directly at the new object instances.

The thick vertical bars (or tall thin rectangles) represent the activation span of objects. During activation, an object is performing an action either directly or through a subordinate procedure. Objects created but not activated exist in time as dashed lines (called *lifelines*). For initial dynamic designs, one may often omit the details of activation and simply draw a vertical lifeline.

As a more involved example, consider the static design diagram in Figure 5-4, which is extracted from Figure 2-26 of Section 2.7 (by omitting the Schema Manager side). Here, Catalog contains a hierarchy of Part objects, which in turn have multiple Attributes.

The sequence diagram for adding a new part to an existing parent part and then adding new attributes to the new part is shown in Figure 5-5. The Client is an object external to the Catalog. Because the Catalog object contains a hierarchy of parts, it needs to find the parent part before creating the new part and adding it to the parent. Subsequently, multiple Attribute objects are created and added to the new part.

UML also has notations that distinguish blocking messages (function calls) and nonblocking messages (queued messages). The default is blocking, which behaves like regular function calls. We do not elaborate on nonblocking messages here.

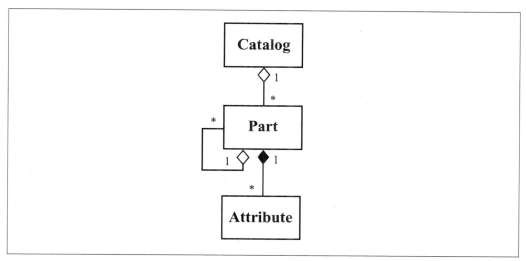

FIGURE 5-4. *The Catalog-related classes extracted from Figure 2-26.*

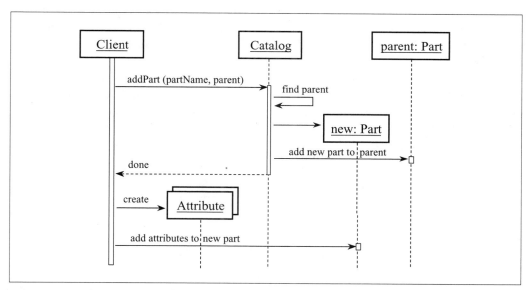

FIGURE 5-5. *The sequence diagram for adding a new part to an existing parent part in a catalog. Note that multiple Attribute objects are created by the Client.*

Sequence diagrams are a type of interaction diagram in UML. The other type is a collaboration diagram. Either one can be used for dynamic modeling, although we use only sequence diagrams in this book because they reveal the sequences in time more directly.

5.3 THE CLIENT/SERVER MODEL AND DISTRIBUTED OBJECTS

Using the sequence diagram, one may introduce a very important concept in software design: the client/server model. As shown in Figure 5-6, a client object invokes a `server` method by sending a message to the server object. The server object executes the corresponding operation and returns the results to the client object.

Obviously, the client/server model is asymmetric. The server passively waits for messages from the client. Except for returning the results of a method invocation, the server does not influence the client in any way.

The design principle of the client/server model is that the server does not reveal any details of the data structure and the implementation of its operations. Hence, all server parameters can only be accessed via operations. The visible behavior of a server object can be defined by an *interface*, which specifies all public operations of the server object. More precisely, the server object implements the interface definition. It is therefore an interface implementation object (denoted by IF Impl).

Taking this one step further, you may have multiple server objects in one or more server components. The client object may invoke methods of these server objects (Figure 5-7). Such separation of objects across a client and one or more servers is a characteristic of the client/server paradigm, and the objects are called *distributed objects*. (Note that they are distributed statically at design time, rather than at runtime.)

The client object and the server objects are statically unrelated. They only interact with each other at runtime. Moreover, they may be implemented in different programming languages (for example, server in C++ and client in Java). At runtime they

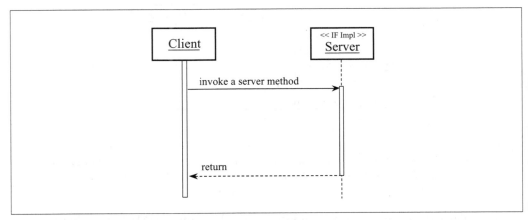

FIGURE 5-6. *The client/server model. Note that Server is an interface implementation (denoted by IF Impl) object, which implements certain interfaces for the client/server interaction.*

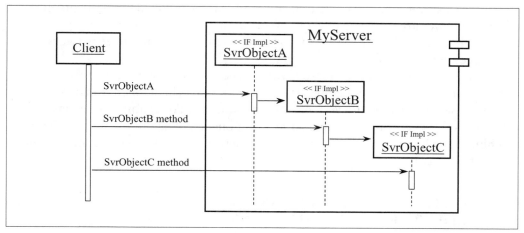

FIGURE 5-7. *Distributed objects in a client/server environment. In this case the server objects (interface implementation objects) are all in one server component (MyServer).*

belong to different address spaces in the same machine or they may even reside in different computers connected by a network (such as the Internet, in Figure 5-8). Because of this, new server objects can only be created by other objects already in the server, and the initial server object (or set of server objects) is created when the server starts up. For example, in Figure 5-7, SrvObjectB is created by SrvObjectA, and SrvObjectC is created by SrvObjectB. In short, a client object cannot directly create server objects.

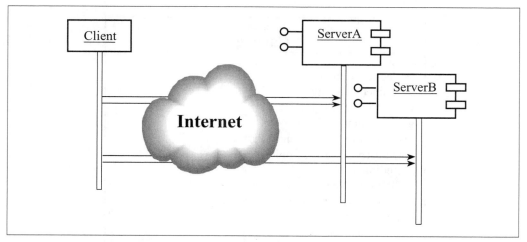

FIGURE 5-8. *Client/servers over the Internet. All method invocations go through the network (the Internet cloud). The server components ServerA and ServerB may contain multiple interface implementation objects.*

Once a server object is created, its methods can be invoked by its clients. If the client and server are connected by a network, all method invocations must go through that network. It is important to keep this in mind to minimize network traffic when designing a client/server system.

Finally, a server object can also invoke objects in other servers. For the duration of the call, the calling object plays the role of a client. Such transparency makes the server architecture very flexible and scalable. For example, one may distribute server objects onto multiple server components, which may run on different machines. The Enterprise JavaBeans (EJB) framework is built on such components (see Section 7.12).

5.4 INTERFACE DEFINITION AND CLIENT/SERVER DEVELOPMENT

For the client to talk to a server, a contract must exist between the two. Such a contract, or *interface definition*, specifies the interface classes and their methods, along with input, output, and return data structures. Figure 5-9 shows the interface definition for the Catalog interface. It is a modified version of the collection manager design in Figure 2-1. We have included only those operations on parts that are directly under Catalog. Note that an interface has only operations and no attributes.

Depending on the interface design strategy, the Part in Figure 5-9 can be another interface class, or it can be a simple data structure (a class with data members only).

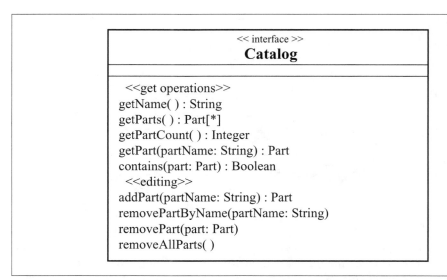

FIGURE 5-9. *The interface definition for the Catalog interface.*

The symbol Part [*] represents a sequence of Part objects. For simplicity we assume that each part has a unique name. Hence, we can use it to locate a particular part with the operations `getPart` and `removePartByName`. (We choose to make all operation names unique so that the interface definition may be applied to a wide range of programming languages.) This example is for illustration only. For a real design you need to consider issues such as recursive operation on the hierarchy of Part objects.

The typical process of developing client and server components is shown in Figure 5-10. After completing the interface definition, an Interface Compiler generates a stub code on the client side and a skeleton code on the server side. The stub code and skeleton code are specific to certain programming languages. Software developers can then separately add detailed code for the client and server, and compile them.

The use of interface definitions has clear advantages. Once an interface is defined, the client and server code can be developed in parallel, as shown in Figure 5-10. As long as the interface remains the same, changes on either the client or the server side will not break the application on either side.

Because interfaces are object oriented, they enjoy all the benefits of object-oriented programming. For instance, they can be extended by subclass interfaces. They can be modified locally without affecting other interfaces or classes. Furthermore, interface definition can be made neutral to programming languages. For example, it can be specified by UML, as in Figure 5-9. This allows the client and server to be implemented in

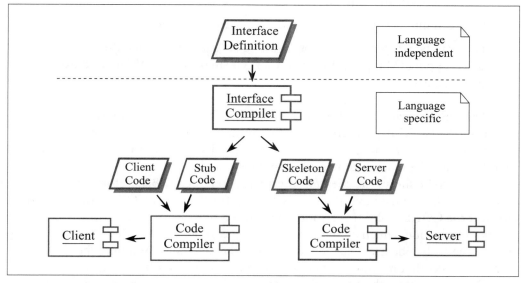

FIGURE 5-10. *The client/server development process, which results in the client and server components. Note that the client and server may be implemented in different programming languages.*

different programming languages, making distributed objects interoperable. In particular, in today's distributed and Internet-centric environments, this technique enables the integration of legacy systems into more modern architectures. To make these a reality, a distributed object infrastructure and an interface definition based on an open standard is indispensable. The following section describes such a standard.

5.5   THE CORBA STANDARD

A widely adopted standard for distributed object architecture is CORBA (Common Object Request Broker Architecture), which was developed by the OMG. With more than 700 member organizations, the OMG is the world's largest software consortium. Since 1989, the mission of the OMG has been the specification of an architecture for an open software bus, called *Object Request Broker* (ORB), on which object components written by different vendors can interoperate across networks and operating systems. The first version of CORBA was adopted by the OMG in 1991, and version 3 was adopted in 1999 [OMG/CORBA 1999]. This section gives an overview of CORBA. For other references, please refer to [Mowbray & Ruh 1997, Orfali et al. 1995, Otte et al. 1995].

   CORBA is based on a client/server model, and therefore all CORBA objects are server-side interface implementation objects. They differ from traditional objects in that

- They can be located anywhere on a network
- They can interact with objects on other computer platforms
- They can be written in any programming language for which there is interface mapping (Mappings for Java, C++, C, SmallTalk, COBOL, and Ada are currently specified.)

The ORB provides an infrastructure for distributed object computing in CORBA. The CORBA standard allows distributed objects to invoke methods of remote objects either statically or dynamically. A client does not need to know in what language the requested objects are implemented.

   Figure 5-11 shows the client/server interaction in CORBA. Before sending a request, the client must have an object reference for the target CORBA object on the server. If the CORBA object is remote (on a different machine), the object reference points to stub code, which contains a proxy object representing a remote server object. The stub code uses the ORB to identify the machine containing the server object and asks that machine's ORB for a connection to the object's server.

   Once connected, the stub code sends the object reference and parameters to the skeleton code via the basic object adaptor (BOA), which helps map the object reference to the target object, and enforces certain object activation policies (for

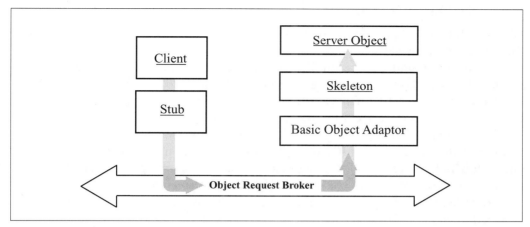

FIGURE 5-11. *Client/server interaction in CORBA.*

example, a thread policy). The skeleton code then transforms the call and parameters into the appropriate implementation-specific format and calls the target server object. Any results or exceptions are returned along the same path.

In this process, the client has no knowledge of the CORBA object's physical location, implementation details, or the type of ORB used. Different ORBs may communicate via the Internet Inter-ORB Protocol (IIOP), which was adopted by the OMG in 1996. IIOP runs on top of Transmission Control Protocol/Internet Protocol (TCP/IP) and is robust, scalable, and transaction oriented. It allows any CORBA client to communicate with any CORBA server object.

The CORBA standard also defines a set of services that provides utilities for distributed object computing. Examples include the following:

- **Naming Service**—Allows a CORBA server to register any of its objects with the Naming Service, assigning each a hierarchical name (for example, company.department.division). The name allows a client to locate the object, regardless of its physical location.

- **Event Service**—Allows any CORBA object to send a message to any number of receivers asynchronously.

- **Security Service**—Provides secured object invocation and message passing.

- **Persistent Service**—Enables CORBA objects to become persistent objects in databases [Sessions 1996].

Finally, a CORBA client itself can contain CORBA server objects, and a CORBA server object may act as a client to other CORBA server objects.

5.6   INTERFACE DEFINITION LANGUAGE

Along with CORBA, the OMG specifies the Interface Definition Language (IDL) as the standard for interface definition. As a standard adopted by the International Organization for Standardization, IDL is a very simple language, with syntax similar to that of C++ or Java. An interface defined by IDL can also be represented by a UML interface class. A CORBA client may invoke only those methods specified in the CORBA object interface using IDL.

IDL is mapped to a programming language to provide access to object interfaces from that language. An IDL compiler translates the interface definition to the client stub and the server skeleton under a specific programming language according to the appropriate mapping. The client and server implementations are then added and compiled to yield the client and server code. This is the same as the process depicted in Figure 5-10.

As an example, we provide the IDL code for the Catalog interface of Figure 5-9:

```
module pdm {

  exception PdmError {
    string message;
  };

  struct Attribute {
    string name;
    double value;
    string unit;
  };

  typedef sequence<Attribute> AttributeList;  // type
    definition

  struct Part {
    string name;
    AttributeList attributes;
    sequence<Part> components;  // a recursive structure
  };

  typedef sequence<Part> PartList;

  interface Catalog {

    // get operations
    string getName();       // name of the Catalog
```

```
    PartList getParts( );   // a list of all parts
    long getPartCount( );   // the number of parts
    Part getPart(in string partName)
      raises (PdmError);
    boolean contains(in Part part);


    // editing operations
    Part addPart(in string partName, in AttributeList
      attributes, in PartList components)
      raises (PdmError);
    void removePartByName(in string partName)
      raises (PdmError);
    void removePart(in Part part)
      raises (PdmError);
    void removeAllParts();
  };


  };
```

As we can see, the IDL syntax is very similar to that of C++. The Catalog interface is part of an interface module named pdm (product data manager). Along with Catalog, two struct types are defined: Attribute and Part. They facilitate the transfer of data as input or return values of the operations. Note that Part is recursive: Its components form a sequence of Parts. An IDL compiler will map these struct types into data structures (for example, C++) or a class without operations (for example, Java).

The operations in the interface are the same as in Figure 5-9 except that two additional input arguments `attributes` and `components` are added to the operation `addPart()`. This is because we have chosen to model Part as a struct type, which does not have any operations for editing its data. We could have modeled Attribute and Part as interfaces, thereby allowing them to have their own operations, such as adding or removing the attributes of a part.

Besides operations and variable types, exceptions can also be defined, as in the PdmError exception. An operation may raise one or more exceptions when an error condition arises. The signature of an operation is therefore defined by its name, parameters, return type, and exceptions. The client code needs to handle both user-defined exceptions and CORBA standard exceptions.

Finally, note that in IDL all operation names in an interface must be unique. Thus, we have used different names for the two remove operations in the previous IDL code.

IDL supports basic (boolean, char, float, double, long, short, string, and so on), compound (struct, including recursive feature), list (sequence), and enumerated (enum) data types. (There are some more types.) Also, an interface can inherit from other interfaces, as in normal object classes. Inheritance is the only static relationship between interfaces. Although in IDL you can define attributes for interfaces, we view this as an implementation issue and generally refrain from including attributes in interfaces.

Tables 5-1 and 5-2 show the IDL-to-Java mapping defined by the OMG [OMG/IDL 1999].

All interfaces are to be implemented by concrete classes, with instances that become CORBA objects. Following the convention in Figure 4-5, we denote the implementation of interface A by A_Impl. Figure 5-12 is a sequence diagram showing a client accessing the CORBA object A_Impl on a server.

TABLE 5-1.   *IDL type-to-Java type mapping.*

IDL TYPE	JAVA TYPE
boolean	boolean
char, wchar	char
octet	byte
string, wstring	java.lang.String
short, unsigned short	short
long, unsigned long	int
long long, unsigned long long	long
float	float
double	double
any	org.omg.CORBA.Any
Object	org.omg.CORBA.Object

TABLE 5-2.   *IDL construct-to-Java construct mapping.*

IDL CONSTRUCT	JAVA CONSTRUCT
module	package
interface	interface*
constant	public static final field or class
enum, struct, union	public final class*
sequence, array	array*
exception	public final class*

With additional helper and holder classes.

The sequence of events in Figure 5-12 are as follows. The main server object initializes an ORB, which in turn starts a BOA. The server then creates the CORBA object A_Impl and sends a message to the BOA indicating that the A_Impl object is ready. After this, the server waits for calls from the client.

Later, the client initializes another ORB and tries to bind to the remote object A (using a marker or server object name). The client ORB communicates with the server ORB, which uses the BOA to obtain a reference to the CORBA object A_Impl. For the client, only the reference to the remote object A is important. This reference allows the client to issue calls to A_Impl's operations.

Other CORBA objects must be created by the main server object or by existing CORBA objects (such as A_Impl) before they can be used by the client.

We note that there are multiple ways to obtain an initial object reference:

1. Use a `bind` call with a server object name as mentioned earlier.

2. Use the CORBA Naming Service, which contains a hierarchy of registered object references and their names.

3. Use a CORBA Interoperable Object Reference, which is a string representation of an object reference and can be retrieved from a local text file, a Web server, or a dedicated socket connection.

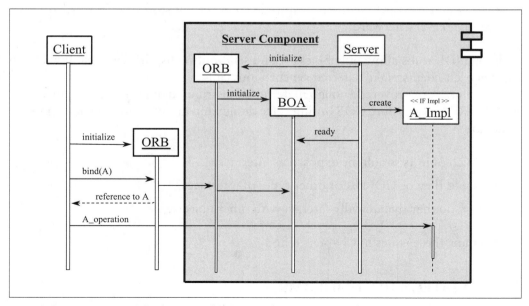

FIGURE 5-12. *A sequence diagram showing a client accessing the CORBA object A_Impl on a server.*

The previous approach of using IDL to define interfaces is called *static* because the interface is fixed before runtime. The other way of invoking CORBA objects is through the Dynamic Invocation Interface. This interface allows a client to access directly the underlying request mechanisms provided by an ORB. Clients may use the Dynamic Invocation Interface to issue requests to server objects without going through an IDL stub. Information about interfaces can instead be obtained through an interface repository maintained on the server.

Similarly, on the server side, the Dynamic Skeleton Interface allows an ORB to deliver requests to a server object that does not have compile-time IDL. Note, however, that the client making the request does not know whether the server object is using static IDL or dynamic skeletons.

Finally, there are different types of calls to server objects:

- **Blocking (synchronous)**—As in normal function calls of programming languages, the client is blocked until the call is completed and the control returns to the client. This is the default option.

- **Send-only (one way)**—The client is not blocked while the server object processes the call.

- **Deferred synchronous**—The caller is allowed to run and polls for the reply later (separate send and receive operations).

- **Store-and-forward**—The call is stored in a persistent store and forwarded to the server afterward.

Although IDL stubs allow only blocking and send-only calls, the Dynamic Invocation Interface lets clients make deferred synchronous calls.

We have now covered enough material on distributed objects implemented with CORBA. Regarding CORBA interface design and architecture, the important issues are

- Which objects should be exposed as interfaces?
- Should they be CORBA or other types of interfaces?
- How do they dynamically interact with other objects?

We examine these issues in Chapters 6 and 7.

5.7   STATECHART DIAGRAMS

If a system or an object may exist in a number of discrete states, we may use a statechart diagram to show the entire life cycle of the system or the object. Specifically, a statechart diagram shows the complete sequence of states that the system or the object undergoes as a result of certain events.

As an example, Figure 5-13 shows a statechart diagram for a book, which may be either in a library or on loan to a borrower. The Book object begins its first state when it is acquired by the library. It may then be checked out, thereby switching to the On Loan state. The book returns to the first state after it is returned. Finally, the Book object ceases to exist when the library discards it.

As we can see, the statechart diagram summarizes the states of a system or an object, along with the transitions between states. These transitions are results of certain events and they typically correspond to certain use cases for the system. For the book, the use cases are acquiring the book, checking it out, returning it to the library, and discarding the book.

A state may also be expanded to substates to reveal more details. This gives rise to nested statecharts, as shown in Figure 5-14. When a book is first acquired by the library, it is a new book and is displayed at the new book shelf. After two weeks, it is moved to the normal book stacks (if it is not checked out already). Notice that all books returned to the library become books in the Normal state.

In summary, a statechart diagram gives an overview or summary of the discrete states of a system or an object. Its transitions correspond to certain use cases for the system.

There is no need to document all objects in a design with statechart diagrams. Rather, we should concentrate on the discrete states of the overall system or certain critical objects. Such statechart diagrams are complementary to use cases or sequence diagrams. They help us to form a complete picture of the system.

Also, we should not overuse nested statechart diagrams. Keep the charts simple and linear if at all possible, and use no more than one level of nesting when needed. Details within a state may be expanded in separate diagrams.

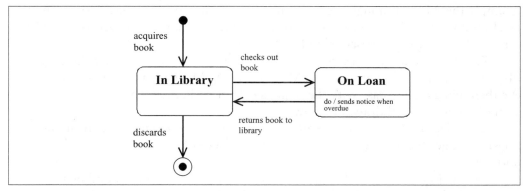

FIGURE 5-13. *A statechart diagram for a book. The "do" statement underneath On Loan describes ongoing activities within that state.*

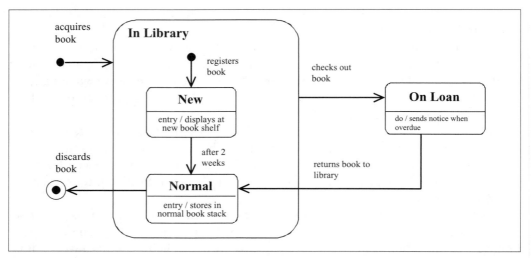

FIGURE 5-14. *A nested statechart diagram for a book, showing two substates when the book is in the library. The "entry" statements describe activities performed when entering a particular state.*

In Section 5.10, we apply statechart diagrams to the object design of the Super-Rent case study. Also, in the case study of EJB, we use statechart diagrams to analyze the life cycle of beans (Section 7.12).

5.8   CASE STUDY: ATM SYSTEM SOFTWARE—PART 3

Now that we have discussed the client/server model and distributed objects, we return to the ATM system software case and perform a dynamic analysis. We first present the use case of a card holder (actor) using an ATM. For the actor, the system is simply the ATM, although there are things happening beyond the ATM. At this level we do not distinguish events occurring at different parts or objects of the ATM system. The use case is presented in Figure 5-15.

Based on the project description in Section 2.10.1, we can identify three main objects in ATM system software: ATM Manager, ATM client, and individual banks. We then refine the use case with the sequence diagram in Figure 5-16. Note that the scenario of a cash withdrawal is shown.

This diagram follows the client/server model. In particular, ATM client and ATM Manager form a client/server pair, whereas ATM Manager and Bank form another.

The ATM client in the diagram represents a client component residing in a remote ATM, rather than the persistent class ATM in Figure 3-21. The Bank object is part of an individual bank server.

Use Case: Performing a transaction at an ATM
Actor: A bank client with a cash card
Description: This use case describes the scenario of a card holder making a transaction at an ATM.
Typical course of events:

ACTOR	SYSTEM
Insert card in ATM.	Request password.
Enter password.	Validate password for card number.
	If valid, prompt card holder for transaction type (obtain information, withdrawal, deposit, transfer).
Select transaction type.	For "obtain information," display account information and prompt card holder for another transaction.
	For others, request amount.
Enter amount.	Process transaction. If successful, display confirmation or dispense cash for withdrawal.
Take cash if it is a withdrawal.	Prompt card holder for another transaction.
Enter "end of use."	Eject cash card.

FIGURE 5-15. *ATM system software use case.*

The ATM Manager in Figure 5-16 is the main server object of the Central Server. It is the exposed interface of the persistent class ATM Manager (a database root in Figure 3-21). The ATM Manager is also a client to the bank server, besides being a server for the ATM client.

These three objects are statically unrelated. In fact, they are physically separated. They interact dynamically when a card holder uses an ATM.

The sequence diagram in Figure 5-16 suggests that two interfaces need to be defined. An ATM Manager interface governs the interaction between the ATM client and the ATM Manager. A Bank interface handles the communication between a bank and the ATM Manager.

Based on the use case analysis and the sequence diagram, we arrive at the following candidate operations for the two interfaces (Table 5-3). (Not all details are defined for the candidate operations. They are refined later.)

Here, CardInfo and AccountInfo are certain data structures carrying the relevant information. We find that the two interfaces (ATM Manager and Bank) share

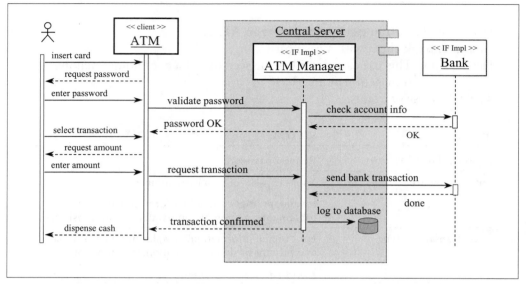

FIGURE 5-16. *Sequence diagram for the ATM system software, showing the scenario of a cash withdrawal. IF Impl stands for interface implementation. Note that only the ATM Manager belongs to the Central Server component. Both ATM client and bank are external to the Central Server.*

TABLE 5-3. *Candidate operations for two interfaces.*

INTERFACE	CANDIDATE OPERATIONS
ATM Manager	<< access operations >>
	login(cardInfo : CardInfo)
	logout( )
	<< operations on an account >>
	getBalance( ) : Float
	getHistory( ) : String
	getAccountInfo( ) : AccountInfo
	deposit(amount : Float) : Float
	withdraw(amount : Float) : Float
	transferTo(accountName : String, amount : Float) : Float
	payBill(receiver : String, amount : Float) : Float
Bank	<< access operations >>
	login(accountInfo : AccountInfo)
	logout(account)

INTERFACE	CANDIDATE OPERATIONS
	<< account management >>
	open(accountInfo : AccountInfo, initialAmount : Float)
	remove(accountInfo : AccountInfo)
	showAccounts( ) : String
	<< operations on an account >>
	getBalance( ) : Float
	getAccountInfo( ) : AccountInfo
	getHistory( ) : String
	deposit(amount : Float) : Float
	withdraw(amount : Float) : Float
	transferTo(accountName : String, amount : Float) : Float
	payBill(receiver : String, amount : Float) : Float

the same operations on accounts and they have similar access operations (`login` and `logout`). The main difference is that ATM Manager is card centric and Bank is account centric. In addition, we have also added some account management operations (`open`, `remove`, `showAccounts`), which are useful for bank operators.

As we refine these interface operations and their organization later, precise interfaces will be defined. Consequently, the server objects ATM Manager and Bank may be refined into more specific server objects. In Chapter 6 we discuss design patterns for interfaces. There we return to this case study and apply some of the patterns.

5.9   CASE STUDY: SHARED WHITEBOARD—PART 3

In this section we examine the use case scenarios for phase I of the shared whiteboard. From the functional requirements in Section 2.11, we arrive at the following use cases:

1. Use the mouse to mark up and annotate the background image.

2. Use the selection boxes to change the style of a markup or annotation.

3. Save and read CGM files.

Use case 1 includes creating, selecting, and moving the markups and annotations. These functions are fulfilled by the operations of the DrawCanvas class in Figure 2-36. In particular, the processMouseEvent and processMouseEvent operations catch the mouse events and perform actions accordingly. These operations involve primarily traditional procedural programming within the DrawCanvas class and are best documented within the implementation code. Here we are more interested in the interaction among several classes, which occur in the last two use cases.

The second use case is rather straightforward and is presented in Figure 5-17.

A sequence diagram for this use case is shown in Figure 5-18, which reveals the interaction between different classes in the shared whiteboard. After the user selects a glyph (a markup or annotation) in the DrawCanvas, the glyph is highlighted. The user then selects a color from the ColorChooser, which then sends the selection to the Main-ButtonBar. The MainButtonBar invokes the setColor operation of DrawCanvas, which in turn sets the color of the selected glyph and refreshes the display.

The third use case (Figure 5-19), saving and reading CGM files, involves a few more steps.

The sequence diagram for saving to a CGM file is shown in Figure 5-20. The DrawCanvas object invokes the class Cgm, which in turn uses CgmTool to convert the glyphs to CGM byte data and save them to a file. The process for reading from a CGM file is similar, except that the conversion from CGM to glyphs is handled inside the class Cgm.

The sequence diagram in Figure 5-20 brings together the two separate sets of classes in Figure 2-35 and Figure 2-38. One reason for separating the two sets is that they can be tested separately. For example, one may include test code in the Cgm class to perform a round-trip test of forward and backward conversion between glyphs and CGM data. The test involves the three classes: Cgm, CgmTool, and Glyph appearing in Figure 2-38. Such modular design and testing is often a good tactic in object-oriented programming.

Use Case: Changing the style of a markup or annotation
Actor: A user of the shared whiteboard
Description: This use case describes the scenario of a user changing a
 markup or annotation.
Typical course of events:

ACTOR	SYSTEM
Select an existing markup or annotation from the DrawCanvas.	Highlight the selected markup or annotation.
Select a color, line thickness, font, or font size from one of the selection boxes.	Change the selected markup or annotation according to the user selection.

FIGURE 5-17. *Shared whiteboard use case.*

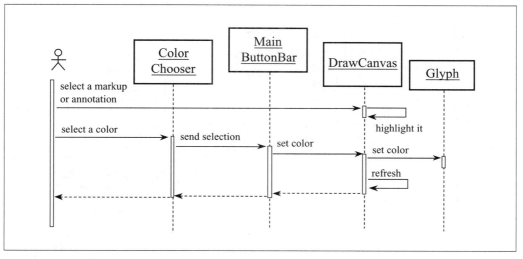

FIGURE 5-18. *The sequence diagram for changing the color of a markup and annotations to a CGM file.*

Use Case: Saving and reading CGM files
Actor: A user of the shared whiteboard
Description: This use case describes the scenario of a user saving the markups and annotations to a CGM file or reading them from a CGM file.
Typical course of events:

ACTOR	SYSTEM
Select Save As from the menu bar.	Pop up a file dialog with a default filename.
Choose a different directory or enter a different filename, then click the Save button.	Close the file dialog. Convert the markups and annotations to CGM byte data and then save them to the specified file.
Select Open from the menu bar.	Pop up a file dialog.
Choose a directory or select a CGM file, then click the Open button.	Close the file dialog. Convert the contents of the CGM file into glyphs and then display them.

FIGURE 5-19. *Shared whiteboard use case.*

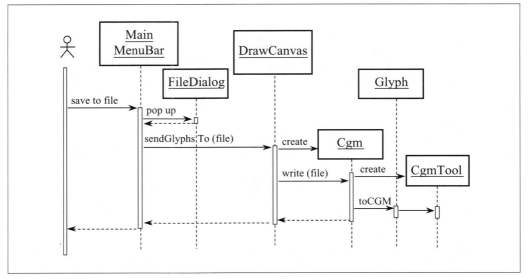

FIGURE 5-20. *The sequence diagram for saving the markups and annotations to a CGM file.*

5.10 CASE STUDY: A RENTAL BUSINESS—PART 2

For the SuperRent system, the rental items (videos, games, and so on) may exist in a number of states. Thus we may use statechart diagrams to gain an overall picture before embarking on sequence diagrams. Figure 5-21 shows the statechart diagram for a rental item in SuperRent. After the item is acquired, it is put in a SuperRent store. The item's state changes to Rented when a member checks it out.

Within the Rented state, there are two substates. A rented item starts in the Normal state, with its store attribute set to null. The system performs a daily check on all rented items. If any item is overdue, it transitions to the Overdue state. The system then sends a notification to the member about the overdue items.

On returning to a store (from a Normal or an Overdue state), an item goes back to the In Store state, with its store attribute set to that particular store.

We note that in the object design (Figure 3-25), the states are actually stored in two classes. The Item class stores the states In Store and Rented using its `store` attribute. The RentalInfo class indicates whether the rental item is Normal or Overdue via the operation `isOverdue` (with data from the `dueDate` attribute).

The statechart diagram suggests several use cases for the SuperRent system:

- Acquiring an item (actor: store operator)

- Checking out an item (actor: store operator)

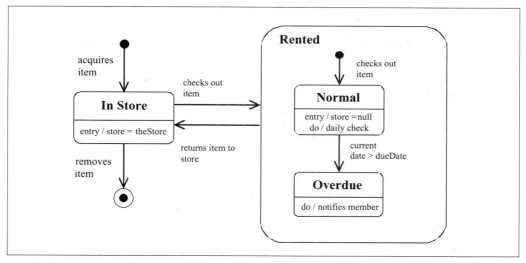

FIGURE 5-21. *The statechart diagram for a rental item in SuperRent.*

- Performing a daily check for overdue items (actor: none; this case is performed by the system as a batch job)
- Checking in a returned item (actor: store operator)
- Removing an item (actor: store operator)

Other use cases not included are various queries (for example, find all items rented by a member, find unpaid or underpaid rentals, and so on), statistical analyses (for example, the top ten most popular videos), and so forth. Next we describe the sequence diagrams for some selected use cases.

Figure 5-22 shows the sequence diagram for checking out a video item. More than one item may be checked out during one rental by repeatedly invoking getItem and addRentalInfo before calling calculateTotalFee on the Rental object. The operation setStore(null) on the Item object changes the state of the item from In Store to Rented.

The sequence diagram for performing a daily check on overdue items is given in Figure 5-23. The SuperRent object acts as an internal actor for the task. It first finds all DueDate objects before the current date and retrieves all RentalInfos in each. It then calls the isOverdue operation on each RentalInfo object. If the operation returns overdue, SuperRent finds the corresponding Member object and sends a notification to the member. If the RentalInfo object is not overdue, it is removed from its parent DueDate object.

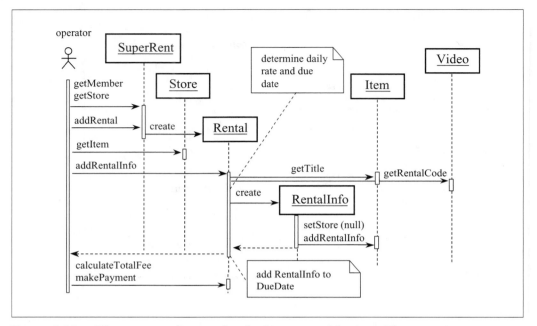

FIGURE 5-22. *The sequence diagram for checking out a video item. The operation* `setStore(null)` *on the Item object changes the state of the item.*

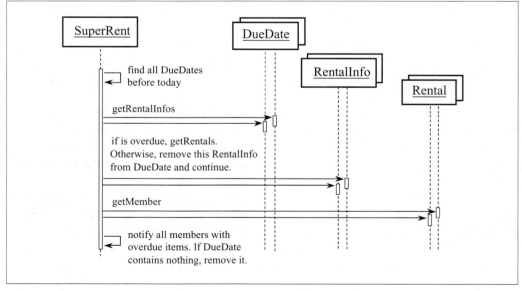

FIGURE 5-23. *The sequence diagram for performing a daily check on overdue items.*

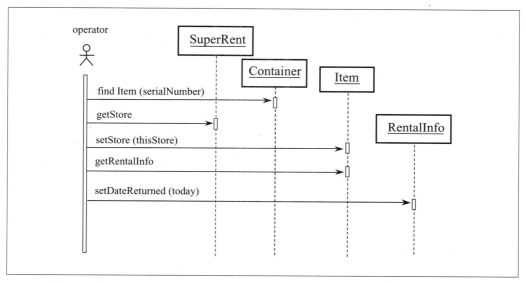

FIGURE 5-24. *The sequence diagram for checking in a returned item.*

Finally, if a DueDate object contains no RentalInfo objects afterward, that means no overdue items exist for that due date. Thus, we may remove the DueDate object from the database root container so that we need not search it again until the next date.

The sequence diagram for checking in a returned item is shown in Figure 5-24. The process simply sets the `store` attribute in the Item object and the dateReturned attribute in the corresponding RentalInfo object. Afterward, the `isOverdue` operation on the RentalInfo object returns false, and `isReturned` returns true.

These diagrams support the major transitions of the statechart diagram in Figure 5-21 and cover the major use cases of SuperRent.

5.11 CASE STUDY: ACCESS CONTROL LISTS—PART 3

Figure 5-25 lists the high-level use cases related to ACLs in a software system. For a user, the privilege request case is handled by the `isPrivilegeGranted()` operation in the ACL class.

For an administrator, the user and group management cases include adding, finding, and deleting users and groups. The privilege setting case includes the following:

- Adding an ACL

- Associating the ACL with an object

- Editing the contents of the ACL (users/groups), including their privileges

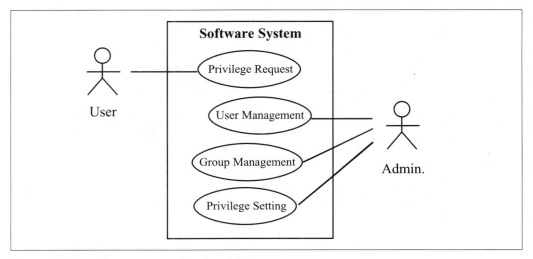

FIGURE 5-25. *The use cases related to ACLs.*

Note that some of these functions may be performed by certain privileged users (such as a project lead). We return to this case study in Section 6.14 to discuss how the ACL can be used.

5.12 EXERCISES

5-1.   Suppose the Trade class in Figure 2-20 is managed by a collection manager (which also creates the Trade objects). Draw and describe the sequence diagrams for the core operations `addTrade(product : String, quantity : Integer, total_price : Double, supplier : Supplier, buyer : Buyer)` and `removeTrade(trade : Trade)`. Note that these core operations ensure referential integrity between a pair of Supplier and Buyer objects.

5-2.   Based on the detailed design for the Part-Property classes (Figure 2-22) in Exercise 2-13, draw a sequence diagram for the operation `addComponent(component : Part, count : Integer)` in the Part class. Note that the count attribute is used in constructing a Property object.

5-3.   Provide a mapping to Java for the Part and Attribute struct types in Section 5.6. Note that an IDL sequence maps to an array, and an IDL module maps to a Java package.

5-4.   Does the construct with an interface in Figure 5-26 make sense? That is, can we replace an association class with an interface? If not, give the reason and suggest an alternative solution.

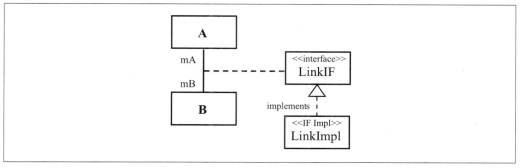

FIGURE 5-26. *Construct for Exercise 5-4.*

5-5.   The design in Figure 5-27 is called the *decorator pattern* [Gamma et al. 1995]. It contains a backward relationship loop. Because the multiplicity is one, the loop forms a simple linked list of objects. The abstract class has an operation `draw()`, which, for the class TextArea, simply prints the text. For the Scroller and Border classes, the `draw()` operation first draws the corresponding graphic decoration and then invokes the `draw()` operation of the next component in the linked list. In this way one can dynamically add decorators to a TextArea object.

Draw a sequence diagram for the `draw()` operation. Also, compare this design with a design using class inheritance.

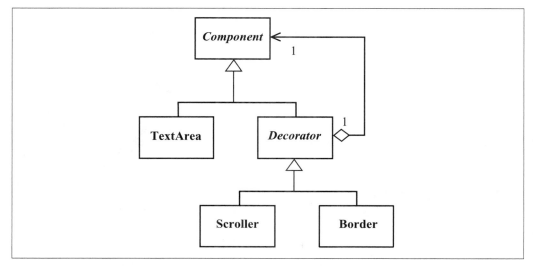

FIGURE 5-27. *Decorator pattern for Exercise 5-5.*

Common Interface Design Patterns

M any of the static design patterns in Chapter 2 can be exposed through interfaces, resulting in various interface design patterns. These patterns can be used within a software component or across components in a client/server environment. To obtain a better perspective, we show in Figure 6-1 three themes of static interface design.

These static design themes appear in various dynamic interface patterns, which we cover in this chapter. (Because an interface cannot hold references to other objects, these three themes cover all possible basic patterns for interfaces.) Later in the chapter we also discuss interface patterns related to CORBA objects.

As in the case of static design patterns, we chose these interface patterns because they appear often in real-life designs. They fulfill specific functions in larger systems and contribute to the overall behaviors of the systems. Most of them are also the equivalents of the irreducible patterns discussed in Section 4.10. Here we begin with some simple interface patterns and gradually build up our repertoire.

6.1   OBJECT WRAPPERS

Object wrappers define object-oriented interfaces for legacy applications that are not object oriented, and enables them to function as true interface implementation objects. Through object wrappers, legacy applications can interact with other distributed objects at the enterprise level. This high-level interoperability is indeed the essence of *enterprise application integration*.

In terms of interface design, an object wrapper is nothing but a basic usage of interfaces. First, we define a wrapper interface, with operations that are those of the legacy application and are made visible to the caller or client. We then implement the interface by making function calls to the legacy code. The sequence diagram for invoking an operation is shown in Figure 6-2.

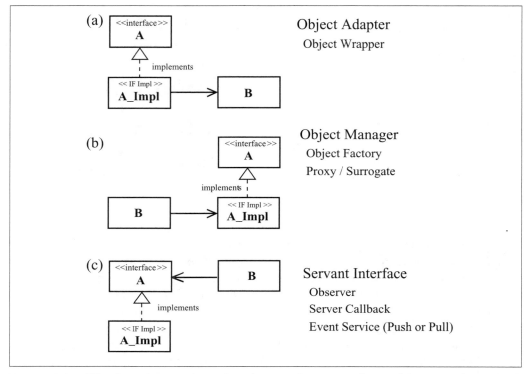

FIGURE 6-1. *The three themes of interface design. These static design themes may be applied to multiple dynamic interface patterns, some of which are listed on the right.*

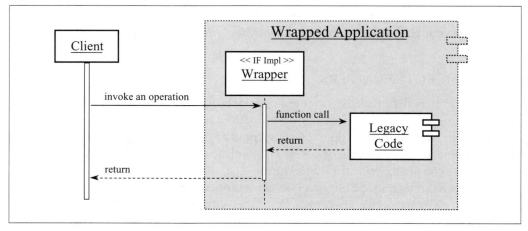

FIGURE 6-2. *Sequence diagram for a wrapper object, which is an implementation of a wrapper interface.*

Note that the legacy code can take various forms. It can be in binary format, such as a dynamic link library, or it can be an external executable that takes some input data and generates results. Object wrappers can be viewed as a degenerate form of object adapters, which we discuss next.

6.2 OBJECT ADAPTERS

The object wrapper concept can be extended to an object adapter, which translates an existing object into a specific or different interface [Gamma et al. 1995]. In this case the object adapter typically contains a reference to the existing object, which is therefore being used as a servant class.

As an example, suppose we have an existing object Mainframe User that has operations specific to mainframe computers. We need to adapt the object to the interface User, which supports the operations `validatePassword(…)` and `changePassword(…)`. The object adapter for Mainframe User is shown in Figure 6-3, in which the implementation class User Impl relays the two operations to the appropriate ones in Mainframe User.

Object adapters can be used as a weak but flexible form of inheritance. Take, for instance, the Mainframe User example in Figure 6-3. If Mainframe User already has the operations `validatePassword(…)` and `changePassword(…)`, we could have inherited it to form the new User class. However, there are other operations in Mainframe User that we want to avoid. In this case the object adapter allows us to use certain operations selectively and omit the others.

This flexible form of inheritance can also be applied to the case of having multiple parent classes. Instead of inheritance, we may treat the existing parent classes as servants for the implementation classes of the new interface. Thus, the methods of the existing classes become available through the new interface. This is actually an effective workaround for multiple inheritance.

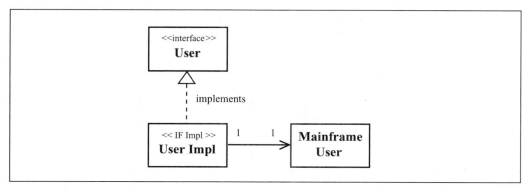

FIGURE 6-3. *An object adapter that adapts the existing Mainframe User to the interface User.*

6.3 OBJECT FACTORIES AND MANAGERS

The collection manager pattern described in Section 2.1 creates an object before adding it to the collection. This behavior of creating objects can be captured by the object factory pattern, with a main function of *creating* objects belonging to a class.

If we add management functions (such as those in a collection manager) to the factory, it then becomes an object manager. Thus, by exposing the operations of a collection manager through interfaces, we arrive at an object manager interface pattern.

Figure 6-4 shows a factory that produces services. The create operation is defined in the Service Factory interface, which creates objects that implement the Service interface. The association between MyService Factory and MyService is needed if the former also manages the latter.

A detailed design of the interfaces for the object factory pattern is shown in Figure 6-5.

One advantage of defining a Service Factory interface is to have a front end for access control. For example, the factory or manager may have a login operation that validates the caller's credentials before creating and returning a service object (Figure 6-6). Thus, login is a secured version of the create operation.

Another advantage of having a Service Factory interface is to allow different service management policies in different implementations when it is used as an object manager.

Finally, in a CORBA context, an object factory is really a CORBA object factory. Both the factory and the objects are defined by IDL. Through the interface, clients can request the factory to create CORBA objects.

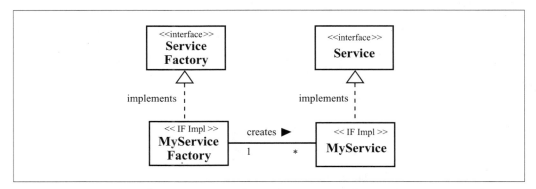

FIGURE 6-4. *An object factory pattern. The implementation class MyService Factory creates service object MyService. If MyService Factory also manages the service objects, then this becomes an object manager pattern.*

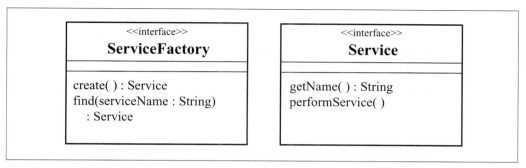

FIGURE 6-5. *Interfaces for the object factory pattern.*

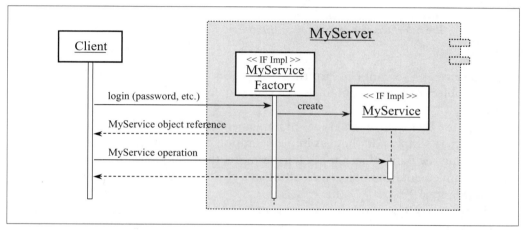

FIGURE 6-6. *Access control with MyService Factory. The* login *operation validates the caller's credentials before creating and returning a MyService object.*

6.4 INTERFACES AS SERVANT CLASSES

As in normal classes, interfaces can also be used as servant classes (see Section 1.7). This is often done to achieve high flexibility.

As an example, let us look at the Bank object in the ATM system software case (Figure 5-16). A bank manages a number of accounts. Thus, the Bank object needs to support an account manager interface named Account Mgr. One approach is to implement the interface within the Bank class, as shown in Figure 6-7a. This will be fine if Bank has only one type of implementation for the Account Mgr interface.

However, a static and fixed interface for the Bank object may be too restrictive. To allow dynamic linkage to an implementation at runtime, we may use the Account

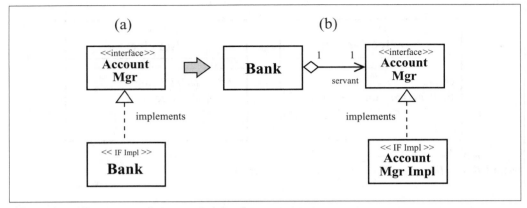

FIGURE 6-7.   *Instead of implementing the Account Mgr interface (a), the Bank class may use the interface as a servant class (b), thereby allowing more flexibility.*

Mgr interface as a servant class for the Bank object. Thus, as shown in Figure 6-7b, the Bank object may now contain an interface implementation object called Account Mgr Impl.

Suppose there are several types of implementations for the interface within a bank. We may simply add them as implementation classes under the interface, without changing the Bank object at all. Furthermore, the Bank object may even contain multiple implementation objects, resulting in a structure similar to the handle-body pattern (Figure 6-8).

In Section 6.8, we find that the servant interface patterns are actually used in CORBA objects.

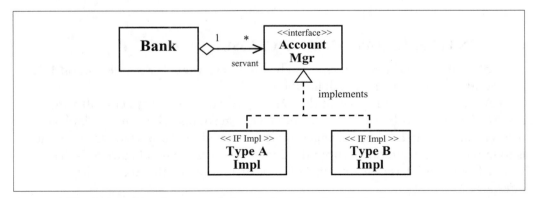

FIGURE 6-8.   *Servant interface extended to the interface handle-body pattern.*

6.5   SERVANT INTERFACES IN EVENT PROCESSING

Events are instances of communication between objects. They can take the form of *direct* events, as in normal method invocations between objects. Alternatively, events can be dispatched through an Event Service or Manager, which allows *indirect* communication between objects.

For each event there are two roles. The *supplier* produces and sends event data, whereas the *consumer* receives and processes the data. Depending on who initiates the transfer of event data, an event can either be of *push* or *pull type*. In a push event, the supplier starts the data transfer. In a pull event, the consumer takes the initiative.

An interface is a natural tool to define the way an event occurs, especially the `push` or `pull` operations. However, before such a `push` or `pull` call can be made, the initiating object must contain the reference to the Consumer or Supplier object. For push events, the consumer can register its implementation object with the supplier. After registration, the supplier holds the Consumer object as a servant class (Figure 6-9a). For pull events, on the other hand, the consumer uses the Supplier object as a servant class to pull the event data (Figure 6-9b).

To obtain a more concrete grasp of using interfaces for events, we next discuss some common design patterns related to event processing.

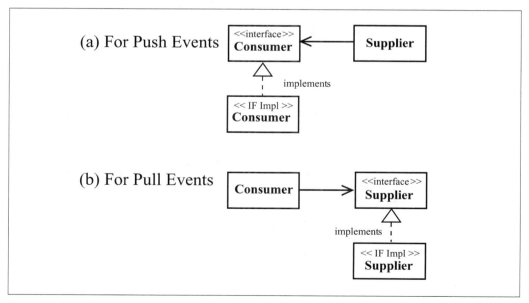

FIGURE 6-9.   *Servant interface patterns for push (a) and pull (b) events.*

6.5.1 SIMPLE EVENT PUSHING AND OBSERVERS

Simple event pushing is a straightforward implementation of the pattern in Figure 6-9a. After an event consumer registers its implementation object with the supplier, the supplier fires events according to certain preset criteria.

As an example, we show the object designs for a Timer and its Listener in Figure 6-10. The Timer holds a Listener interface (the Consumer object) as a servant class. The link is established during the construction of a Timer object. After the construction, the `start` operation is called. After a specified delay time, the Timer object will fire an event by calling the `processEvent` operation of the Listener's implementation object (ListenerImpl).

The Timer can, for example, be used to time out and close down a pop-up dialog window or to start up a separate process after a delay.

The simple event pushing pattern can be generalized to allow multiple listeners or observers. The result is known as the *observer pattern* [Gamma et al. 1995], which defines a one-to-many dependency between an observable and observers.

The observer pattern shown in Figure 6-11 involves two interfaces: the Observer and the Observable. The implementation class ObserverImpl first obtains a reference to an observable (for example, via a collection manager). It then calls `addObserver()` to add itself to the list of observers, thereby establishing a link from ObservableImpl to Observer. When an event of interest occurs, the ObservableImpl object goes through the observer list to invoke the `update()` operation. (We note that the observer pattern of [Gamma et al. 1995] also includes an extra step of pulling data from ObservableImpl.)

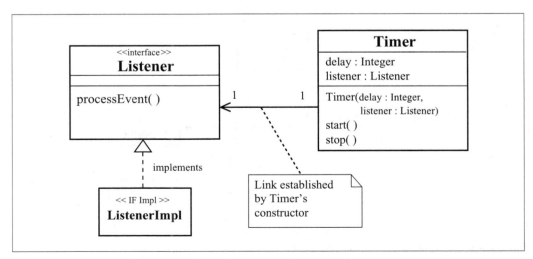

FIGURE 6-10. *A timer as a simple push event supplier.*

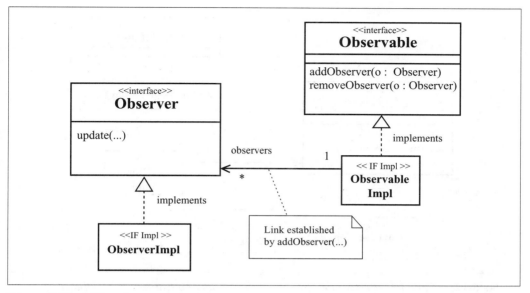

FIGURE 6-11. *The observer pattern.*

6.5.2 CALLBACKS FROM SERVER OBJECTS

In a client/server context, callbacks are push events initiated by a server object directly against a client. Before such an event can be sent, the client must pass a client-side object reference to the server object, thereby allowing the server to make callbacks to the client. A callback is really an observer pattern applied to the client/server context.

Figure 6-12 shows a chat room application using callback. In this application, each ChatUser is a client to the central ChatRoom server object. The callback operation is `send(message)` in the ChatUser interface. On startup, the client program signs on to the chat room server, which can subsequently invoke the callback operation to broadcast messages to all registered users. Note that the links from the server to the ChatUser objects are established only during the `signOn` calls.

The callback pattern may also be used within a programming component. An example is event-based parsing of XML documents. Events are sent from the parser to a user application whenever the parser reaches certain boundaries or elements in a document. For details, please refer to Exercise 6-4.

6.5.3 SUBSCRIPTION AND NOTIFICATION

In a subscription and notification service, consumers first subscribe to certain types of events. Later, event suppliers push the events to an event manager, which in turn may

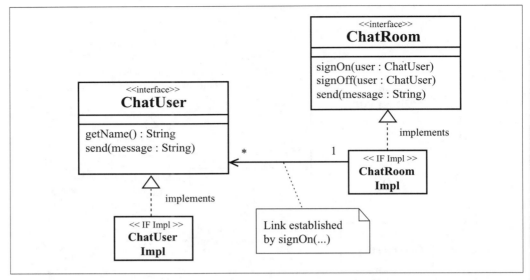

FIGURE 6-12. *Callback interface design for the chat room application. The callback operation is* send(...) *in the ChatUser interface. (The class ChatUser << IF Impl>> must first obtain a reference to the ChatRoom interface to invoke ChatRoom's operations. This association is not shown here to avoid confusion.)*

push the event data to the consumers, or may wait for the consumers to pull the event data.

To allow asynchronous event processing, the event manager must store the events in holders, because multiple events can be sent from a supplier to a consumer. An event holder may contain more than one event, each of which may be in a different state (New, Sent, and so on).

An event holder may be modeled as an association class between a consumer and a supplier. Figure 6-13 illustrates these object relationships.

Next we mutate the seed design in Figure 6-13 to include a Subscriber (consumer) interface and an Event Producer interface (supplier). The producer's implementation object periodically invokes the processEvent operation (the push call) on each subscriber. Unsent events are pushed to the subscribers during such calls. The resulting interface design is shown in Figure 6-14. With the EventHolder, the design can handle push events asynchronously.

Figure 6-15 displays a sequence diagram for the event subscription and notification processes under the interface design pattern of Figure 6-14. A subscriber subscribes to a certain type of event through a producer, which in turn creates an EventHolder for the subscriber. Note that from Figure 6-14, the producer contains a set of event holders, through which it reaches the subscribers.

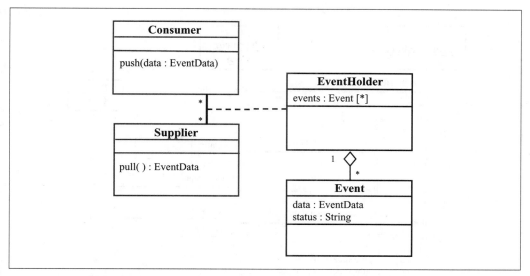

FIGURE 6-13. *Class relationships related to a subscription and notification service. The class EventHolder is modeled as an association class between a Supplier and a Consumer. Also shown in Consumer and Supplier are the generic* push *and* pull *operations.*

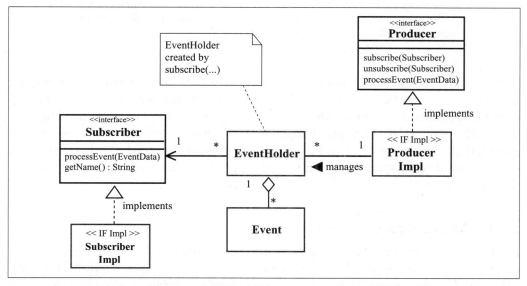

FIGURE 6-14. *Interface design pattern for a subscription and notification service that can handle push events asynchronously. The design combines Figure 6-9a and Figure 6-13, and applies the scheme in Figure 2-21 for a binary association class.*

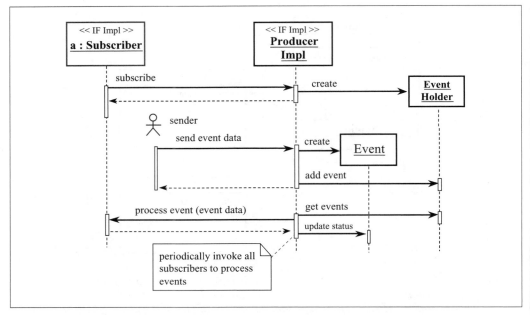

FIGURE 6-15. *A sequence diagram for the subscription and notification processes under the interface design pattern of Figure 6-14. A subscriber subscribes to a certain type of event through a producer. The producer periodically checks for new incoming events and pushes them to the subscribers via the* process event *calls.*

A sender sends event data to the producer, which creates a new Event object and stores it in the event holders. The producer periodically checks for new, incoming events and pushes them to the subscribers via the processEvent operation. The push calls on the subscribers may happen asynchronously with the receipt of the event data. Whenever a processEvent operation returns successfully, that status of the event in the corresponding event holder is updated. This completes the life cycle of an event object in the subscription and notification service.

6.5.4 MODEL-VIEW-CONTROLLER

Model-View-Controller (MVC) is an effective design pattern for GUIs. It became popular along with the SmallTalk language in the 1980s [Goldberg & Robson 1989]. MVC emphasizes a modular approach to user interface design by separating user input, data model, and presentation. As shown in Figure 6-16, the static design is divided into three parts: controllers that accept user inputs, an application-specific model that contains the core functionality and data, and different views of the model.

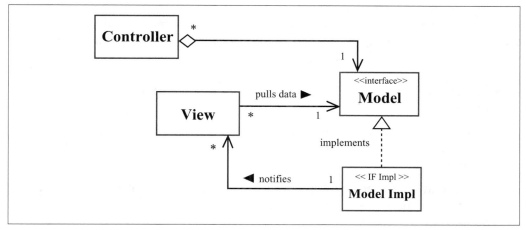

FIGURE 6-16. *The MVC interface design pattern. The View objects are observers to Model.*

The MVC pattern uses an interesting combination of both push and pull events. When a user input is received, the controller directly invokes methods or pushes events to the model (for example, updating certain data elements in the model). After the model is updated, it notifies or pushes an event to all of its views. If a certain view cares about the aspect that has changed, it can get the update by pulling relevant data from the model. Thus, the views are observers to the model. The sequence diagram for this interaction is shown in Figure 6-17.

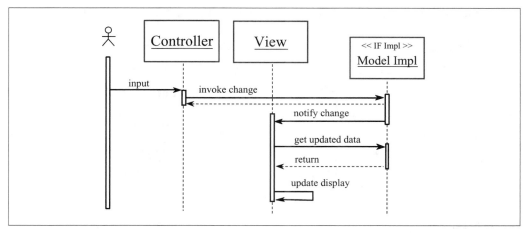

FIGURE 6-17. *A sequence diagram for events in the MVC pattern. A case with only one user, one controller, and one view is shown here.*

Notice that at no time does the model send data directly to the view. It only contains a list of views that should be notified when there is a update to the model. In fact, the model does not care what data a particular view is interested in. This design pattern brings about several advantages:

- The views and the model can be tested separately, which makes debugging easier.

- Changes in the model (by using a new implementation for the Model interface) will not affect the views. Similarly, changing the views will not affect the model either.

- The design can support multiple views on the same model. Any updates on the model data will be broadcast to all views, thereby synchronizing the views with the model.

The essence of MVC is separation of data from presentation. This philosophy can actually be applied to system-level architectures. We return to this topic in Section 7.3.2 within the client/server context.

6.6   RELATIONSHIP LOOPS WITH INTERFACES

Now that we have discussed the basic interface design patterns, we are in a position to explore other interesting variations. As in normal classes, relationship loops with interfaces can be constructed. For example, in Figure 6-1c, if we identify class B with class A_Impl, then we arrive at the relationship loop shown in Figure 6-18a.

Such a construct can be used, for example, to expose the Part objects in Figure 5-4 to clients. We first define a Part interface with all public operations. We then

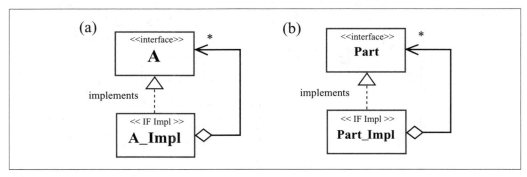

FIGURE 6-18.   *Relationship loops (a, b) with interfaces. The structure is similar to the backward containment loop of Figure 2-6a and can be viewed as a variation of the third theme in Figure 6-1.*

implement the interface with the class Part_Impl, which contains a collection of Part interfaces, as shown in Figure 6-18b. The case study of the shared whiteboard also involves such a relationship loop (see Section 6.13).

Because interfaces cannot contain member variables, forward relationship loops similar to the one in Figure 2-6b do not exist.

6.7   INHERITANCE LADDERS

Interfaces can be used to identify a restricted subset of the operations of a class. Similarly, an inheritance tree of interfaces can specify layers of operations for a corresponding tree of implementation classes. Figure 6-19 shows that the User IF and Admin IF interfaces control certain operations of the User and Admin classes respectively.

The horizontal lines of implementation and the vertical inheritance together form a ladderlike structure, which we call an *inheritance ladder*. Such constructs are useful when exposing a set of operations from internal objects to external clients. Again, we find such patterns in CORBA objects.

6.8   CORBA OBJECTS

This section is a detailed exposition of CORBA objects and their dynamic behavior. Because CORBA is a mature standard, the underlying interface design patterns may be considered archetypes for others.

Figure 6-20 shows the CORBA object tree related to an IDL interface A. The interface A and the abstract class A_Impl_Base are both generated by the IDL

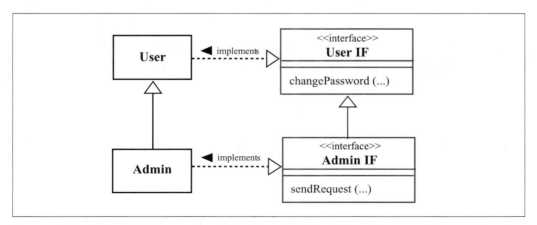

FIGURE 6-19.   *The inheritance tree of User IF and Admin IF interfaces specifies a restricted set of operations for the User and Admin classes. They form an inheritance ladder.*

compiler. A_Impl_Base contains skeleton code to be executed on the server side. The actual implementation for interface A's operations are in A_Impl, which is an interface implementation class coded by the programmers.

The interface CORBA Object (which in Java is org.omg.CORBA.Object) is the root of the inheritance tree. It defines a CORBA object reference that identifies the same CORBA object for all method invocations on the object.

The abstract class Object Impl (which in Java is the class org.omg.CORBA. portable.ObjectImpl) is the superclass for client stubs and object implementations. It provides a default implementation for the CORBA Object interface. All methods are forwarded to a servant or delegate object, which can be implemented by a specific ORB.

To create a CORBA object, one instantiates the class A_Impl and notifies the BOA that the object is ready, as shown in Figure 5-12. With this approach, however, the implementation class A_Impl is tightly coupled to the skeleton code (the Skeleton class through inheritance). To decouple the two, we may apply the servant interface approach of Section 6.4. In CORBA, this is called a TIE approach.

The CORBA objects in the TIE approach are shown in Figure 6-21. A new class A_TIE is introduced, which holds a servant interface A_Op. The interface A_Op is identical to interface A except it does not inherit from the base CORBA

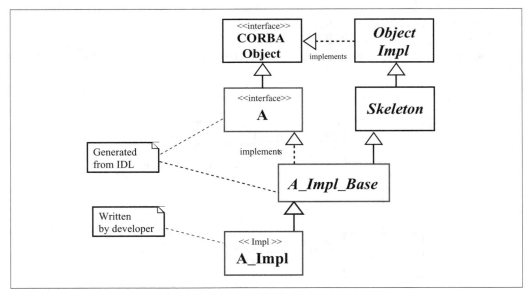

FIGURE 6-20.   *The CORBA object tree for an IDL interface A. The interface CORBA Object, and abstract classes Object Impl and Skeleton are provided by a CORBA-compliant library. A and A_Impl_Base are generated by an IDL compiler. A_Impl is written by the developers.*

Object interface. The implementation class A_Impl is now completely detached from the skeleton code. Both A_TIE and A_Op are generated by an IDL compiler.

At runtime a main server object first creates an A_Impl object and then creates an A_TIE object using the A_Impl object as an input argument. In this way the TIE object is dynamically tied to the interface implementation A_Impl. Any invocation of A's operation will always go through the TIE object before reaching the A_Impl object. The sequence diagram for this process is given in Figure 6-22.

The TIE approach is especially helpful when there is inheritance between interfaces. To appreciate this point, we first examine the interface inheritance and the related CORBA objects in the original approach (Figure 6-20).

As can be seen from Figure 6-23, the B classes inherit A's operations through interface B. If B_Impl was a subclass of A_Impl, multiple inheritance by B_Impl would be necessary. Thus, in a programming language that prohibits multiple inheritance (such as Java), a different approach is needed to preserve the inheritance relationship between A_Impl and B_Impl (which allows us to reuse the implementation in A_Impl).

With the TIE approach, on the other hand, the class B_TIE inherits A's operations through interface B (Figure 6-24). And in B_TIE, all inherited A operations and

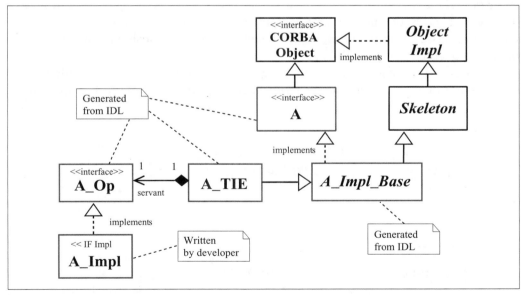

FIGURE 6-21. *CORBA objects using the TIE approach. The interface A_Op serves as a servant to the class A_TIE. (This is a strong ownership of the interface A_Op by the A_TIE class. Hence the black diamond.)*

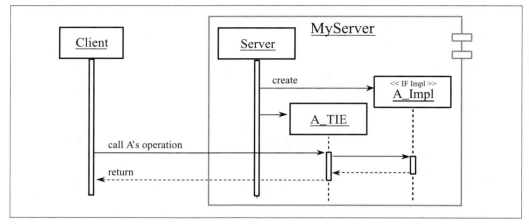

FIGURE 6-22. *The sequence diagram for invoking a CORBA object using the TIE approach. Note that all client calls must go through the A_TIE object first.*

B operations are implemented by delegating the calls to the servant interface B_Op. B_Impl now exists in a decoupled structure (Figure 6-25), and can therefore inherit from A_Impl without resulting in multiple inheritance.

The implementation classes and the servant interfaces A_Op and B_Op form an inheritance ladder (Figure 6-25). Because interface A_Op has the same operations as interface A, and B_Op has the same as B, they stipulate the behavior of the implementation classes A_Impl and B_Impl. The inheritance relationship from A to B is maintained from A_Impl to B_Impl.

In short, the TIE approach uses the servant interface pattern to decouple the implementation classes from the skeleton classes. The trade-off of the TIE approach

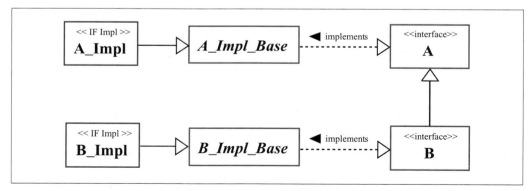

FIGURE 6-23. *Interface inheritance and the related CORBA objects in the original approach. (Some superclasses like Skeleton are omitted from the figure.)*

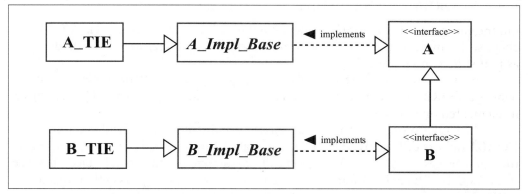

FIGURE 6-24. *Interface inheritance and the related CORBA objects in the TIE approach. Note that there is no inheritance between A_Impl_Base and B_Impl_Base, or between A_TIE and B_TIE.*

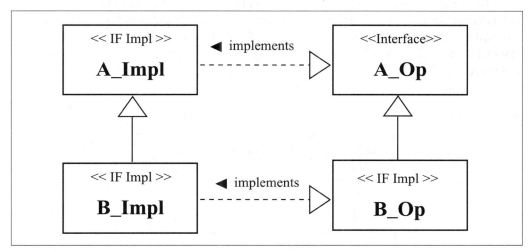

FIGURE 6-25. *An inheritance ladder of CORBA objects.*

is the additional TIE objects, which occupy dynamic memory and add an extra indirection for all client calls to CORBA objects.

Because the choice between the two approaches is an implementation detail, we will omit the detailed differences between them in our subsequent static and dynamic diagrams. In particular, only interface implementation objects such as A_Impl will be shown. The TIE objects will be hidden from the pictures for simplicity, even though the actual implementation may use them.

6.9 CORBA CLIENT STUBS

On the client side, an inheritance ladder similar to Figure 6-25 exists. The CORBA client stubs implement the corresponding interfaces and therefore form a ladder such as that shown in Figure 6-26.

For the client, the interface CORBA Object (org.omg.CORBA.Object in Java) defines a CORBA object reference, which is a handle for a particular CORBA object implemented on a server.

The CORBA object reference is "smart" because it handles local and remote CORBA objects differently. If the CORBA object is local (in other words, running in the same process as the client), method calls are directed to the actual object instance. If the CORBA object is remote, the reference points to a stub (proxy) that uses the ORB machinery to make a remote invocation on the CORBA object.

For the implementation from a specific CORBA software vendor, the class Object Impl and the interface CORBA Object in Figure 6-26 may actually be subclasses of the corresponding superclasses defined by the CORBA standard.

Because all remote calls always go through a client stub, one may enrich the behavior of the client by replacing a standard stub with its subclass. Suppose we have an interface A and its stub Stub A. We may define MyStub A, which is a subclass of Stub A. The detailed sequence diagram of a client using MyStub A is given in Figure 6-27.

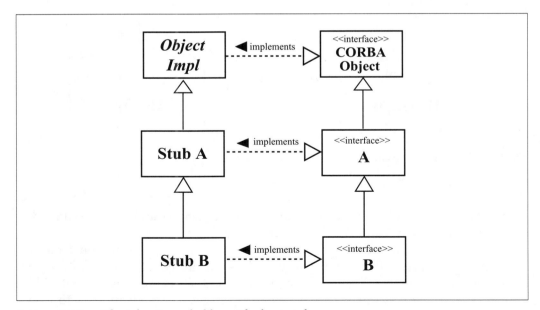

FIGURE 6-26. *The inheritance ladder with client stubs.*

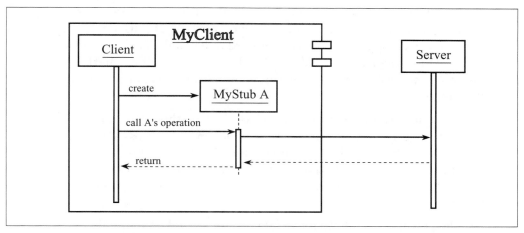

FIGURE 6-27.   *A CORBA client with a customized stub MyStub A. The class MyStub A is a subclass of Stub A, which implements the interface A.*

Some uses of MyStub A are the following:

- **Client cache to improve performance**—MyStub A may contain private member variables that store a snapshot of data returned from the server. Client access to these data is local to the client as long as the data are valid. There are several strategies to ensure that the snapshot data are valid. For example, the data may be considered valid if the time elapsed from the last update is smaller than a certain period. When they expire, a call is made to the server to obtain an update. Alternatively, one may use a callback mechanism so that the server may update the client cache actively.

- **Client activity log**—MyStub A may output the client activities to a log file, which may be sent back to the server periodically if desired. The client log alleviates the burden on the server of keeping track of the activities of all its clients.

6.10   TACTICS IN DESIGNING DISTRIBUTED OBJECTS*

To achieve good performance on systems with distributed objects, additional factors such as network latency and interface organization must be taken into account. In general, the following three tactics offer a good start:

1. **Limit the number of bind calls to interfaces**—As we discussed in Section 5.6, to use a remote object, a client must obtain an initial object reference.

This can be done through a `bind` call, a CORBA Naming Service, or a string representation of the object reference. Such `bind` calls are, however, expensive because socket connections need to be established. To improve performance, we may consolidate related interfaces into one interface, organize interfaces by functional group, or use the object factory pattern (Section 6.3).

2. **Limit the number of remote invocations**—Each method invocation on a remote object is a remote invocation, which may go across a network, becoming the bottleneck of the application. To alleviate this, we may use client stubs (Section 6.9) to cache certain information or to group a sequence of calls into a single interface operation (coarse-grained function).

3. **Use the pull approach for passing large amounts of data to multiple places**—With this approach, the data sender first notifies the data consumers that the data are available. It is then up to the consumers to decide whether to pull the data, thereby avoiding a long wait in pushing the data to one consumer after another. This interaction is the same as that between Model and View in the MVC pattern (Figure 6-17).

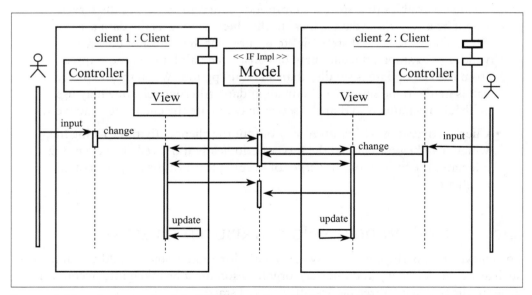

FIGURE 6-28.   *An example of the MVC pattern applied to multiple users across a network. Here the two clients are on different machines. They go through a network to access the Model object on a separate server machine, thus introducing network latency.*

Finally, in dynamic design, one needs to consider network latency between distributed objects. For example, the MVC pattern may be applied to multiple users across a network. An example is shown in Figure 6-28, in which two clients interact with one Model object that resides on a separate server machine.

The design in Figure 6-28 can be applied to collaborative applications, such as a shared whiteboard. However, with this design a user may wait a long time before seeing any changes made locally. This is because all changes must first go to the Model object, which in turn relays the change data to the View objects via a push/pull mechanism. At least three calls across the network are made for each change, thus introducing network latency even for local changes. A possible remedy is to include the complete MVC pattern in each client component and to add a central coordinator to synchronize all clients (see Exercise 6-8).

6.11 PROXY AND SURROGATE OBJECTS

The TIE objects in Section 6.8 play the role of surrogates or proxies for the corresponding implementation objects. Likewise, the client stubs in Section 6.9 are also proxies of their CORBA server objects. In general, a proxy is a representation of a target object that is hidden from the client. The proxy implements a set of operations defined by an externally visible interface, whereas the target implements a similar but possibly different set of operations (Figure 6-29). Because of this, certain operations of the target object can be hidden from the client for security or other purposes.

The proxy may control the access to the target object, for example, by checking the access request against the predefined privileges in an ACL (see Section 5.11). The proxy may also manage the target object by creating, modifying, and removing it on behalf of the calling object or client. (Notice the similarity between Figure 6-29 and the object factory/manager pattern in Figure 6-4.)

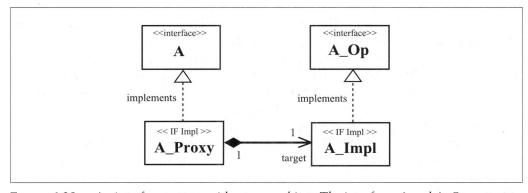

FIGURE 6-29. *An interface pattern with a proxy object. The interfaces A and A_Op are usually similar but may be different.*

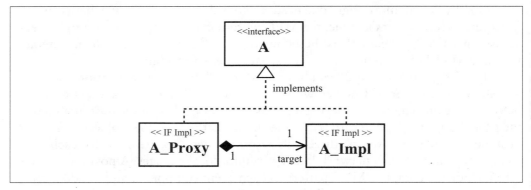

FIGURE 6-30. *An interface pattern with a tightly defined proxy object.*

Proxy objects also appear in layered systems (see Section 7.4). For example, objects in the interface layer of Figure 7-10 (the full-exposure approach) are, effectively, proxies of their corresponding persistent objects.

Finally, under certain circumstances, it may be desirable to couple the two interfaces in Figure 6-29 tightly. Figure 6-30 gives a design in which both the proxy and target objects implement the same interface. This is in fact the standard proxy pattern described in [Gamma et al. 1995].

6.12 CASE STUDY: ATM SYSTEM SOFTWARE—PART 4

We now return to the ATM system software case and carry out a detailed interface design. We start with the bank interfaces. As we described in part 3 of this case (Section 5.8), the bank operations include access control, account management, and operations on an account. A bank needs to manage multiple accounts and control the access to them. Naturally the object manager pattern of Section 6.3 provides a good model for this case. Figure 6-31 shows the bank module (or package), which consists of two interfaces, AccountIF and AccountMgrIF.

The interface AccountIF contains three `get` operations and four simple transaction operations (Figure 6-32). A transaction returns a Float number, indicating the updated account balance after the transaction. AccountInfo is a data structure containing account name, number, password, and so forth.

The interface AccountMgrIF contains access operations and account management operations (Figure 6-33). For example, the `open` operation opens an account with an initial amount and returns an AccountIF object. Similarly, `login` returns an AccountIF object for an existing account after verifying the account information.

Next we turn to the ATM Manager interfaces. Again we may use the object manager pattern, which yields two interfaces: SessionIF and SessionMgrIF. SessionIF

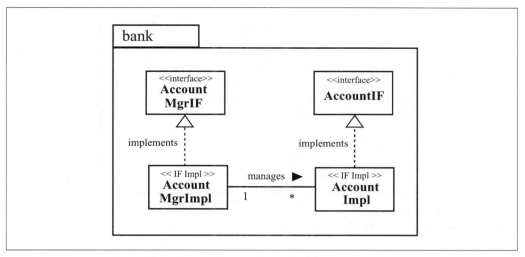

FIGURE 6-31.   *The bank module interfaces and their implementation classes. The suffix IF indicates an interface.*

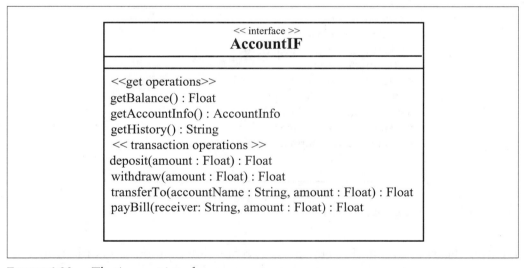

FIGURE 6-32.   *The Account interface.*

(Figure 6-34) represents a cash card usage session. Its definition is actually the same as AccountIF, because it relays the client calls to an AccountIF object at a bank.

Each card in use always has exactly one session, and each session connects to one account at any time. However, multiple cards or sessions may connect to the same account (the server object AccountImpl) simultaneously. To ensure that these

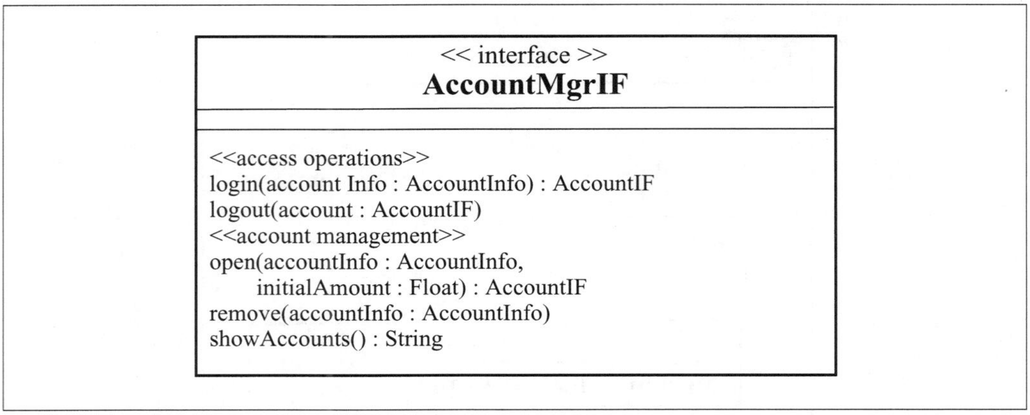

```
                        << interface >>
                         AccountMgrIF

        <<access operations>>
        login(account Info : AccountInfo) : AccountIF
        logout(account : AccountIF)
        <<account management>>
        open(accountInfo : AccountInfo,
             initialAmount : Float) : AccountIF
        remove(accountInfo : AccountInfo)
        showAccounts() : String
```

FIGURE 6-33. *The Account Manager interface.*

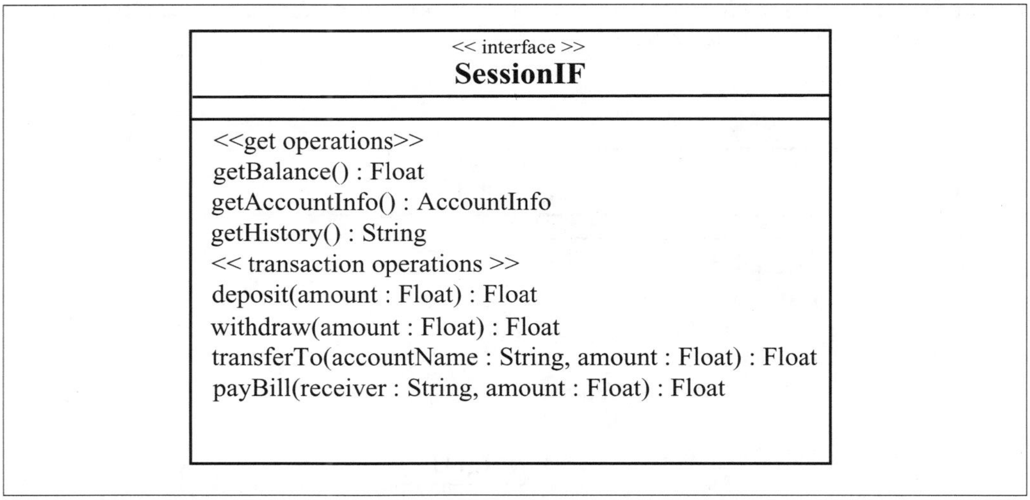

```
                        << interface >>
                          SessionIF

        <<get operations>>
        getBalance() : Float
        getAccountInfo() : AccountInfo
        getHistory() : String
        << transaction operations >>
        deposit(amount : Float) : Float
        withdraw(amount : Float) : Float
        transferTo(accountName : String, amount : Float) : Float
        payBill(receiver : String, amount : Float) : Float
```

FIGURE 6-34. *The Session interface.*

multiple clients of AccountImpl update the account information in an orderly manner, we need to enforce a synchronized update rule. This is achieved by declaring all the transaction operations "synchronized" in the AccountImpl class, as shown in Figure 6-35.

The UML property "synchronized" in Figure 6-35 carries the same meaning as in Java: Before a client thread invokes a transaction, it will try to obtain an exclusive lock for the object instance of AccountImpl. The transaction proceeds only if the lock is obtained. Otherwise, it will wait for the lock to become available (when another client thread releases the lock).

Because each bank has its own programming interface to its main database machine, the implementation of AccountImpl may differ from bank to bank. The definition of AccountIF in Figure 6-32 ensures that they all can communicate with the ATM system. This is a typical strategy for enterprise application integration.

Finally, the interface SessionMgrIF (Figure 6-36) contains access operations (`login` and `logout`). Its implementation class may have session management operations but they need not be exposed to the client (because the client is not allowed to manage sessions).

```
                        AccountImpl

  balance : Float
  accountInfo : AccountInfo
  history : String

  <<get operations>>
  getBalance() : Float
  getAccountInfo() : AccountInfo
  getHistory() : String
  << transaction operations >>
  deposit(amount : Float) : Float {synchronized}
  withdraw(amount : Float) : Float {synchronized}
  transferTo(accountName : String, amount : Float) : Float {synchronized}
  payBill(receiver : String, amount : Float) : Float {synchronized}
```

FIGURE 6-35. *The AccountImpl class. Note that all the transaction operations carry the UML property "synchronized."*

```
                      << interface >>
                      SessionMgrIF

    << access operations >>
    login(cardInfo : CardInfo) : SessionIF
    logout(session : SessionIF)
```

FIGURE 6-36. *The Session Manager interface. Only access operations are exposed here.*

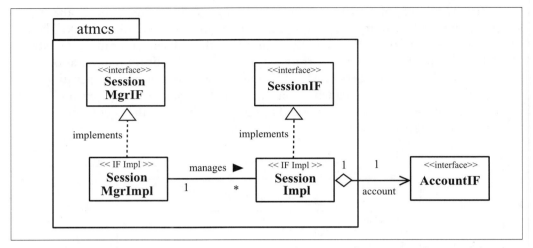

FIGURE 6-37.   *The ATM Central Server (atmcs) package contains two interfaces and their implementation classes. Note that AccountIF is used as a servant class to relay transaction requests. The suffix IF indicates an interface.*

During the implementation of SessionIF, one may use the interface AccountIF as a servant class to relay transaction requests. SessionIF and its implementation thus becomes an object adapter to the Account object. The design is shown in Figure 6-37. Note that the interfaces in the ATM Central Server (atmcs) package are refined from the ATM Manager in Figure 5-16.

To verify that all requirements in Section 2.10.1 are properly captured, we set up a requirement trace table (Table 6-1). The design features from this and previous parts of the case study are included in the table, showing that all the requirements are indeed fulfilled.

TABLE 6-1.   *The requirement trace table for the ATM system software design, showing design features fulfilling enumerated requirements.*

REQUIREMENT	DESIGN FEATURE
1. Adequate records of all ATM usage and transactions [*static*]	Records are kept by the persistent Transaction object and related persistent objects (Figure 3-21).
2. Security measures [*dynamic*]	Provided by the `login` operation in the interface SessionMgrIF (Figure 6-36).
3. Concurrent access to the same account [*dynamic*]	The account server object (AccountImpl) may be used by multiple clients with synchronized thread operations (Figure 6-35).
4. Future inclusion of cashier stations, Internet clients, and so forth [*static*]	Cashier stations, Internet clients, and so forth are modeled as subclasses of an abstract class Agent and can be added in the future (Figure 2-33).

Based on the two packages of interfaces (bank and atmcs), one can build a simulated bank server and an ATM Central Server with just the interface layer.

6.13   CASE STUDY: SHARED WHITEBOARD—PART 4

Continuing the shared whiteboard development into phase II, we first need to define the interface between different instances of the shared whiteboard. Before we do this, let us review the major requirements for phase II from Section 2.11:

- Sharing of a background image, markups, and annotations with multiple shared whiteboards in a collaboration group (requirement 2.5 for phase II)

- Connection to and disconnection from a collaboration group (requirement 2.6 for phase II)

These requirements can actually be divided into two levels. First, we need an infrastructure for connecting multiple shared whiteboards to form a collaboration group. The infrastructure also manages the members in a group, including their disconnection from the group. Second, we need to enable the collaboration group to share a background image, markups, and annotations in some orderly fashion.

Because such a system is new to us, we like to develop a rapid prototype to prove the concept before enhancing it with full capabilities. This is often a good strategy in real-life projects. One advantage of this approach is that it can be pursued in parallel to the mainstream whiteboard development. Lessons learned from the rapid prototype can be directly applied to the full shared whiteboard later.

6.13.1   MessagePort—An Infrastructure
for a Collaboration Group

The rapid prototype we will develop is called MessagePort, which provides the infrastructure for a collaboration group to exchange textual messages. Once this prototype is operational, we can easily upgrade it to an ImagePort for exchanging image data.

As for shared whiteboards, any user running MessagePort may join an existing group by connecting to *anyone* in the group. Also, any user in a group may disconnect without affecting the ongoing collaboration.

The former requirement suggests that all MessagePorts are equivalent. Hence, all connections between two MessagePorts must be bidirectional. To establish such a bidirectional connection, the operation `connect(...)` must include calling (local) MessagePortIF as an input argument. This allows the remote MessagePort to call the `connect(...)` operation on the local port to establish the backward connection.

The design for the interface MessagePortIF is shown in Figure 6-38. The identifier UserInfo is a data structure containing the address (username and host) of the local MessagePort user. Most operations have UserInfo as an argument so that the caller can be identified. The operation `getUserInfo` returns the user information about the server MessagePort. The operation `disconnect` disconnects the input MessagePort from the server.

Because a MessagePort may be connected to an existing group via any member in the group, the messages for the group must be propagated to all members by relaying through multiple MessagePorts (rather than broadcasting from a central MessagePort). Thus, besides the message, the operation `propagateMessage` also takes UserInfo as an argument to avoid sending the message back to the caller (which will result in an infinite loop).

Finally, the operation `getUserInfoList` returns a full list of all users in the group. This operation, like `propagateMessage`, is a propagating operation.

Regarding the object design, we envision that the implementation class of MessagePort contains a set of MessagePortIF object references (the remote MessagePorts). These connections represent both the MessagePorts that connect to the local one and the MessagePorts with which the local port joins. The core design thus includes a relationship loop with an interface, as shown in Figure 6-39. The relationship loop between MessagePortIF and MessagePortImpl allows messages to propagate across the entire group.

Finally, the MessagePort class is rather interesting in that it serves as both a client and a controller to its local MessagePortImpl server object. MessagePort's bidirectional link to MessagePortImpl allows it to invoke interface operations

```
                << interface >>
                MessagePortIF

<<connection operations>>
connect(portIF : MessagePortIF , userInfo : UserInfo)
disconnect(userInfo : UserInfo)

<< get operations >>
getUserInfo() : UserUnfo
getUserInfoList(userInfo : UserInfo) : UserInfo [*]

<< propagate operation >>
propagateMessage(message : String, userInfo : UserInfo)
```

FIGURE 6-38. *The interface MessagePortIF. Here, UserInfo is a data structure containing the address of the local MessagePort user.*

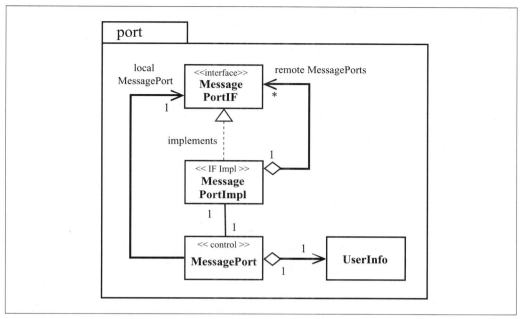

FIGURE 6-39. *The object design for MessagePort, showing a relationship loop with an inter-face. The class MessagePort serves as a control class for MessagePortImpl. All classes are defined within the package port.*

(such as `propagateMessage`) through its local server object and to process the messages received by MessagePortImpl. MessagePort maintains a unidirectional association with MessagePortIF, which is needed as an argument when connecting to a remote MessagePort. The MessagePort class also contains a UserInfo data structure for identifying the local MessagePort.

The detailed design for the class MessagePortImpl is shown in Figure 6-40. Besides the operations defined in Figure 6-38, `getConnectedPorts` returns the MessagePortIFs connected to the local port (the server object). The operation `findMessagePortIF` uses the input address as a key to find a MessagePortIF from the set of connected ports (contained in portIFs).

Figure 6-41 shows the MessagePort class design. The constructor takes an address string (containing the username and host machine of the local user) and creates a MessagePortImpl object and a MessagePortIF object. Their object references are stored as attributes in the class.

The `connect` operation connects the local port to the MessagePort at the input address, and `disconnect` removes the local port from an existing group. The operation `sendMessage` sends a message to all users in a group using `propagateMessage` in MessagePortImpl. On the other hand, `showMessage` displays the input message at

```
                    << IF Impl >>
                   MessagePortImpl

   port : MessagePort
   portIFs : MessagePortIF [*]

   << constructor >>
   MessagePortImpl(port : MessagePort)
   << connection operations >>
   connect(portIF : MessagePortIF , userInfo : UserInfo)
   disconnect(userInfo : UserInfo)
   << set, get, and propagate operations >>
   setMessagePort(port : MessagePort)
   getNumberOfConnectedPorts() : Integer
   getConnectedPorts() : MessagePortIF [*]
   getUserInfo() : User Info
   getUserInfoList(userInfo : UserInfo) : UserInfo [*]
   findMessagePortIF(address : String) : MessagePortIF
   propagateMessage(message : String, userInfo : UserInfo)
```

FIGURE 6-40. *The implementation class MessagePortImpl. The address string contains the username and host machine of a user. It is used as a key to find a MessagePortIF from the set portIFs.*

```
                     << control >>
                     MessagePort

   userInfo : UserInfo
   portIF : MessagePortIF
   portImpl : MessagePortImpl

   << constructor >>
   MessagePort(address : String)
   << connection operations >>
   connect(address : String) : MessagePortIF
   disconnect( )
   << get and send operations >>
   getMessagePortIF() : MessagePortIF
   getNumberOfConnectedPorts() : Integer
   getUserInfo() : User Info
   sendMessage(message : String)
   showMessage(message : String)
```

FIGURE 6-41. *The control class MessagePort. The address string contains the username and host machine of a user.*

the local port. The class MessagePort also reproduces some of the `get` operations in MessagePortImpl for convenience.

In summary, the MessagePort prototype provides three major functions: connect to a group, propagate messages to a group, and disconnect from a group. Next we examine the sequence diagrams for these functions.

6.13.2 SEQUENCE DIAGRAMS FOR MESSAGEPORT

Figure 6-42 shows the sequence diagram for connecting to a remote MessagePort from a local one. The user enters an address for the remote port. The local MessagePort (the control object) attempts to bind to the remote address. If successful, it then retrieves a list of user information already in the collaboration group. For each item in the list, the control object ensures that it is *not* already connected to the local port (using the `findMessagePortIF` operation). This avoids forming a loop connection, which will result in an infinite loop of message propagation.

After all members in the collaboration group are checked, the local control object invokes the `connect` operation on both the local and the remote MessagePortImpl server objects. These two calls establish a bidirectional connection between the two.

The sequence diagram for sending messages to all users in a group is given in Figure 6-43. On receiving a message from the user, the local control object invokes

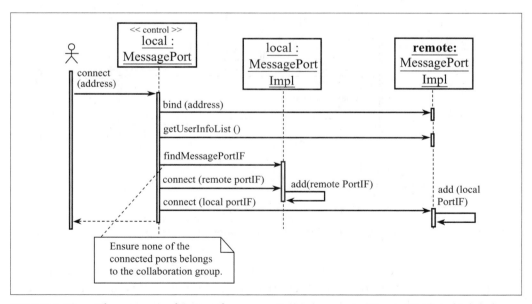

FIGURE 6-42. *The sequence diagram for connecting to a remote MessagePort (which belongs to a collaboration group) from a local one.*

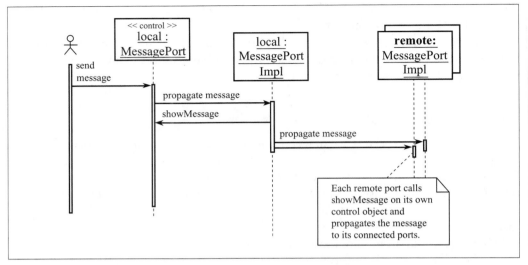

FIGURE 6-43. *The sequence diagram for sending messages to a group.*

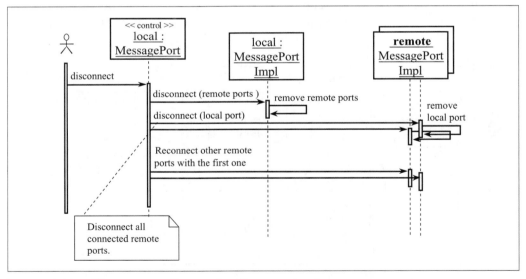

FIGURE 6-44. *The sequence diagram for disconnecting from a group.*

the `propagateMessage` operation on the local MessagePortImpl object. The message is first displayed by a call to the local control object (echoing). It is then propagated to all the remote MessagePortImpl objects connected to the local one.

At each remote MessagePortImpl object, the message is first displayed via its local control object. It is then further propagated to all its connected ports.

In this way the message will eventually reach all members in the collaboration group.

When any member in a group disconnects from the group, it must ensure that the ongoing collaboration is not disrupted. As shown in Figure 6-44, after the local port disconnects from all the remote ones (that are originally connected to the local port), it invokes the `connect` operation to reconnect all remote ports to one of the originally connected ports (such as the first one). This allows the remote ports to communicate with the collaboration group normally.

These three sequence diagrams constitute the major functions of the MessagePort infrastructure. In the next part of this case study, we will upgrade it to include image data exchange and to integrate it with the mainstream shared whiteboard design.

6.14   CASE STUDY: ACCESS CONTROL LISTS—PART 4

Object-level access control differs from system access control (such as the login process) in that each object may be individually controlled via an ACL. Thus, to utilize an ACL, one must link it to those objects being controlled. To begin, we define an ACL interface with the operation `isPrivilegeGranted(user : User, requestedPrivilege : Privilege) : Boolean`, where `user` is the user requesting the input privilege. The interface may be implemented by either one of our two ACL designs.

Next, an abstract class Accessible is constructed. It uses the ACL interface as a servant and contains the operation `isPrivilegeGranted`. In this way, any class inheriting Accessible is now controlled by the ACL. The design is shown in Figure 6-45, which is in fact the handle-body pattern with interface in Figure 6-8. Notice that multiple objects may link to the same ACL.

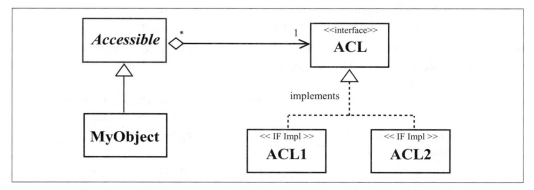

FIGURE 6-45.   *The interface design for ACL using the handle-body pattern of Figure 6-8. This allows either one of the ACL designs (ACL1 or ACL2) to be the implementation.*

ACLs are typically used to control persistent objects. The ACL implementation classes are also persistent objects. In systems with interface and persistent layers (see Section 7.4.1), the operation isPrivilegeGranted is usually invoked from the interface layer on behalf of the accessing user. Each access operation in the interface layer maps to a privilege defined for the system. For example, a write function requires a write privilege, a read function needs at least a read privilege, and so forth.

In systems with large numbers of persistent objects, it may not be practical to tie each one to an ACL. In this case we may control the objects by categories or by access control groups.

6.15   EXERCISES

6-1.   Design a universal resource locator (URL) service factory by combining the object factory pattern in Figure 6-4 and the inheritance ladder. The URL service factory creates and manages URL services, which take URLs and return their contents to the client.

Follow these steps. First, give the IDL file for a general service factory that, besides the create operation, also includes the management methods find, remove, and showAll. The service interface should have a generic performService operation that takes a generic (of type "any") input argument and returns a generic output variable. Second, design a partial implementation of the interfaces and a full implementation for the URL service factory and URL service.

6-2.   Draw a sequence diagram for the Timer and its Listener in Figure 6-10. Include the construction of a Timer and an event that close a window dialog.

6-3.   For the chat room application shown in Figure 6-12, draw a sequence diagram including activities such as user sign-on, callbacks from server, and so forth. Include two ChatUser clients in the diagram.

6-4.   The Simple API for XML (SAX) is a simple event-based application program interface (API) for parsing XML documents (see http://www.megginson.com/SAX/ for more information). SAX defines a set of interfaces, including DocumentHandler, ErrorHandler (to be implemented by the user's application), and Parser (to be implemented by a specific XML parser). These three interfaces and some of their operations are shown in Figure 6-46.

To use SAX, a user must find a SAX-compliant XML parser and write his/her own classes that handle the callbacks from the parser. For example, startDocument indicates the beginning of a document.

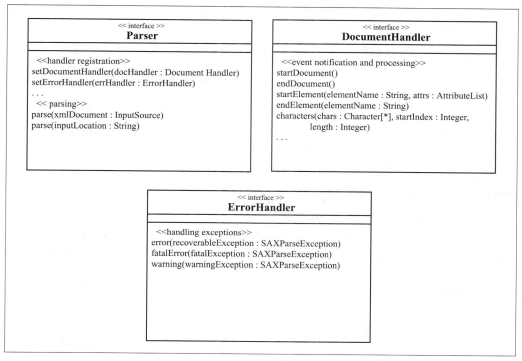

FIGURE 6-46. *SAX interfaces for Exercise 6-4.*

Similarly, the callback `startElement` signifies the beginning of an element. It also passes in the element name (which is #text in the case of a text element) and the associated list of attributes.

Based on this information, draw a design diagram for a SAX application including the interfaces in Figure 6-46 and their implementation classes. Also, draw a sequence diagram showing a simple parsing without errors.

6-5. Study the documentation for the following classes in the Java library: java.util.EventListener, java.awt.event.ActionListener, java.awt. AWTEventMulticaster, and java.awt.Button. The first two Listener classes are interfaces. AWTEventMulticaster is a class that dispatches AWT events in a multicast fashion. The Button class is a graphic component that can trigger an action event.

Suppose we want to have a class MyPanel to listen to the action events from a button. Draw a design diagram in short form, including all the classes and interfaces mentioned. *(Hint: Use the constructor of AWTEventMulticaster to infer what member variables it has.)*

To register a MyPanel object as a listener, the method `addActionListener` in the Button object must be invoked with the MyPanel object as the argument. For simplicity, we assume that the object is the only listener. In this case `addActionListener` calls the `add` method in AWTEventMulticaster and then sets a member variable of the Button object to point to the MyPanel object. Draw a sequence diagram showing the registration and the subsequent event processing. Note: You may look at the Java source code to find out more details.

6-6.   Expose the XML object model in Figure 2-29 through interfaces.

6-7.   Expand Figure 6-17 to include multiple views for the MVC pattern.

6-8.   Modify the diagram in Figure 6-28 by including the complete MVC pattern in each client component and adding a central server to synchronize all clients. Draw the corresponding static design in short form. Draw a sequence diagram for two clients and the server. You may omit the detailed process within each client.

6-9.   In Java, remote method invocation (RMI) provides capabilities similar to CORBA. Study the documentation on RMI and some simple code examples. Then, for an interface A, draw the RMI server-side object tree and the client-side objects (see Figures 6-19 and 6-25 for CORBA). Comment on the similarities and differences.

C H A P T E R 7

Object-Oriented Architecture

Software architecture grows out of algorithms, data structures, and object-level designs. It is an abstraction of system implementation that describes the overall system structure, decomposition of functionality into components, the nature and properties of these components, interfaces, and communication protocols between components, and the overarching tactics and rules. A software system architecture diagram serves as the common ground for people from different backgrounds (developers, users, project managers) to discuss and analyze jointly the high-level properties of the system with regard to its requirements.

Other architectural issues include relationships and constraints between components, external interfaces, overall access control and security, and strategies for scaling and performance. A good software system requires a sound and integrated architecture. Architectural integrity is like color coordination in paintings: It underpins the ultimate success of the system. In addition, an architecture also determines a wide range of system characteristics, such as cost-effectiveness, interoperability, scalability, and so forth.

The distinction between architecture and design is not absolute. In architecture we are more concerned with the coordination between components, overall system performance, and scaling properties. In design we focus on the details within a component, an interface, or a subsystem. However, it may happen that problems arising from design (such as a poorly performing interface) may force a revision of the architecture.

Object-oriented architectures differ from traditional ones by emphasizing the allocation of distributed objects, components and their interfaces, persistent objects, and object-based communication. Different architectures are needed for different requirements and constraints. In this chapter we focus on the common patterns in object-oriented architectures. The study of such patterns allows us to

- Communicate the high-level properties of a particular architecture to people of different backgrounds

- Recognize the frameworks or patterns that can be reused in other systems, either as variations or mixtures

- Make informed decisions on architectural alternatives based on a thorough understanding of their properties

We begin with a description of our notations for architecture diagrams.

7.1   NOTATIONS FOR ARCHITECTURE DIAGRAMS

In terms of graphic notations for software architectures, there is as yet no standard style in the real world. In our opinion, such a standard may not be practical, because architecture diagrams are used by a wide range of people, from marketing, managerial, to technical. Consequently, people have used a widely divergent set of icons, blocks, and connectors to describe the organization and properties of software systems. Many of these graphics are specific to their own systems.

Here, for our architecture diagrams, we adopt a more engineering (although rather plain-looking) style, one that is based on the UML *deployment diagram*. You can certainly make these architecture diagrams more attractive by using other graphic icons.

In UML, a deployment diagram is a graph of nodes connected by communication channels (connectors). It shows the configuration of runtime processing elements. A node is a runtime physical object that has processing capability. It may contain component instances and other physical things such as databases. Those components live or run on the node. An example is shown by the Server node in Figure 7-1.

As we discussed in Section 4.7, components are deployable parts of implementation (or, runtime manifestations of code units). They may contain multiple object instances. However, these object instances are typically hidden in architecture diagrams. Thus, we generally go down only to the component level in our architecture diagrams.

In UML, when one component uses the services of another component, a dependency notation can be indicated. In our architecture diagrams, however, we prefer to use connectors in place of dependency notations because they convey the dynamic behavior of the system.

The notation for connectors is simply lines connecting nodes or components. The lines represent communication paths (for procedure calls, operation invocations, event triggers, and so on) between nodes or components. The default communication is bidirectional. Arrows can be used to indicate unidirectional links. Components can

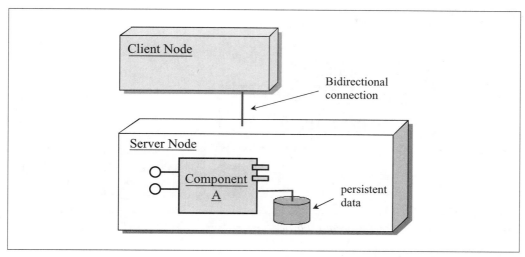

FIGURE 7-1. *An example architecture diagram. Nodes are denoted by cubical blocks. A connector between the two nodes indicates bidirectional communication. The cylinder represents a database containing persistent data.*

exist without being contained by a node. In this case it can be connected directly to other components or nodes. Components and nodes represent conceptually similar runtime code in a system. We do not try to make a clear distinction between them and may even use them interchangeably.

7.2   PROCEDURAL PROCESSING SYSTEMS

Procedural processing systems center around algorithms and data structures. They are like pipelines or filters. Each process takes some inputs, processes them, and generates outputs. Data flow from one process to the next in one direction. An example is shown in Figure 7-2.

Typical uses of such an architecture are data/image processing, modeling and simulation, mathematical solution, and so forth. Take, for example, a simulation system. It may have a preprocessor, which reads in data and converts them to certain formats. The output from the preprocessor is piped to a solver, which solves a set of model equations and outputs the results. Finally, a postprocessor packages the data into formats suitable for plotting or other visualization tools. These three components are shown in Figure 7-3. The connectors between different processing components are unidirectional data pipelines. Note that the components may reside in different machines.

The three processing components are augmented by a user interface/controller and a System Services node. The user interface/controller handles all user requests

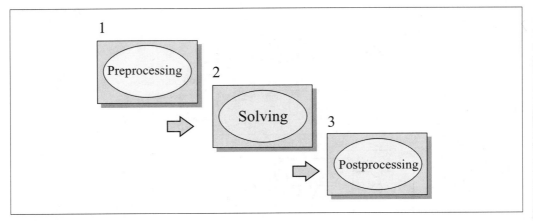

FIGURE 7-2. *Processes in a procedural processing system.*

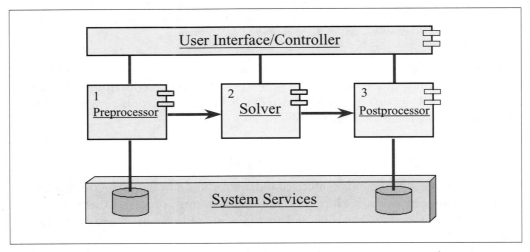

FIGURE 7-3. *An architecture for a simulation system. The System Services node contains databases indicated by the cylinders.*

and relays them to the appropriate components. It presents a unified interface to the user and allows the user to control and monitor the full cycle of a simulation. The System Services node provides services such as data management and interfaces with external tools.

The most important characteristic in this architecture is the unidirectional data flow in the pipelines between the processing components. Many scaled-down versions of such an architecture may have only a primitive user interface besides the core processing components.

The advantages of this architecture include the following:

- The overall behavior is a simple composition of individual processing components.

- The processing components can be reused easily if the input and output data are compatible.

- The system can be easily extended by adding new processing components.

- The system can be run in massively parallel computers (of either shared memory or distributed memory type).

The limitations of this architecture include the following:

- It primarily operates in a batch mode and is not suitable for interactive applications.

- The management of corresponding input and output data sets may be a challenge because of different formats or data storage requirements.

7.3 CLIENT/SERVER SYSTEMS

To simplify development and maintenance of complex applications, we separate centralized, monolithic systems into more manageable components or nodes. At the design level, this leads to the client/server model described in Section 5.3. The corresponding architecture is the client/server system. In a simple client/server system, an application is partitioned into a client and a server. The client handles the presentation and the server handles low-level functions and database access. The server typically contains multiple server objects and may serve multiple clients, as shown in Figure 7-4.

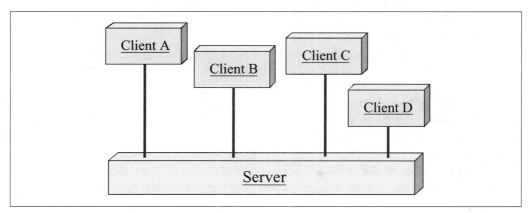

FIGURE 7-4. *A client/server system with four clients.*

The business logic may be handled by the client or by the server, depending on the implementation strategy. Clients communicate with the server via certain protocols, such as HTTP (Hypertext Transfer Protocol) or CORBA/IIOP.

The advantages of this architecture are the following:

- The clients can be detached from the server, allowing remote access and separate code development.

- One server may serve multiple clients.

The limitations of this architecture are the following:

- Client/server communication relies on a network, which may become the bottleneck of performance (except in the case of a client/server colocated on the same machine).

- Changes on the server side require changes on the client side if the interface definition is changed. When there is a large number of clients, keeping them up to date becomes a difficult task. This is especially serious for enterprise applications that support thousands of users.

The first limitation suggests that we should minimize remote invocation from clients. For example, groups of operations may be bundled together and processed in one remote request. Such tactics on distributed object design have been discussed in Section 6.10.

The second limitation may be alleviated by introducing *thin clients*, which have a standardized interface definition and presentation framework. A prominent example is a Web browser, which is based on HTTP and HTML standards. Web applications developed for such thin clients are free from the burden of maintaining client software (provided the HTTP and HTML standards remain the same). (Section 7.3.1 covers this topic.)

Alternatively, the same objective can by achieved by using *dynamic object distribution* or *object transportation,* by which we mean part or all of the objects are actually transported to the client when a client application starts up. This is the same principle as Java Applets, which in reality require a preinstalled and consistent set of libraries on the client side. (Given the fluid nature of today's software evolution, this may not always be the case.)

In most large systems, the speed of the servers affects significantly the overall performance of the system. This is because the servers are shared by multiple users. To increase server efficiency, you may use the following techniques (not a complete list):

- Shift some workload to the clients (for example, doing certain consistency checks on the client side).

- Increase database transaction throughput by bundling queries together.

The hardware and management costs of the system are also lowered when the efficiency of the servers is increased.

When the number of users goes up to thousands or more, the server side can be expanded to have multiple servers. This naturally leads to systems with more than one tier of service nodes. We cover this topic in Section 7.5.

7.3.1 "Thin Clients" and Object IDs

An important class of client/server system is the ubiquitous *Web browsers,* which are also referred to as *thin clients.* Although the browser software itself may take up many megabytes of disk spaces, browsers are still considered thin. This is because to construct a GUI, the server only needs to send some structured data to the client, rather than a full program. Such structured data are defined by two standards: HTTP and HTML [HTTP and HTML].

HTML is concerned with the format or presentation of contents, whereas HTTP is a message-based data exchange protocol that defines the interface between an HTTP server (Web server) and its clients (Web browsers). As such, HTTP is not an object-oriented protocol. Hence, a certain software component is needed in the Web server to flatten the object structures in the back-end application and to convert messages from the clients to method invocations for objects.

This, of course, is not an ideal situation for object-oriented applications in the back end. However, historic development has proved that this simple protocol is highly popular. Our task, then, is to find a way to identify objects between the servers and the thin clients. Another issue of thin client/Web server systems is the separation of data from presentation, which we cover in Section 7.3.2.

Our focus here is on Web-based applications, which differ from simple Web sites in that they provide interactive services to clients rather than static or semidynamic contents. For example, a Web banking client allows users to see their account balances, make transfers, or pay bills. The characteristics of a Web-based application are the following:

- The user interacts with objects in the server via a thin client.

- The application uses a small number of views for unlimited data (such as the amounts of bill payments).

Figure 7-5 shows the interaction between a thin client and a Web server for a Web-based application. First the client connects to the Web site, which returns an

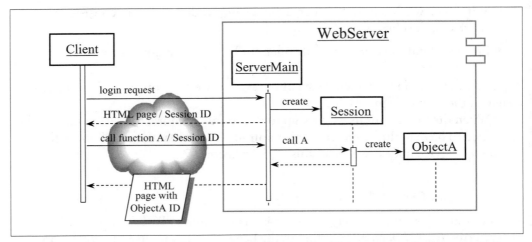

FIGURE 7-5. *Communication between a thin client and a Web server on the Internet (indicated by the cloud). ServerMain represents the main function that processes requests for the Web application. The Session ID and Object ID uniquely identify the objects on the server side.*

HTML page with a login form (this step is not shown in the figure). After filling out the form, the client sends a login request to the Web server.

At this point the server invokes the Web application's main function (ServerMain), which processes *all* requests from the client. After validating the password, ServerMain creates a Session object for the client. The Session object lasts for the duration of the client's interactive session. It encapsulates all operations available to the client. It may also handle access control for those operations based on the client's credentials. Such a design on the server side is nothing but the object factory and object manager patterns (see Section 6.3).

Now the difference is that because HTTP is not object oriented, a string (or a long integer) of Session ID must be sent back to the client along with the HTML page. The Session ID is an object ID for identifying the Session object associated with the client. Hence, it plays the role of an object reference in an object-oriented interface. To achieve an interface, the Session ID needs to be stored in the client and made accessible for every request to the server during the session. (The ID is typically stored as a text string, called a *cookie* in a client machine.)

Similarly, if a function call creates an object that needs to be identified by the client, a unique object ID (such as a hash code) must be returned along with an HTML page. Such IDs are often embedded in the HTML page (or client-side scripts) and are sent to the server with the client's next request.

The Session ID also plays the role of a secured token because it varies from session to session. The ServerMain function actively manages the Session objects and

IDs. For example, if a session is inactive for a certain time, it should be deleted automatically. As a result, the token becomes invalid and the user must login again at the next connection. ServerMain can limit the number of concurrent sessions (by any one user or by all users). It may also keep a record of all the activities in a session.

The Web applications usually take the form of *Servlets* (which are Java code invoked by a Web server or an associated *Servlet engine*), server-side scripts (for example, Visual Basic script, Javascript), or CGI (Common Gateway Interface) programs (such as PERL code or executables). These programs control what should be done in response to user requests and how the data from the back-end objects are presented to the users. In this context, an effective approach is the MVC framework, which is discussed next.

7.3.2 WEB APPLICATIONS USING THE MVC FRAMEWORK

The MVC framework provides an effective approach for implementing Web-based applications. Although the details may vary, the essence is the separation of data from presentation.

Figure 7-6 shows a Web-based application using the MVC framework. On the server side, the ServerMain object represents the main function that processes requests for the application. The Template object contains an HTML page template, which defines a view for the application. DataSet contains the data model. Objects related to security control are omitted in the figure.

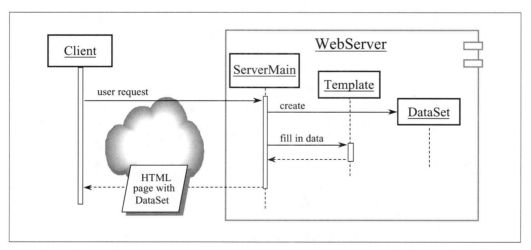

FIGURE 7-6. *A Web-based application using the MVC framework. ServerMain represents the main function that processes requests for the application. Template contains an HTML page template. DataSet contains the data model. The Internet is indicated by the cloud.*

After receiving a user request, ServerMain creates a DataSet object based on the data retrieved from some back-end databases (not shown in Figure 7-6). The DataSet object contains all the data needed for the view, which is defined by an HTML page template in the Template object. ServerMain then fills in the variables in the page template and returns the altered page to the client. Note that instead of having the template to pull data from the server, the data are returned to the client along with the template. This is different from the standard MVC framework and helps to avoid network latency problems.

An example template page is shown in Figure 7-7, in which the variables are denoted by `${variable_name}`. Their values are obtained from the DataSet object in the server. To make a payment, a user enters the amount, selects a vendor, and then clicks the Make Payment button. The server processes the request and returns a new page with a new balance. The Show Recent Payments button brings up another view with a list of all recent payments.

Note that besides having ServerMain as the controller, the template page may actually contain some controls to be performed on the client side. For example, when a user hits the Make Payment button in Figure 7-7, the page can verify that the value in the Pay input field is a legitimate number and is below the current balance. This can be done using client-side scripts before sending the payment request to the server.

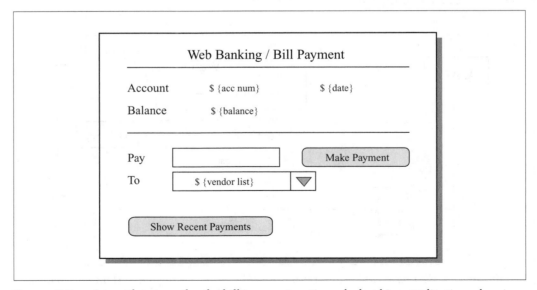

FIGURE 7-7. *A template page for the bill payment section of a banking application, showing the template variables in the form* `${variable_name}`. *The page can be constructed easily with HTML.*

In summary, the MVC framework is applied to Web-based applications as follows:

- **Model**—The model is defined by a DataSet object in the server. It is created by a server-side controller using data from databases or other objects.

- **View**—A view is defined by a template page, such as an HTML page with certain variables. The page is totally separate from the controller and can be viewed as a stand-alone page with a thin client. For template pages containing client-side controls, they can be developed, tested, and modified independently of the controller. This allows front-end development to be conducted in parallel with server-side development. The interface between a view and a model is the set of template variables or a DataSet object in a client-side script.

- **Controller**—The main controller resides in the server (such as a Servlet). It responds to client requests, invokes other objects to process the requests, fills the template page with updated data, and returns the resulting page to clients. A secondary controller may be included in the template page to perform client-side validation and other manipulation of views. This controller has no network latency, thereby greatly enhancing the efficiency of the application. The template page in this case will contain both presentation information (such as HTML) and client-side scripts (such as Javascript).

7.4   LAYERED SYSTEMS

Layers refer to logical groups of objects within a component or a node. Layered systems typically appear in servers, in which each inner layer provides services to its immediate outer layer. For example, in Figure 7-8, the interface functions call the

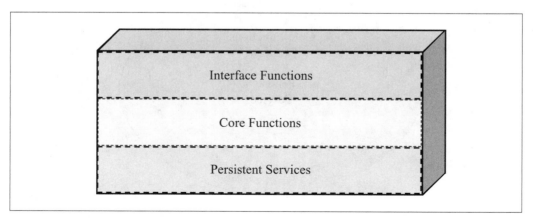

FIGURE 7-8.   *A node with three layers.*

core functions to perform tasks. The core functions in turn use the persistent services to make objects persistent.

Layered systems are also drawn in nested ellipses, such as those presented in Figure 7-9. This picture clearly shows that services and functions inside the interface layer are hidden from the external world. Note that each layer may contain a set of objects that works coherently to provide the services. Communication between layers is typically through direct function calls, defined by an API. It may also occur through object references across layers.

The advantages of this architecture are the following:

- It promotes layers of design abstraction, allowing a complex problem to be decomposed into several layers of functions.

- It allows easy control of internal functions and services that should not be exposed to the external world. Only objects in the interface layer are visible as interface classes.

- New operations can be introduced in the interface layer. These are often combined operations from the core or persistent layers. For example, frequently used queries involving multiple calls to the server can be grouped into one function call. This helps improve system performance.

- A layer may be reused if the interface is compatible. A self-contained layer may also be deployed as a separate node.

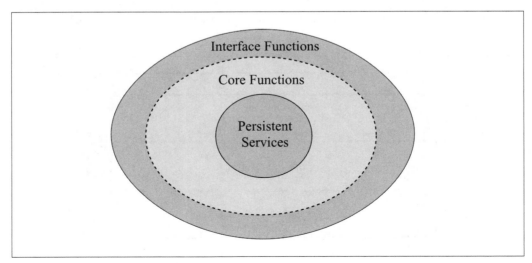

FIGURE 7-9. *Another notation for a layered system.*

The limitations of this architecture are the following:

- Layering may degrade system performance because interface functions may need to go through several layers to invoke the operations in the inner layers.

- Standardizing layer interfaces may lead to cumbersome and inefficient function calls.

Layered architectures are found mostly in application servers, database systems, layered communication protocols (such as CORBA/IIOP), and operating systems. They are often used together with other types of architectures.

7.4.1 LAYERING WITH SERVANT OBJECTS

One strategy in layering is to treat the persistent classes as servant classes to the interface implementation classes. Figure 7-10 shows the objects related to the Catalog hierarchy of Figure 5-4 in two layers: the interface layer (in which only the implementation classes are shown) and the persistent layer. Each interface implementation class (an interface object with IF Impl) is associated with one persistent class. The

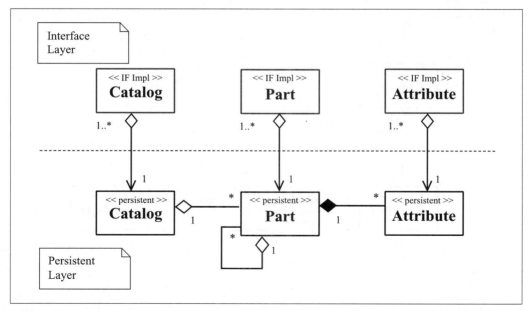

FIGURE 7-10. *Persistent servant objects in a double-layer design. In this example, every persistent object is exposed through one or more objects in the interface layer (full-exposure approach).*

interface object is created after the corresponding persistent object is created or retrieved from the database.

In this particular design, each persistent object is exposed through one or more objects in the interface layer. This includes all public operations of the persistent classes. These operations are defined as the operations of the interfaces. The implementation classes simply relay them to those in the persistent classes. Thus, objects in the interface layer of Figure 7-10 are, effectively, proxy objects of their corresponding persistent objects.

Such full exposure of all persistent objects gives the clients to the interfaces full control of all persistent objects. The interface implementation is straightforward. Access control or security can be performed in the interface layer. However, such full exposure may be undesirable for security and other reasons. For example, if the persistent layer has many objects, a large number of interfaces will be created. A single query from a client may hop through several server objects, which will slow down the execution. Thus, as a good practice, the inner layer should expose only those objects and operations necessary for the outer layer.

Figure 7-11 shows an example of using only one interface to access the Catalog hierarchy. This may be adequate when only a limited set of catalog functions (coarse-grained

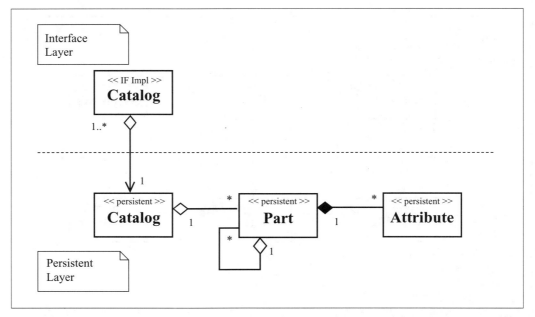

FIGURE 7-11. *Persistent servant objects in a double-layer design. In this example, only one class of interface objects is used to access operations in the persistent objects (single-exposure approach). This results in better control and performance.*

functions) are needed. Each operation invocation now involves only one call to the server object, thereby reducing network traffic and enhancing performance. The interface definition for such a design can be found in Section 5.6, where Part and Attribute appear as data structures in the interface definition.

In reality, some persistent objects are exposed to the interface layer whereas others are hidden. Such partial exposure gives us sufficient capability with flexible access control and reasonable performance. Objects in the interface layer may also arise from dynamic analyses. In this case, you may need to match the objects in the two layers. The ATM Central Server case provides such an example (see Section 7.9).

The implementation classes in the interface layer usually handle the following important functions in all relevant operations:

- **Security and access control**—Ensures that a persistent object can only be accessed by users with the right privileges.

- **Transaction**—Guarantees changes made to a persistent object fulfill the ACID requirements (see Section 3.1).

- **Synchronization**—Prevents different threads from interfering with one another during transactions. This is important because in either Figure 7-10 or Figure 7-11, each persistent object may be affected by more than one interface object (which typically belong to different threads). Certain concurrency policies are needed to ensure that changes to the persistent object are made in a synchronized manner. For example, concurrent access to the persistent object from different threads may be prohibited.

7.5   THREE-TIER AND MULTI-TIER SYSTEMS

Unlike layers, which reside inside components or nodes, tiers are physically distributed components or nodes. A client/server system has two tiers, the client and the server. In a three-tier system, there are two pairs of client/servers (Figure 7-12). The first tier is usually a Database Management node. The second or middle tier typically handles business logic or application-specific computation. It is a client to the first tier. It also serves as a server to the third tier, which includes a number of clients.

The third tier, or user-interface tier, handles user interaction. Its design focus is on efficient user interface and accessibility in an enterprise. The client software can either be a regular or thin client, depending on the requirements. Different user interfaces may also be provided to different types of users, who may access the same Business Logic node.

The Business Logic node in the middle tier may contain multiple components, each of which handles a specific service (such as security, search, and event services). These components are in turn made up of business objects, which are, for example, CORBA

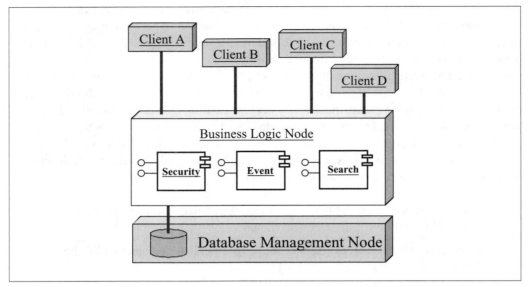

FIGURE 7-12. *A three-tier architecture has two client/server pairs.*

objects if CORBA is used for communication between the third and second tiers. The business objects perform business functions and invoke the methods in the first tier.

Generalizing this to multi-tier systems, n-1 pairs of client/servers may chain together to form an n-tier system. For example, we may add a Web server and thin clients to the three-tier system to obtain the four-tier system in Figure 7-13. The Web server handles any Web browsers (thin clients) in the Internet. It translates HTTP requests into method invocations in the Business Logic node (the second tier). On the other hand, regular clients (such as Client A) in the internal or virtual private network may still connect directly to the second-tier node. These clients typically perform more involved business operations.

The advantages of this architecture are the following:

- The system is easy to maintain and extend because different groups of functions are distributed across several tiers of server.

- It allows hierarchical control of functions from the lower tiers to the upper tiers and similarly different levels of services to clients of different tiers.

- It enables enterprise-level integration, typically by connecting the middle tiers with other enterprise systems.

- It is highly scalable to handle a large number of concurrent clients. This can be achieved by clustering with a pool of servers.

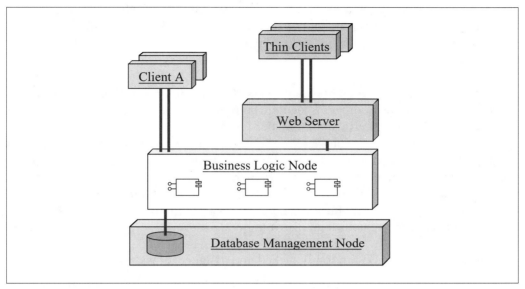

FIGURE 7-13. *A four-tier architecture with both regular and thin clients.*

The limitations of this architecture are the following:

- More than one communication protocol is involved between the client/server pairs. For example, in a four-tier system, these may include HTTP between thin clients and the Web server, CORBA/IIOP between the Web server and the Business Logic node, and SQL between the Business Logic and the Database Management nodes. Hence, a wide range of expertise is needed when implementing such systems.

- Performance tuning of the system becomes more difficult because data may travel through multiple nodes (which may be in machines with different platforms and operating systems) before reaching the clients.

7.5.1 CLUSTERING AND SERIALIZING

To scale up a multi-tier system to handle a large number of clients, we may use a set of server nodes, which cooperate with each other to provide services to clients. Two approaches may be employed:

1. Each replicated server node provides the same functionality, and a client may use any one of them. We call this technique *clustering*.

2. Each server component provides a specialized function. A client request may start with one server, followed by other servers. This is reminiscent of the procedural processing system in Section 7.2 and may be called *serializing*.

In clustering, client requests are processed in parallel, and is therefore most appropriate for a large number of clients who perform similar tasks.

An example of clustering in a four-tier system is shown in Figure 7-14. A large number of thin clients go through a Web server to use the components in the Business Logic nodes. Three identical nodes are shown in the figure. They all obtain data from the Database Management node in the first tier.

In the architecture in Figure 7-14, the Web server determines how the work is distributed evenly across the Business Logic nodes to minimize users' wait time. This can be achieved using various load distribution algorithms:

- **Random**—A node is randomly picked and assigned a task.

- **Round-robin**—One node is selected after another in a cyclical fashion.

- **Load balanced**—The node with the least workload is chosen.

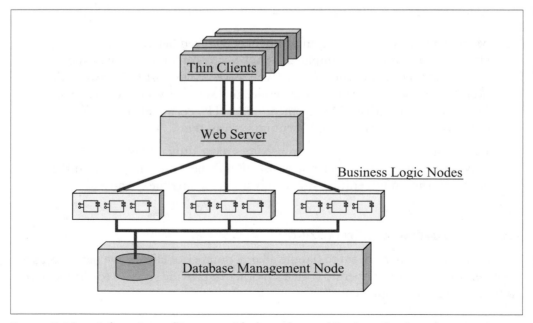

FIGURE 7-14.   *A four-tier architecture with three clustered Business Logic nodes may serve a large number of thin clients.*

- **Multiple queues**—Client requests are divided into several categories, each associated with one or more nodes. Requests of the same category wait in the same queue. This technique may be used when certain requests require more processing power than others. A special queue may be set up with a more powerful machine to process these requests.

Serializing is typically used together with clustering to provide specialized services. For example, Figure 7-15 is a variation of Figure 7-14. It uses two serialized nodes to handle security and load balancing. When a client request comes in, the security node checks its credentials. The dispatcher then determines which Business Logic node should be used and returns a reference or pointer for an object in that node to the client object in the Web server. From this point on, the client object in the Web server talks directly with the chosen Business Logic node to complete the process.

The same technique can be applied to Web servers so that they can handle a large number of Web clients. However, because each Web server is directly accessible to all clients, a security check must be performed at each server. Exercise 7-1 deals with this topic.

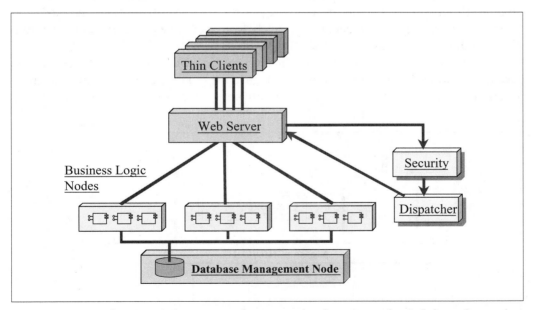

FIGURE 7-15. *A four-tier architecture with two serialized service nodes and three clustered Business Logic nodes. After the security check, the dispatcher balances the load by selecting a Business Logic Node and returning its reference to the client object in the Web server.*

7.6 AGENTS

From a component point of view, agents are simply servers. They wait quietly for requests or messages from clients. When an agent receives a request, it processes the request, returns the results, and then waits for the next request.

From an architecture point of view, agents can simulate actors in a workflow-oriented enterprise. For example, in an application processing environment, Agent 1 may check the integrity of the application. Then, if everything is in order, Agent 2 will log the application and process financial information such as application fees. Other agents will then perform work on different parts of the application.

Each agent may be fully automatic or may have a human in the loop. The workflow may follow a rigid process or it may vary according to the application. A controller is needed to coordinate such agent activities, which may occur in a parallel or serial fashion. This flexibility requires that clients, agents, and other server nodes share a common communication channel.

Figure 7-16 shows an agent architecture with one Controller node and three agents. The message bus or ORB is the common communication channel, which transports either messages or method invocations.

The agents can be single nodes or they can be tiered systems (such as Agents 1 and 2 in Figure 7-16). When a particular client connects to an agent, they form a virtual multi-tier system. Furthermore, one agent may connect to another agent as a client. Thus, the agents and clients effectively form a complex web of communication through the message bus.

To emphasize the importance of the message bus, we may draw the agent architecture in a looplike fashion, as shown in Figure 7-17. The message bus may be an internal network or it may be a virtual private network across the globe.

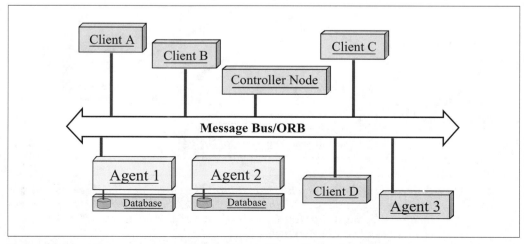

FIGURE 7-16. *An agent architecture with one Controller node and three agents.*

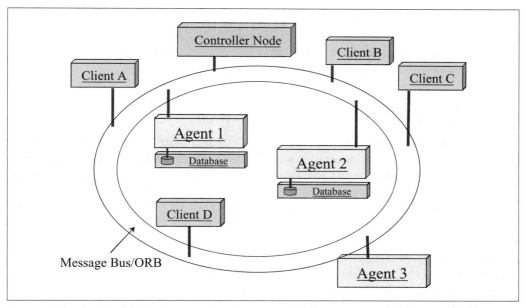

FIGURE 7-17. *An agent architecture with one Controller node and three agents. The message bus or ORB is shown as a loop.*

The advantages of this architecture are the following:

- It allows high flexibility in processing complex tasks that require the attention of multiple agents.

- The system can be built incrementally and can accommodate gradual transition from a previous system.

- The system is easy to maintain and extend because different groups of functions are distributed across agents.

- It can be easily combined with multi-tier systems, enabling enterprise-level integration and achieving high scalability.

The limitations of this architecture are the following:

- Security issues require special and early attention because all activities are exposed through the message bus or ORB. Any encryption or authentication will impose an extra burden on the network and will affect overall system performance.

- Enterprisewide planning becomes crucial because a single communication protocol must be adopted for the message bus or ORB to make the whole system work. For enterprises with legacy systems, this implies that extra effort is needed to wrap the old systems with the selected protocol.

- Performance tuning of the system may be difficult because processing occurs in multiple agents in various orders.

7.7   AGGREGATIONS AND FEDERATIONS

Another way of forming an enterprise system is to aggregate a number of identical or compatible nodes into a connected group (Figure 7-18). Structurally, this is the same as the recursive aggregation in Figure 2-3a. From any one node you may reach all the other nodes by walking through the aggregation. As an enterprise software system, the group of nodes share something in common (such as a common view) through a common communication protocol.

For example, in a chat room or conferencing application, each user may join the conference by connecting to anyone already in the conference (the aggregation). All users share the contents of the conference. When a user sends a message, it propagates to the entire group by going through all the branches.

The design of the software at each node only needs to consider the interface between two nodes. This is because messages are sent from one sender to one receiver. Furthermore, only one interface design is needed for the entire system.

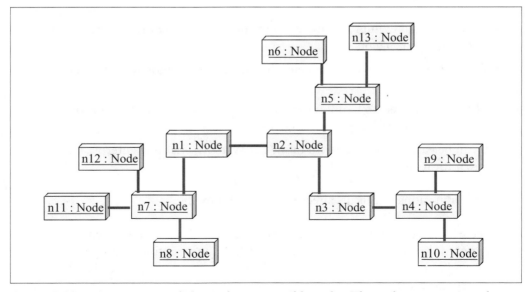

FIGURE 7-18.   *An aggregate of identical or compatible nodes. The nodes communicate by a common protocol. The node numbers indicate the order in which the nodes join the aggregate.*

To join an aggregation, a new node may connect to any one node already in the group. Likewise, the new node can leave the group at any time. However, other nodes connected to the group via that node will lose their connection. Thus, in Figure 7-18, if node n5 leaves the group, nodes n6 and n13 will be lost. To overcome this problem, the software should reconnect the orphan nodes to the group appropriately when their aggregate node disconnects from the group.

Going one step further, each node may have a number of subnodes. In this case we promote the original nodes to *hubs*. A group of hubs may form an aggregate as before, whereas the subnodes only connect to its parent hubs. Such a federation topology is illustrated in Figure 7-19.

There are many possible incarnations of the federation architecture. For instance, the hubs can be server nodes and the subnodes can be client nodes. Each server may have its own local database. By aggregating the servers, an enterprise-wide database is formed. Although each client connects to its own local hub, it can access the entire enterprise database, which is physically distributed but logically integrated. Such an architecture is a central theme of many enterprise data management systems.

The hub-to-hub or server-to-server communication protocol may be different from that between a hub and its subnodes (although they may share the same

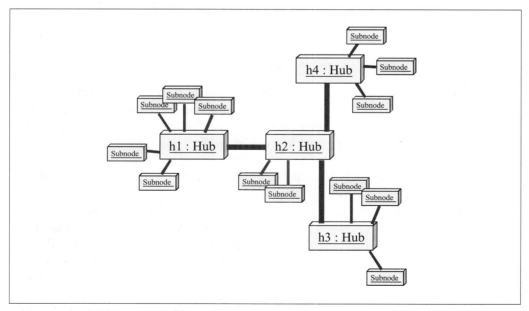

FIGURE 7-19. *A federation architecture containing an aggregate of hubs, each with its own satellite subnodes. The communication protocol between the hubs (the thick connectors) may be different from that between a hub and its subnodes (the thin connectors).*

network, such as the Internet). Each hub may also enforce its own security policies and expose only certain parts of its local system to the federation.

The advantages of the aggregation and federation architectures are the following:

- A large-scale system may be formed from small and reusable nodes. The nodes share a common integrated view of the entire system, which is physically distributed.

- Each node is relatively simple and needs only to interact with one or a few interfaces.

- The structure is very flexible and decentralized, leaving strong control by local nodes or hubs.

The limitations of these architectures are the following:

- An aggregation is not necessarily an optimized network. Message propagation may be slow because the message needs to pass through many nodes.

- An aggregation is prone to single-point failure. The failure of a key connection may impact a large subset.

- If the nodes are not identical and their number is large, maintaining them may be become a burden.

7.8   ARCHITECTURAL PATTERNS IN UML*

This section provides a more abstract coverage of the architectures described in Section 7.7. The architecture diagrams in that section are actually instances of certain architectural patterns, which are more generic descriptions of classes of architectures. Here we attempt to specify these architectural patterns using the UML notations.

To do this, we treat the nodes and connectors in our architecture diagrams as instances of two UML classes: Node and Connector. Some of the attributes for these classes are shown in Figure 7-20.

For a Node, the attributes are its name and platform. For a Connector, they include the name, the two nodes it connects, the direction of data flow (for example, bidirectional, from node 1 to node 2), and the communication protocol (HTTP, CORBA/IIOP, and so on). Connector typically appears as an association class for Node. In what follows we use the UML stereotypes <<Node>> and <<Connector>> to represent these two types of classes.

The architectural pattern for procedural processing systems is shown in Figure 7-21. A GUI connects to a number of processing units (Processor), which utilize services from the common service unit (Service).

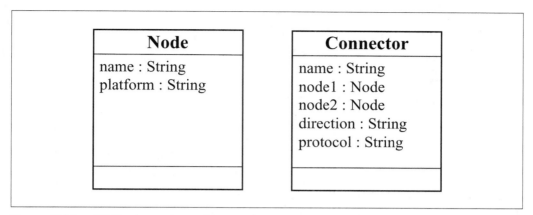

FIGURE 7-20. *UML classes for architectural patterns.*

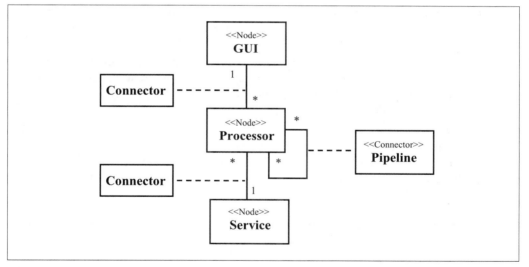

FIGURE 7-21. *The architectural pattern for procedural processing systems. Pipeline is a uni-directional connector.*

The Processors in general form a network (see the Node network in Figure 2-4). The Processors run their processes according to a certain prescribed order. When a Processor finishes its run, its outputs are sent to its downstream Processors through a Pipeline, which is a unidirectional connector.

Figure 7-22 shows the architectural pattern for multi-tier systems. Starting from the Client node, each Tier connects to the next one in a linked list fashion. (We omit the situation of having clusters of nodes.) The last Tier in the link is typically a

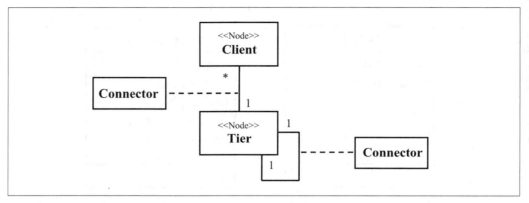

FIGURE 7-22. *The architectural pattern for multi-tier systems.*

Database Management node. The Connectors between different Tiers usually employ different protocols. For example, for thin clients, the protocol is HTTP. For thick clients, it may be CORBA/IIOP.

The architectural pattern for aggregation and federation systems is depicted in Figure 7-23. The hubs themselves form an aggregation because each hub may be connected to a set of other hubs. If there are subnodes attached to the hubs, then a federation system results. Hub-to-hub communication may use a different protocol from that between a hub and a subnode.

For systems with agents, the architectural pattern has a Connector in the center (Figure 7-24). A set of Agents and Clients may connect to it. There is also a Controller to coordinate the work of the Agents.

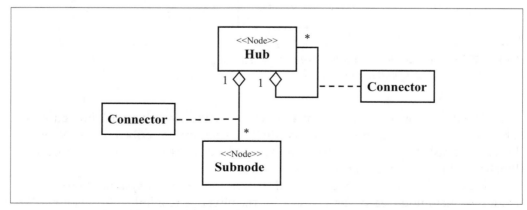

FIGURE 7-23. *The architectural pattern for aggregation and federation systems.*

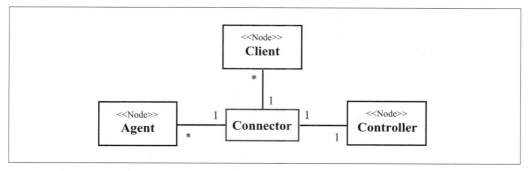

FIGURE 7-24.   *The architectural pattern for systems with agents.*

7.9   CASE STUDY: ATM SYSTEM SOFTWARE—PART 5

In this final part of the case study we bring together everything from the previous parts and discuss the architecture of the ATM system software. We have built the design from the ground up, so the composition of the architecture is now rather straightforward.

First we go back to the sequence diagram in Figure 5-16, which shows that there are three things in the system: the ATM clients, the Central Server, and the banks. For completeness we add the Bank Database node to each bank. This results in a four-tier architecture for the ATM system software, shown in Figure 7-25.

In this architecture, the ATM clients talk to the interfaces at the ATM Central Server component. These interfaces (SessionMgr and Session) are identified in the atmcs package of Figure 6-37. The interfaces in the bank package of Figure 6-31 (AccountMgr and Account) are in turn used by the Session implementation object in the Central Server to access the accounts.

The ATM Central Server has its own persistent data or database, which for now is included as part of the Server. Each bank has a separate database node to handle the account data.

One can also add a Web interface to the ATM Central Server, as in Figure 7-13. The Web Server handles thin clients and contains controllers that acts as clients to the ATM Central Server. One may apply the MVC framework of Section 7.3.2 to implement this Web application. An example is given by the iBank sample application (see the preface of this book for reference to the sample code).

As indicated in Figure 7-26, the architecture allows a large number of ATM clients accessing multiple bank servers. The ATM Central Server becomes the unifying mechanism for all banks. On the other hand, with a large number of clients, it may become a bottleneck to the operation of the entire ATM system.

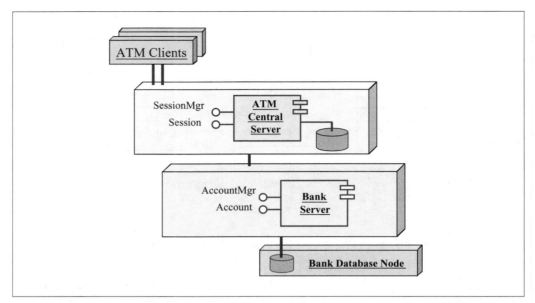

FIGURE 7-25. *Four-tier architecture of the ATM system software. The ATM clients use the interfaces at the ATM Central Server, which in turn uses those of the Bank Server.*

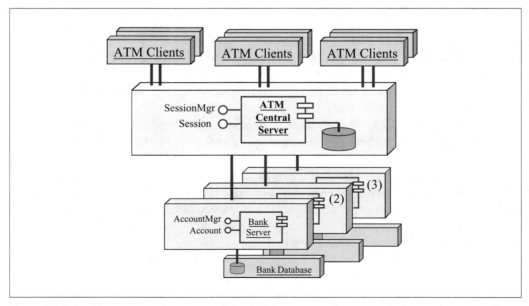

FIGURE 7-26. *Four-tier architecture of the ATM system software, indicating a large number of ATM clients accessing multiple bank servers.*

Now that we have a prescription of the system architecture, let's investigate further the details in each node. The Bank Database node in Figure 7-25 is assumed to be given (which is most likely a relational database). It determines the actual implementation of the bank server component. The ATM clients use the SessionMgr and Session interfaces in the Central Server node, which also has its own persistent data. Next we elaborate the layered structure in the Central Server node.

The objects in the Central Server node can be organized into two layers: interface and persistent. Because we have identified the interface design in Figure 6-37, we may use it to refine the persistent object design in Figure 3-21.

The first thing we notice from these two designs is that they do not quite match each other. The implementation class SessionMgrImpl in Figure 6-37 corresponds to the database root ATMManager in Figure 3-21. However, SessionImpl has no counterpart in the persistent layer. Because each client to the Central Server has a handle to SessionImpl to execute transactions, we may simply insert a Session class into the persistent layer to manage the transactions within a session. This gives rise to the design in Figure 7-27.

Next we apply the servant object approach from Section 7.4.1 to connect the two layers. The result is shown in Figure 7-28 (only two persistent objects are shown).

With this layered design, we may refine the sequence diagram in Figure 5-16 to include interaction with objects in the two layers. For the use case of ATM transaction in Section 5.8, the following objects in the persistent layer are affected: ATMManager, Session, Transaction, and DailyLog.

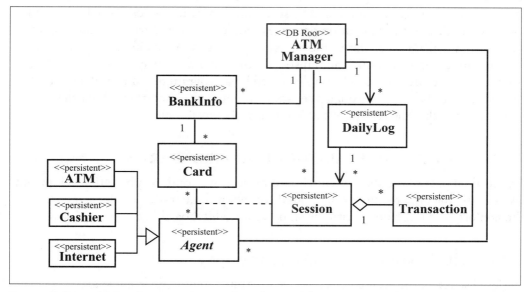

FIGURE 7-27.   *Object design in the persistent layer of the ATM Central Server.*

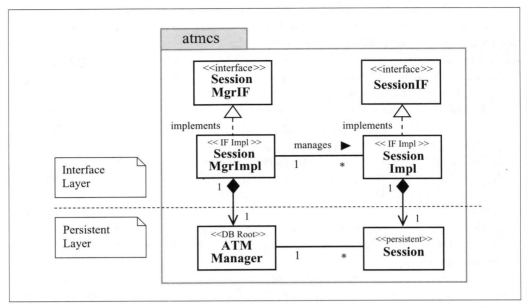

FIGURE 7-28. *The interface and persistent layers of the ATM Central Server. The package atmcs contains objects in the interface layer. Only two persistent objects are shown in the persistent layer.*

Other objects in the persistent layer (such as BankInfo, Card, ATM, and so on) are actually created and maintained by some administration processes, which we have not discussed. The administration processes should be covered with one or more use cases, from which we can derive the necessary functions. Although not explicit from the system requirements, such administrative functions are always needed. In terms of system architecture, they can be implemented by a program that directly manipulates the persistent objects, or through a separate administration interface. After that, we can safely say that the ATM Central Server is fully functional.

7.10 CASE STUDY: SHARED WHITEBOARD—PART 5

In this final part of the shared whiteboard project, we continue phase II development. We discuss the architecture of the shared whiteboard, upgrade the MessagePort to ImagePort, and integrate it with the stand-alone whiteboard.

7.10.1 THE SHARED WHITEBOARD AGGREGATION

When discussing the architecture, we are interested in how different shared whiteboards connect to each other. Reviewing the object design for MessagePort in Figure 6-39, we find that its relationship loop is in fact the same as the hub-to-hub aggregation depicted in Figure 7-23. The classes MessagePortImpl and MessagePort combined form the equivalent of a hub. The connector is a communication bus based on certain protocol, such as CORBA/IIOP. The multiplicity of one on the aggregate side of the relationship loop is guaranteed by forbidding loop connection (see Section 6.13.1).

It is beneficial to investigate how a MessagePort can dynamically join and leave a group. In Figure 7-29a we show two instances of a collaboration group. The one on the left has labels p1 to p9, whereas the one on the lower right contains four MessagePorts. The second group (or any new MessagePort in general) can join the first group by connecting to any port in that group. Such is the case in Figure 7-29b, where port pB is connected to p5.

After the two groups are joined, additional connections between them, such as p1-pA in Figure 7-29b, are forbidden. This prevents loop connections, which could result in infinite cyclical propagation of messages.

Also, when a MessagePort disconnects from a group, it must ensure that other ports connected to it will communicate with the group properly. For example, when port p3 in Figure 7-29a leaves its group, one of the connected ports (such as p8) is selected randomly as the new point of contact. The other connected ports are reconnected to this port, resulting in the configuration in Figure 7-29b.

We note that all these features were already covered by the MessagePort prototype developed in Section 6.13.1. Here we cast them in the context of the aggregation architecture to gain a more thorough understanding of the whole picture. More importantly, we have shown that the MessagePort prototype does provide the communication infrastructure for the shared whiteboards.

7.10.2 IMAGE EXCHANGE FORMATS AND POLICIES

Before carrying out the object design, we need to decide on two things: the format for image data exchange and the policies on such exchanges.

In general, to exchange objects one needs to serialize them into streams of data. Our image data include the pixels for the background image, and the markups and annotations. Because the pixels are readily available from DrawCanvas of the shared whiteboard, we may put them into an array. This avoids the difficulty of dealing with different image file formats if we were to send the original image files.

For the markups and annotations, because we already have the capability of converting them into CGM data, which are arrays of bytes, we can simply use the CGM data as the exchange format.

For the MessagePort we may simply stack the messages from multiple users. However, in a shared whiteboard such a practice will quickly lead to an unreadable

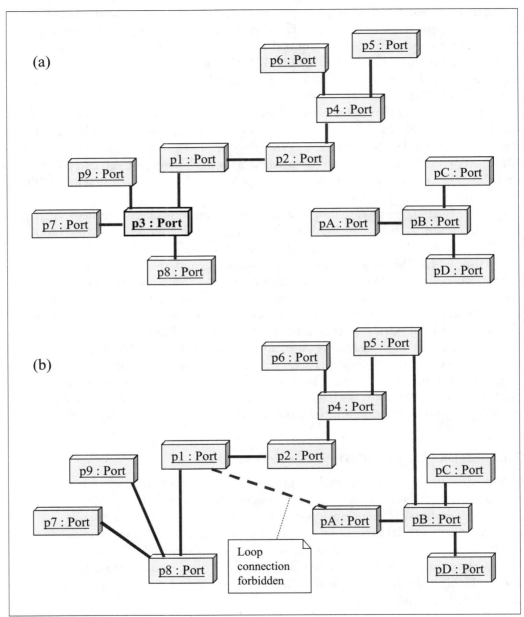

FIGURE 7-29. *The dynamics of collaboration groups consisting of ports. The two groups in (a) are joined by connecting ports pB with p5. Also, port p3 in (a) leaves its group, resulting in reconnected ports around p8 in (b). Loop connections such as p1-pA in (b) are forbidden.*

drawing because the markups from all users are shown together. This subtle difference prompts us to establish certain policies for the orderly exchange of image data.

Although such policies are not explicitly called for by the requirements in Section 2.11, they are nevertheless important in developing a robust shared whiteboard application. Such is often the case in real-life projects, in which the initial customer requirements need to be augmented with such provisions or revised with additional requirements.

For a collaboration group, we introduce the concept of *leadership*. A collaboration group can have no more than one leader (although none may exist). The group leader has the privilege of sending image data to the entire group, whereas others can only draw markups and make annotations on their own whiteboard, in addition to seeing the image data from the leader. This is similar to a group discussion in a meeting room, where only one person is allowed to draw on the whiteboard.

Anyone in the group can request to become a leader. We enforce the policy that a leadership request must be granted by the current leader (although the leadership may be granted automatically). If no leader exists in the group, the request is automatically granted. This avoids the situation in which more than one member tries to send different image data to the group.

When one group joins another one, as is the case in Figure 7-29, we may have one leader in each group and therefore the joint group may end up with two leaders. To be compliant with our single-leader policy, we stipulate that the joining port must secure itself as a leader for its own group before joining the target group, and afterward it must give up its leadership. Thus, for example, in Figure 7-29b port pB must become a leader of its own group before joining the other group.

After joining the target group, members of the old group will receive images from the joint group leader, who is also the leader of the target group. (Of course any one in the joint group can request leadership from the joint group leader.)

To sum up, we have established the following policies for image exchange for collaboration groups:

- No more than one leader can be present in a collaboration group.

- Only the group leader can send images to the entire group.

- Requests for leadership must be granted by the current leader. If no leader exists in the group, the request is automatically granted.

- Only the leader can take the group and merge it with a target group. The leader of the target group assumes leadership for the joint group afterward.

We note that these policies may also be applied to other types of aggregation or federation architectures in which shared data are disseminated from one source at a time.

7.10.3   THE INTERFACE AND CONTROL LAYERS

Based on the MessagePort prototype, we are now ready to transit to ImagePort, which is a subclass of MessagePort. Figure 7-30 gives the object design for the port package, which contains objects in both the interface and the control layers.

Each class for the MessagePort has a corresponding subclass for the ImagePort. Specifically, ImagePortIF defines the interface, ImagePortImpl implements the interface, and ImagePort acts as a controller for image communication. As subclasses, the ImagePort classes reuse operations and attributes from the MessagePort classes, thereby greatly accelerating the additional development. The classes in the interface layer form an inheritance ladder.

The design for the interface ImagePortIF is given in Figure 7-31, along with the Image structure. The pixels of an image are represented by an integer (with 4 bytes that contain alpha, red, green, and blue signals respectively). The operation `getImage` simply returns the Image at the ImagePort server.

The operation `propagateImage` propagates the input image to the group. However, unlike `propagateMessage` in the MessagePort prototype, this operation does not echo the image back to the initial sender (because it is already on the sender's screen). This again is a subtle difference between sharing images and sharing messages.

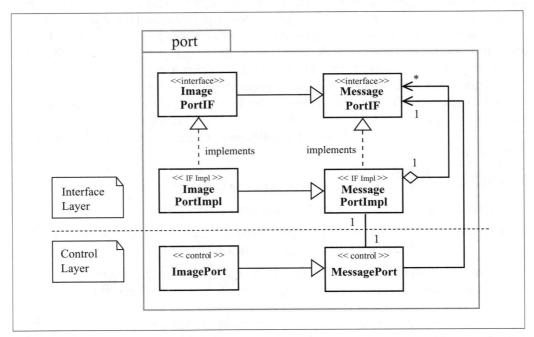

FIGURE 7-30.   *The interface and control layers in the port package. Note that only one link goes across the two layers.*

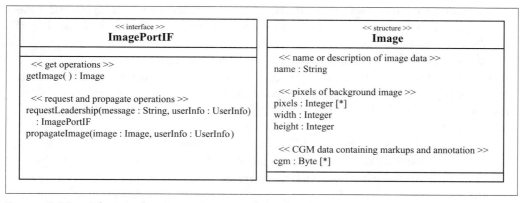

FIGURE 7-31. *The interface ImagePortIF and the data structure Image.*

The interface also includes `requestLeadership`, which is needed to implement the policies in Section 7.10.2, thereby maintaining an orderly image exchange. The operation carries a message argument from the initial requester.

The implementation class ImagePortImpl (Figure 7-32) contains a Boolean flag to indicate whether the server object is a group leader (the flag is initially true). Its constructor takes an input ImagePort, which is stored in the port attribute of the superclass MessagePort. The operation `findImagePortIF` returns the ImagePortIF object for the input address. It actually calls the superclass's `findMessagePortIF`

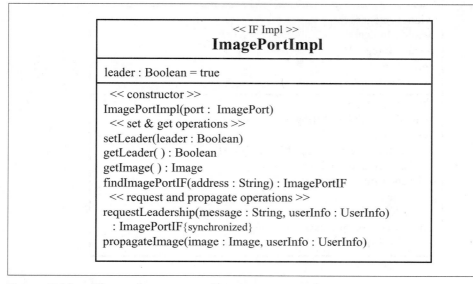

FIGURE 7-32. *The implementation class ImagePortImpl.*

operation and then narrows the returning object reference into an ImagePortIF object (this is typically done by calling a narrow operation associated with the ImagePortIF or its helper class).

If the server object is a group leader, the operation `requestLeadership` in ImagePortImpl will call the corresponding operation in the control object to request the leadership. Otherwise, it simply propagates the call to its connected ports. Notice that this operation has the UML property "synchronized," which we discuss in Section 7.10.4.

The control class ImagePort in Figure 7-33 contains the image data and a reference to a DrawCanvas object, which allow an ImagePort object to exchange images with its shared whiteboard's DrawCanvas. The operation `setImage` populates the image data in ImagePort and triggers DrawCanvas to display the image (including the markups and annotations). Specifically, DrawCanvas uses the operations `getImageFrom` and `getGlyphsFrom` in Figure 2-36 to get the image data and display them.

The operation `setLeader` attempts to secure the local port as a leader by calling `requestLeadership` in ImagePortImpl, which will subsequently propagate the request to the group. On the other hand, the operation `requestLeadership` in the ImagePort class (Figure 7-33) responds to calls from ImagePortImpl and decides

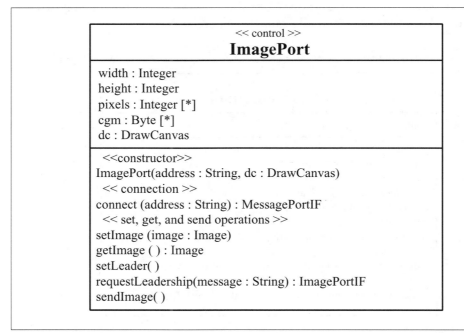

FIGURE 7-33. *The control object ImagePort.*

whether to grant leadership to the requester (for example, by popping up a user dialog window). This operation is called only if the local port is a leader in the group.

The operation `connect` in Figure 7-33 overrides the one in the MessagePort class. As shown by the sequence diagram in Figure 7-34, the operation first ensures that the local ImagePort is a leader of its own local group by calling `setLeader` (which may request leadership from other members of the local group). If that is successful, it then invokes the `connect` operation in the superclass MessagePort. After establishing a connection, the local ImagePort retrieves the image data from the remote ImagePort and sends them to its local group. Finally, the local ImagePort gives up its leadership as prescribed by the policies in Section 7.10.2.

To send the image data contained in the control object to the entire group, `sendImage` may be used. This operation actually first tries to make the local port a leader in the group (using `setLeader`) before invoking `propagateImage` at the local ImagePortImpl object. On receiving the image data, the remote ImagePortImpl objects set the image data at the control objects, which in turn send the image to their own DrawCanvas for display. The corresponding sequence diagram is shown in Figure 7-35.

The sequence diagram for ImagePort to disconnect from a group is the same as in Figure 6-44.

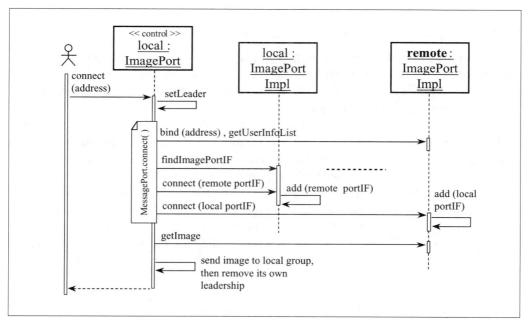

FIGURE 7-34.   *The sequence diagram for connecting a local ImagePort to a remote one. The process reuses the* `connect` *operation in the superclass MessagePort.*

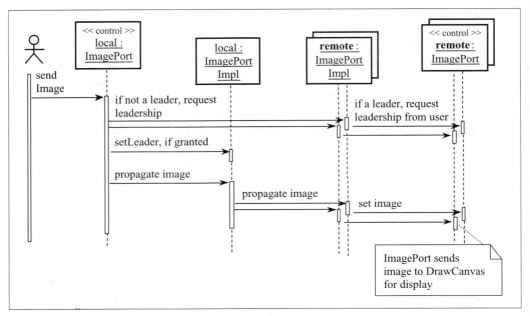

FIGURE 7-35.   *The sequence diagram for ImagePort to send an image to the group.*

7.10.4 SYNCHRONIZATION AND RELATED ISSUES*

An ImagePort by itself is a leader of its own (the Boolean leader is initially true in the implementation class ImagePortImpl of Figure 7-32). When it joins another Image-Port, it gives up its leadership according to the policies. In this way an aggregate of ImagePorts will have only one leader.

However, before sending image data, an ImagePort tries to make itself a group leader first, as shown in Figure 7-35. If more than one ImagePort makes such requests simultaneously, we need to ensure that the leadership is transferred from one to another in an orderly fashion so that the group has only one leader at all times.

The uniqueness of leadership is guaranteed by the UML property *synchronized* on the operation requestLeadership in Figure 7-32. It means that before a client executes the operation, it will try to obtain an exclusive lock for the object instance of ImagePortImpl. The execution proceeds only if the lock is obtained. Otherwise, it will wait for the lock to become available (when another client belonging to a differ-ent thread releases the lock).

Within the aggregation architecture, one can show that such synchronized execution does guarantee that the group has a unique leader. For example, in Figure 7-36, the requester at port p9 is waiting for the group leader at port p6 to grant leadership. During this time, the ports p9, p8, p1, p2, p4, and p6 are all

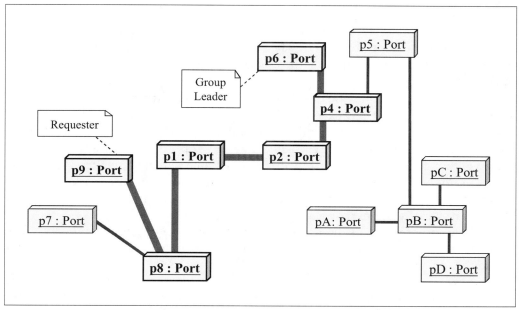

FIGURE 7-36. *The synchronized execution of a leader request in progress. The highlighted ports in the group connect the requester to the group leader. They are all locked during the synchronized execution. Other requests for leadership must wait for that process to finish.*

locked by the synchronized execution. Requests for leadership from other ports, such as p5, will need to wait for that one to finish (or time out automatically). Afterward, either p9 becomes a new leader or p6 remains the leader. The request from p5 or pB will then go through port p4 to request leadership from the current leader.

This type of synchronization is often needed to ensure that the states of objects change in an orderly fashion when multiple clients invoke the same operation in a multithreaded environment.

With synchronization operations, there is a possibility that a deadlock may occur, for example, when a port (call it portA) requests leadership from another port (portB), which is in the process of obtaining leadership from other ports. Not finding the existing leader from the other ports, portB later contacts portA to get leadership. This results in a deadlock because portB is waiting for portA to complete the request and vice versa.

To break the deadlock, we may either time out the synchronization execution or let the operation be executed as usual when a deadlock is detected (as is the case in which portA and portB are waiting for each other).

7.10.5 TRACE TABLE FOR REQUIREMENTS

Finally, to verify that all requirements in Section 2.11 are captured, we complete a requirements trace table (Table 7-1). The design features from this and previous parts of the case study are all included in the table, showing that all the requirements are indeed satisfied.

We note that there are other issues when implementing the design. For example, a certain port in a group may experience network problems during a collaboration session. The program should detect this and should gracefully drop the port from the list or try to reconnect to it. The `requestLeadership` operation in MessagePort should automatically grant leadership after a preset time so that an unattended Image-Port does not block the process. Also, DrawCanvas should distinguish markups sent by remote ports from the ones drawn locally. This allows users to make markups locally and at the same time participate in the collaboration.

These and other issues did not appear explicitly in the original requirements for the shared whiteboard. We should review them with the customer

TABLE 7-1. *The requirement trace table for the shared whiteboard, showing that the design features fulfill all the requirements.*

REQUIREMENT	DESIGN FEATURE
2.1. Background image (phase I)	Given by the image attribute in the DrawCanvas class (Figure 2-36).
2.2. Text annotations and graphic markups (phase I)	Provided by the Glyph class, which allows different types of markups and annotations (Figure 2-37).
2.3. Create, select, move, and change annotations and markups (phase I)	Provided by the `display` and `editing` operations in the DrawCanvas class (Figures 2-36, 5-17, and 5-19).
2.4. Save and read annotations and markups to CGM file (phase I)	Enabled by the operations in the DrawCanvas class, with help from the CGM utilities in Figure 2-38.
2.5. Sharing of a background image, markups, and annotations with multiple shared whiteboards in a collaboration group (phase II)	Provided by the ImagePort and MessagePort classes. The orderly exchange of image data is guaranteed by the policies described in Section 7.10.2.
2.6. Connection to and disconnection from a collaboration group (phase II)	Provided by the infrastructure of the MessagePort prototype (Section 6.13.1).
2.7. Some new types of markup (phase II)	New glyph types may be added to the Glyph class. The CGM utility classes also need to support the new types.
3.1. User interfaces following the Windows standards	Described by the user interface in Figure 2-34 and the object model in Figure 2-35.

and either refine the requirements or document the solutions in the software design document.

In summary, we have gone through a rather detailed discussion for the two phases of the shared whiteboard development. The first phase involves the stand-alone whiteboard, for which the emphasis is the design of graphic elements and drawing functions. For the second phase, the rapid prototype of MessagePort proves to be very useful. The design of the prototype can actually be reused through inheritance.

Our development process in this case study is linear. In reality, though, system architecture and object design often go through several iterations. Certain issues, such as the representation for image data and markups, will affect both phases. It is advantageous to have them settled early during the development process.

7.11 CASE STUDY: A RENTAL BUSINESS—PART 3

We developed the database design for SuperRent by gathering information from our friend informally. Although formality is not necessary among friends, it is still a good practice to summarize the requirements for the design in an organized way. Further-more, we need to find out system-level requirements that allow us to make a system design. The complete list of requirements is presented in Table 7-2, along with rele-vant design features and notes.

Requirements 1 through 5 can be accommodated by the existing design. Requirements 6 and 7 are system-level requirements. They have strong implications on the system architecture.

Requirement 7 suggests that the catalog data be exposed through a Web server. Thus, we need to add software components to the Web server to access the back-end database. These components should also handle user requests and queries. Going one step further, they will enable new customers to join SuperRent as members at the Web site.

At this point we are pondering whether the same components may be used to allow store operator access through a Web browser. Given our experience with the ATM Central Server, we feel that we can implement a similar access control mecha-nism in a Web interface, so that only store operators with sufficient privileges can per-form a predefined set of business processes (such as check out, check in, and so on).

There are other issues, such as integration with cashier terminals, encrypted transaction data for additional security, and so forth, but we omit them for brevity here.

Figure 7-37 shows a four-tier architecture for the SuperRent system. The thin clients connect to the Web server through HTTP. Inside the Business Logic node are service components, such as Servlets or server-side scripts. These components play

TABLE 7-2. *Rental business system requirements.*

REQUIREMENT	DESIGN FEATURES/NOTES
1. Includes a database that captures all needed information for SuperRent and allows members to rent items from any store and return them to any store.	Persistent object design using the association class, the collection manager, and container patterns (Figure 3-25)
2. Supports the following business processes performed by store operators: • Acquiring an item • Checking out an item • Checking in a returned item • Removing an item	The sequence diagrams in Section 5.10 handle checking out and checking in items. Acquiring and removing items can be treated similarly.
3. Provides a daily report of rented items.	The DailyLog class allows us to find rentals by date quickly (Figure 3-25).
4. Performs a daily check for overdue items.	The sequence diagram in Figure 5-23
5. Provides rental statistics for each title, including top ten and bottom ten titles, monthly rental volumes at all stores, and so forth	These can be implemented as operations in the SuperRent class.
6. Allows operators at different stores to access the central database securely and to perform business processes.	Different stores may access the central database via a private network or the open Internet with additional security measures.
7. Allows members to browse through the catalog from SuperRent's Web site.	This suggests that the catalog data be exposed through a Web server.

the role of a controller in the MVC framework (see Section 7.3.2). The Web server communicates with these components through some internal protocol or by direction function calls.

Next in the chain is the Database Management node. The service components talk to this node through, for example

- JDBC (Java Database Connectivity)
- ODBC (Open Database Connectivity)
- Direct API calls

The first two are used for relational databases, whereas the last one is more common for object-oriented databases.

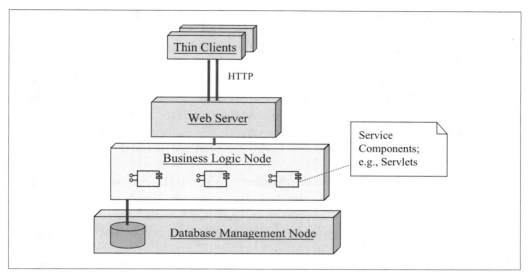

FIGURE 7-37. *A four-tier architecture for the SuperRent system.*

7.12 CASE STUDY: THE ENTERPRISE JAVABEANS FRAMEWORK

The Enterprise JavaBeans (EJB) standard is an emerging framework for distributed objects. It is specifically designed for the application domain of transaction processing in a high-volume, mission-critical environment. As in other frameworks, the EJB framework provides a family of interdependent components and objects that can be extended and adapted to a wide range of applications within its own domain. Specifically, EJB provides a component architecture that facilitates the development of enterprise applications with distributed objects.

Although EJB is by definition Java specific, we believe that it is a good reference for other frameworks of distributed object computing and therefore deserves a thorough study. This case study is by no means a comprehensive discussion of EJB. We skip many implementation details to focus on the object-oriented mechanisms of the EJB framework. For complete coverage of application development using EJB, see [Monson-Haefel 2000, Roman 1999]. Because we have covered the CORBA standard in detail, we use CORBA as a reference frame in studying EJB. We point out the salient features provided by EJB that are absent in CORBA.

7.12.1 STATIC STRUCTURES

Each component in EJB is a distributed object. Hence, as for a CORBA object, an EJB component has an interface and an implementation class. In addition, it has a factory interface for managing the life cycle of the components. Here for convenience we use the term *bean* to denote such an EJB component. In Figure 7-38 we use a Part bean to illustrate the static design of the EJB framework (see Figure 7-10 for objects related to Part).

The Remote interface is the superclass of all remotely visible interfaces in Java. The interfaces EJBHome and PartHome together define the life cycle operations for the beans, including `create`, `find`, and `remove`. The interface PartIF specifies the operations specific to a Part object, such as `getName`, `setName`, and so forth. The interface Part combines these operations with the bean access operations from EJBObject.

The interfaces PartHome and Part constitute the interfaces of the bean factory and the bean respectively. The bean itself is implemented by the class PartBean, which is similar to an implementation class in CORBA. Besides implementing the operations in PartIF, PartBean also implements notification callback operations from EntityBean and PartHome. Typical callbacks are `ejbCreate`, `ejbPostCreate`, `ejbActivate`, `ejbPassivate`, and so forth. Notice also that EntityBean is a special type of EnterpriseBean. The other type is SessionBean. Different types of beans have different life cycles. We discuss their significance in Section 7.12.2.

For users (or, more precisely, developers) of the EJB framework, the Part bean is defined by PartHome, PartIF, and PartBean. Details of these objects are shown in Figures 7-39 and 7-40. Note that PartBean implements two callbacks—`ejbCreate`, and `ejbPostCreate`—from PartHome, in addition to the callbacks from EntityBean

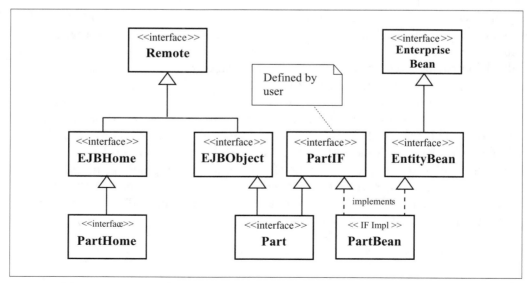

FIGURE 7-38. *A static object design in the EJB framework. All Part-specific classes are defined by the user. Together they define an EJB component of Part.*

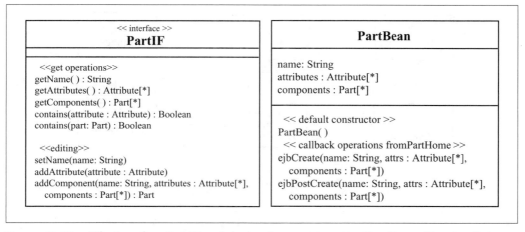

FIGURE 7-39. *The interface PartHome, which defines the* create *and* find *operations. We assume that each Part object is uniquely identified by its name.*

<< interface >> **PartIF**	**PartBean**

<<get operations>>
getName( ) : String
getAttributes( ) : Attribute[*]
getComponents( ) : Part[*]
contains(attribute : Attribute) : Boolean
contains(part: Part) : Boolean
 	
<<editing>>
setName(name: String)
addAttribute(attribute : Attribute)
addComponent(name: String, attributes : Attribute[*],
   components : Part[*]) : Part
	name: String
	attributes : Attribute[*]
	components : Part[*]
	
	<< default constructor >>
	PartBean( )
	<< callback operations fromPartHome >>
	ejbCreate(name: String, attrs : Attribute[*],
	   components : Part[*])
	ejbPostCreate(name: String, attrs : Attribute[*],
	   components : Part[*])

FIGURE 7-40. *The interface PartIF and the implementation class PartBean. (For simplicity, not all operations are listed in PartIF.)*

and the operations from PartIF. Also, the interface Part simply inherits the operations from EJBObject and PartIF, and is not shown here.

Once the bean is defined, the next step is to deploy the bean to an EJB container along with the appropriate configuration. The EJB container manages the bean and provides valuable services. Often, such a container is part of the distributed object infrastructure within an *EJB server*. Through their EJB containers,

EJB servers provide services such as persistence, transaction management, security, and concurrency.

Different EJB servers from different vendors may use different mechanisms to fulfill the container's functions. Users need not know the details of these mechanisms and may treat the EJB container as a "magic box." Here we discuss some representative mechanisms for performing such bean magic. (A specific EJB server may use a combination of different mechanisms.)

On deployment of the Part bean, the EJB container examines the interfaces and generates the implementation classes PartEJBHome and PartEJBObject. The object structure of the Part bean is shown in Figure 7-41. Clearly, PartEJBHome, PartEJBObject, and their interfaces form an object factory pattern as in Figure 6-4. PartEJBObject is similar to the TIE object in CORBA. It is a proxy object of its servant class PartBean (see Figure 6-29) and is visible to the client.

The EJB container also generates PartBeanManager (or some component with similar function) to create and manage a pool of PartBeans. Because of this, PartBean is not allowed to have constructors other than a default one.

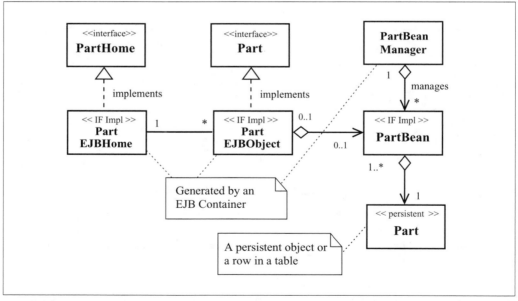

FIGURE 7-41. *A representative object structure for the Part bean after deployment in an EJB container. The PartBeanManager manages a pool of PartBeans. The persistent Part class represents a persistent object or a row of data in a relational table, which typically resides in a separate database server. Note that a PartBean may or may not be linked to a PartEJBObject.*

TABLE 7-3. *Comparison of object structures in EJB and CORBA.*

EJB	CORBA
PartEJBHome	Object factory for Part (optional)
PartIF	PartIF (interface in an IDL file)
Part (interface)	None
PartEJBObject	Part_TIE
PartBean	Part_Impl

Finally, PartBean points to a persistent Part object in the persistent layer, which can be captured by an object-oriented database or a relational database. In the latter case, the persistent Part object corresponds to a row in a table. An EJB server often provides a mechanism or a wizard to map an object to a relational table. The primary key of the table is used as a persistent ID for the bean.

We note that the object structure in Figure 7-41 is only representative. The actual structure used in a particular EJB server may be different.

To compare the object structures in CORBA and in EJB, we list the corresponding objects for the Part bean in Table 7-3. Note that in CORBA, Part_Impl has the same life cycle as Part_TIE, whereas in EJB, PartBean can be detached from PartE-JBObject. Also, PartEJBObject always has its factory PartEJBHome.

From Table 7-3 we find that CORBA and EJB obviously have many similar static structures. How do we benefit from using an EJB server then? The answer lies mostly in the active management of beans by an EJB container. This brings up the topic of resource management, which is not provided by typical CORBA infrastructures.

7.12.2 RESOURCE MANAGEMENT STRATEGIES

An enterprise system needs to handle large numbers of objects and clients. A key to the success of such systems is resource management. One general strategy is to limit the number of in-memory objects and recycle them to serve multiple clients. To do this, we must have a good handle on the life cycle of these objects.

The EJB framework supports several types of beans with different life cycles and provides resource management through several mechanisms. We have introduced *entity beans,* which are representations of persistent objects. Entity beans are usually shared by multiple clients. In large databases, the number of entity beans can be huge.

There are also *session beans,* which encapsulate processes invoked by clients. Furthermore, a *stateful session bean* keeps track of the state of a process (for example, different stages in an online order) so that its client can use the bean several times before discarding it. Obviously, each stateful session bean can only serve a single

TABLE 7-4. *Bean state and resource management strategies.*

BEAN TYPE	STATES AFTER CREATION	RESOURCE MANAGEMENT STRATEGY
Entity beans	Pooled/Ready	Instance pooling with database synchronization
Stateful session beans	Ready/Passive	Passivation to secondary storage
Stateless session beans	Ready	Instance pooling

client throughout its life cycle. A *stateless session bean,* on the other hand, finishes its work at each invocation (similar to an operation innovation). It therefore can be reused to serve other clients. For systems with a large number of users, the number of session beans can be large.

The states and resource management strategies for different types of beans are listed in Table 7-4.

In *instance pooling,* a small number of bean instances are created and actively managed to serve multiple clients. Beans that finish their tasks are recycled to the instance pool. This allows a small number of beans to serve a large number of clients. This simple strategy is sufficient for stateless session beans.

For entity beans, database synchronization ensures that the bean's persistent attributes are consistent with the corresponding fields in the database. EJB servers also use *connection pooling* so that multiple access to the same database is performed using less frequent connections. This increases the throughput and boosts overall system performance.

When they become inactive, stateful session beans are moved to secondary storage and are then evicted from memory. This passivation process helps conserve resources in the system. The inactive beans remain in secondary storage until they are activated.

Of the three strategies, the one for entity beans is the most sophisticated. Next we use our standard dynamic modeling techniques to discuss the life cycle of entity beans.

7.12.3 DYNAMIC BEHAVIORS OF ENTITY BEANS

Recall that in CORBA the TIE object has a strong compositional relationship with its target object (see Figure 6-21). PartBean, on the other hand, may or may not be linked to a PartEJBObject. This flexibility allows the beans to have a different life cycle from PartEJBObject. The life cycle of an entity bean is depicted in Figure 7-42.

All entity beans are created by an EJB container. They are kept in a pool of beans until clients request them. At that point they enter the Ready state to respond to client requests. After a certain duration of inactivity, entity beans in the ready state

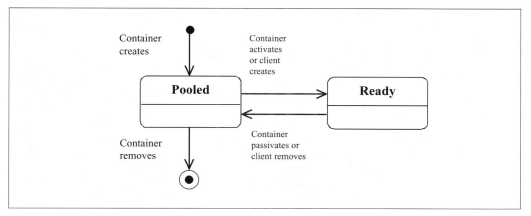

FIGURE 7-42.   *The life cycle of an entity bean.*

may be put back in the pool by the EJB container. This is called *passivation*. Other EJB servers may define a maximal number of beans. When that number is reached, the least recently used bean is passivated so that it can perform new services.

The clients may remove an entity bean in the Ready state explicitly, which also makes the bean go back to the pool. Notice that clients have no direct access to the bean pool. Thus, to the clients, beans in the pool do not exist. Clients only create or remove EJBObjects.

Next, we investigate the dynamic behaviors of the entity beans using sequence diagrams. Figure 7-43 shows the sequence diagram of a client creating a Part bean. Note that the bean instances (such as pb1 and pb2) are created by the PartBeanManager and are kept in a bean pool when the EJB server starts up. When the client invokes the create operation, PartEJBHome selects one instance from the pool (with the help of PartBeanManager), invokes its callback operation ejbCreate, and then inserts the corresponding record into the database. When this is done, PartEJBHome creates a PartEJBObject and associates it with the selected bean instance (pb1 in our case). It then invokes the callback ejbPostCreat of the bean instance and returns the object reference of the PartEJBObject.

After this process, the bean enters the Ready state and is ready for client requests. As shown in Figure 7-44, the client invokes an operation through PartEJBObject. This is similar to operation invocation in CORBA, in which a client invokes operations of Part_Impl via the Part_TIE object.

After the invocation, the EJB container may decide to passivate the bean to conserve resources. This passivation process is also shown in Figure 7-44. PartBeanManager first calls ejbStore of the bean instance, obtains its attributes, updates the corresponding records in the database, and then calls ejbPassivate of the bean. Afterward, the bean returns to the Pooled state.

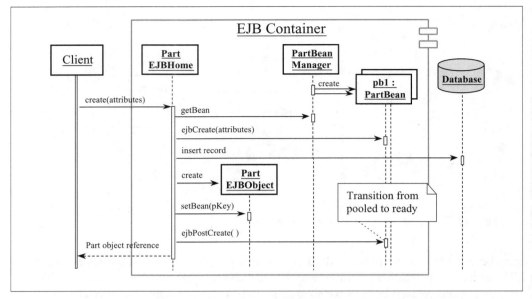

FIGURE 7-43. *A client creating an entity bean. Here, pKey stands for the primary key of the corresponding record in the database table.*

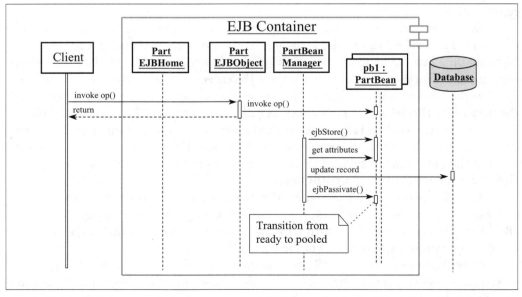

FIGURE 7-44. *A client invoking an operation of an entity bean in the Ready state. Also shown is the passivation process of the bean by the EJB container. The bean returns to the Pooled state after passivation.*

PartEJBHome may also have a find operation defined, which takes a primary key and returns the corresponding Part object reference. Inside the EJB container, this involves selecting a bean instance from the pool, creating a PartEJBObject, and assigning the bean to the PartEJBObject (Figure 7-45). Notice that the bean instance is not activated until the client actually invokes one of its operations. This can be called *just-in-time activation.*

As shown in Figure 7-45, when the client invokes an operation of the bean, the bean goes through an activation process, which is the reverse of the passivation process in Figure 7-44. Note that a different bean instance from the one in Figure 7-44 may be used. Thus, a client may be served by more than one bean over time.

If a client removes an entity bean, the corresponding record in the database is also deleted. However, the bean instance in use merely returns to the pool. Removal of beans from the pool is controlled by the EJB container. It happens, for example, when the server shuts down.

In summary, EJB servers use object factory, servant class, and collection manager patterns to manage actively the life cycle of beans. For the Part bean, the three objects that are generated by an EJB container—PartEJBHome, PartEJBObject, and PartBeanManager—cooperate to perform resource management.

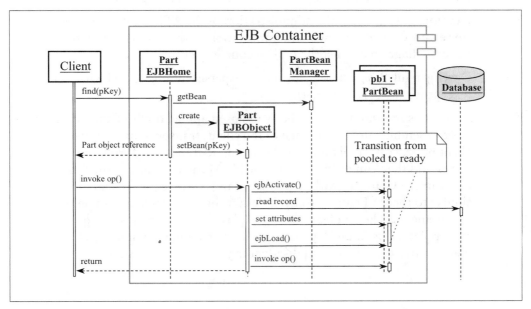

FIGURE 7-45. *Finding a bean and invoking its operation. Here, pKey stands for the primary key of the corresponding record in the database table. Note that the bean instance pb2 (behind pb1) is selected to perform the operation.*

Different strategies are used for different types of beans, with the overall goal of conserving system resources. These, together with other value-added services, such as mapping to relational tables, transaction, security, and concurrency, enable EJB servers to handle large number of users and large databases in an enterprise environment.

7.13 EXERCISES

7-1. Draw a four-tier architecture with a cluster of Web servers, each having one Business Logic node connecting to the same Database Management node. Use the clustering and serializing techniques in Figure 7-15 to handle load balancing and security. Note that because each Web server is directly accessible to all clients, a security check must be performed at each server. Draw a sequence diagram with two thin clients, one gateway Web server, one Security node, and two clustered Web servers. (Omit the Business Logic nodes in this drawing.) Comment on the advantages and disadvantages of this architecture.

7-2. Refine the sequence diagram in Figure 5-16 to include interaction with objects in the interface and persistent layers of the ATM Central Server. For simplicity, the DailyLog object may be omitted from the diagram.

7-3. Develop a use case for the administration of the ATM Central Server (for example, adding new bank information to the server). Draw the use case diagram and list the typical course of events.

7-4. Develop a full design in long form for the persistent objects in Figure 7-27 (except for the class Internet).

7-5. Consider some variations of the Web-based application in Figure 7-6. Besides sending an HTML page to the client, transport an Applet to the client node. (An Applet is a small executable transported from the server and then run on the client. The HTML page contains the link to the Applet.) Come up with two designs and draw sequence diagrams similar to that in Figure 7-6. Each design should be able to handle two requirements: The Applet needs to display data known at start up, and the Applet needs to display real-time data changing dynamically. Comment on the advantages and disadvantages of the two designs.

CHAPTER 8

Summaries and Notes

8.1 CHAPTER 1 SUMMARY AND NOTES

An *object class* is the abstract descriptor of a set of *object instances*, which share the same attributes, operations, and relationships with other objects. Objects *encapsulate* their attributes and operations, thereby isolating their properties from other objects except through specific operations.

The term *object* is often used to indicate either an object class or an object instance. The creation of an object instance is called *instantiation*.

The *Unified Modeling Language* is a general-purpose modeling language designed to specify, visualize, and document a software system.

An *association* defines a relationship between two or more classes. A *link* is the realization of such a relationship among object instances. Links can have properties that belong to all object instances in the association.

Aggregation is a special form of binary association in which a class is a part of or a component of another class (the aggregate). *Composition* is a strong form of aggregation in which the component is an integral part of the whole aggregate, which cannot exist without its components. Operations on an aggregate often propagate to its parts. The distinction between normal association, aggregation, and composition may be left blurred during the initial phase of object design.

A subclass extends its superclass by inheriting the attributes and operations of the superclass (*inheritance*) and by adding new ones to its own (*extension*). The subclass describes a set of object instances that inherit all behaviors from the superclass (except for those that are altered by or hidden from the subclass). The key to a correct inheritance relationship is to ensure that the subclass is a *special type* of the superclass (is-a or type-of relationship). A subclass can alter the behavior of its superclass by adding new operations or by overriding the inherited operations with new implementations.

Compared with inheritance, delegation to a *servant class* is often the preferred way of reusing an existing class because it does not require a type-of relationship between the master and the servant classes. Furthermore, unlike inheritance, the master class does not need to adopt all behaviors of the servant class.

Polymorphism allows us to issue the same command to different objects in an inheritance tree and to invoke the operation implementation specific to the object classes. The *substitution principle* states that we can invoke polymorphic operations of a subclass using an object reference belonging to its superclass.

8.2   CHAPTER 2 SUMMARY AND NOTES

Static design focuses on the structural relationships between classes and ignores their dynamic or time-dependent behavior. *Common patterns* are composed of a few interconnected classes to provide a set of functions. They are the building blocks that frequently appear in more complex designs.

A *collection manager* manages a collection of objects, including the creation and removal of those objects. *Object containers,* on the other hand, only contain objects but do not create them.

Self-containing classes may form linked lists, hierarchies, or networks of objects. *Relationship loops* form when two or more classes are related by both association (including aggregation and composition) and inheritance. They typically result in treelike hierarchies of objects, implying recursive operations.

Inheritance from classes involved in a relationship loop may lead to complex and unexpected relationships among the subclasses. Such designs should be simplified or avoided.

Relationship fission is a technique for analyzing complex loop relationships. It decomposes relationship loops into two separate diagrams, one for aggregation and one for inheritance.

An *association class* is an abstraction of links among classes. It encapsulates the link properties and the operations on them. The association class belongs to all classes participating in an association. A *binary association class* between two classes may be implemented as a normal class associated with the two classes.

The *handle-body pattern* allows an object to select or combine different roles or properties flexibly, which are categorized into mutually exclusive subclasses. The *dynamic schema* pattern can classify objects into categories according to their attributes without modifying the object design.

A *shared object pool* has a limited set of objects that are used simultaneously in multiple contexts. This pattern allows effective reuse of objects.

The object model of a well-formed XML document contains a relationship loop, which gives rise to nested aggregation structures. Relationship fission may be used to map object models into *XML object models*, which define the structure of the XML documents.

8.3   CHAPTER 3 SUMMARY AND NOTES

Persistent objects are representations of objects that exist independently of the processes that create them. Persistent objects are managed by *DBMSs*, which perform work in units called *transactions* (such as read or write). Transactions satisfy the so-called *ACID requirements*.

Database roots are the starting points of an object-oriented database. They are often top-level objects such as collection managers or containers, from which one can navigate to all other objects in the database.

A collection that contains all the instances of a class is called the *extent* of the class. It is typically referenced by a class-scope variable and is often used as a database root.

Persistence-enabled objects are initially transient objects and can later become persistent in a database. DBMSs manage the migration from transient to persistent objects transparently, using processes such as *transitive persistence*. For unused persistent objects (*orphan objects*), DBMSs provide garbage collection utilities to find and destroy them.

In mapping persistent objects to relational tables, a class generally maps to one table. The columns (fields) correspond to the attributes of the class, whereas the rows (records) correspond to the instances of the class. Conceptually, a table is like an extent for persistent objects. The standard "one class/one table" mapping rules are summarized in Table 3-2.

To optimize an object-oriented database, we can *partition an object extent* into subextents with a set of keys. The keys serve as presorted indices that direct us quickly to a small set of relevant objects.

To optimize object-relational mapping, we may *combine tables* that share the same primary key. This allows us to take advantage of the fast operations (such as ad hoc queries) within a table.

8.4 CHAPTER 4 SUMMARY AND NOTES

An *abstract class* is a superclass of at least one other class, but it may not instantiate any objects itself.

Multiple inheritance should be avoided because it is prone to conflicts between superclasses. We typically may use servant classes (*delegation*) to prune away multiple inheritance.

An *interface* specifies only the operations of a class visible to the external world without revealing its internal structure or implementation. Interfaces cannot be instantiated. Formally, an interface is similar to an abstract class with only abstract operations and no attributes. Table 8-1 contrasts the two.

An *inner class* is local and contained within an outer class. The life span of an inner class object is completely subordinate to its outer class object.

A *collection* is a group of objects. Depending on whether the elements have indexing and ordering, and whether duplicate or null elements are allowed, different types of collections are identified. Examples include Sets, Bags, Dictionaries, Maps, Lists, Sequences, and Arrays. Table 4-1 summarizes their behavior.

TABLE 8-1. *Comparison of interfaces and abstract classes.*

INTERFACES	ABSTRACT CLASSES
Define a set of operations that must be implemented by a implementation class.	Define member variables and operations that can be implemented by a subclass.
May be used to control the behavior of implementation objects within the same runtime process.	Typically used for organizing class hierarchies. Enable overall object management across subclasses.
May also be used for defining interfaces between software components.	Has no meaning beyond a software component.

Packages are containers to organize and manage object model elements such as classes. There may be dependency between different packages.

A *component* represents a piece of software implementation that can be deployed and used in a system. A component may support certain interfaces by implementing them. A *node* is a runtime physical object that has processing capability.

Irreducible patterns are the minimal building blocks in an object design that carry a self-contained set of functions. In analyzing object designs, one may first identify the irreducible patterns, then analyze the relationships and functions provided by these patterns. The findings of this *reverse engineering* process may be compared with the original requirements. This often helps improve design.

8.5   CHAPTER 5 SUMMARY AND NOTES

Dynamic modeling describes the pattern of communication between objects. Such dynamic behavior can be derived from use case analyses and can be documented with object sequence diagrams.

A *use case* presents a sequence of events for an end-to-end process between a system and its user (called an *actor*). A use case is documented as a list of actions taken by the actor and the system.

The UML *use case diagrams* help organize use cases into groups. A UML *sequence diagram* depicts a set of message exchanges among object instances in a use case.

In the *client/server model,* a client object invokes a server operation by sending a message to the server object, which subsequently executes the operation and returns the results to the client object. An *interface* specifies all public operations of the server object. An *interface definition* serves as the contract between a client and a server.

Distributed objects are distributed statically at design time across the clients and servers. They may be implemented in different programming languages. At runtime they belong to different address spaces or they may reside in different computers.

CORBA is a widely adopted open standard for distributed object architecture. It includes the *Interface Definition Language* and a set of services for distributed object computing. Interfaces are implemented by *implementation classes*, with instances that become *CORBA objects* in servers.

The *ORB* provides mechanisms by which clients can transparently use *object references* to invoke the operations of CORBA objects. The initial object references can be obtained by a client through direct binding, the CORBA Naming Service, or a string representation of an object reference.

A *statechart diagram* gives an overview or summary of the discrete states of a system or an object. Its transitions typically correspond to some use cases for the system.

8.5.1 NOTES ON CORBA-COM INTEROPERABILITY

CORBA also defines mappings to and from Microsoft's Component Object Model (COM) and Object Linking and Embedding (OLE) Automation. They enable communication between Microsoft desktop products and CORBA clients or servers. For example, a GUI written in Visual Basic can use OLE Automation to access a CORBA server, which may be written in C++.

Compared with CORBA, OLE Automation relies less heavily on interface definition. It uses arrays of function pointers and their layout to determine how data are communicated. OLE Automation supports pointers to interfaces, but not object references, as does CORBA. An OLE Automation object can have multiple interfaces, but supports only single inheritance. (CORBA supports multiple inheritance.)

8.6   CHAPTER 6 SUMMARY AND NOTES

Many of the static design patterns can be exposed through interfaces, resulting in various *interface design patterns*.

Object wrappers define object-oriented interfaces for legacy applications and enable them to function as server objects. An *object adapter* translates an existing object into a specific or different interface. The existing object is typically used as a servant class. Object adapters can be used as a weak but flexible form of inheritance.

The main function of an *object factory* is to create objects. An *object manager* also manages the objects it created. Object factories and managers are often used to control client access.

Servant interfaces are used to achieve high flexibility in interface design. Servant interfaces often appear in push or pul! event processing such as the *observer pattern* (simple event pushing from one observable to many observers), *callbacks* (push events initiated by a server object directly against a client), *subscription and notification,* and GUIs under the *MVC pattern.*

Relationship loops with interfaces can be used to expose relationship loops in static design.

The inheritance tree of a set of interfaces and their corresponding implementation classes form an *inheritance ladder,* which exposes layers of operations to clients.

CORBA objects and their superclasses make use of the inheritance ladder and servant interface patterns to enable designs for distributed objects. On the client side, one may extend the CORBA client stubs to provide additional functionality.

Network latency and interface design are important factors that affect the performance of distributed objects. Some tactics for achieving good performance are to limit the number of bind calls to interfaces, to limit the number of remote invocations, and to use the pull approach for passing large amounts of data to multiple places.

A *proxy object* is a representation of a target object that is hidden from the client. The proxy implements a set of operations defined by an externally visible interface, whereas the target implements a similar but possibly different set of operations.

8.7   CHAPTER 7 SUMMARY AND NOTES

Software architecture is an abstraction of system implementation that describes the overall system structure, decomposition of functionality into components, the nature and properties of these components, interfaces and communication protocols between components, and the overarching tactics and rules. A good software system requires a sound and integrated architecture.

A UML *deployment diagram* is a graph of nodes connected by communication channels (*connectors*). A *node* is a runtime physical object that has processing capability. It may contain component instances and other physical things such as databases.

Our *architecture diagrams* are based on the UML deployment diagrams, showing nodes, components, and connectors.

The common architectural patterns are

- *Procedural systems* containing processing units and pipelines
- *Client/server systems* across a network, including thin clients/Web servers
- *Layered systems* with different layers of functionality
- *Multi-tier systems* that serve end users through a chain of client/server pairs (They include systems with server clustering and serializing.)
- *Agent systems* containing distributed software agents that cooperate with one another to perform tasks
- *Aggregation* of nodes that shares something in common using a common communication protocol (A *federation* system is an aggregation of nodes with each node having its own satellite subnodes.)

These patterns can be represented generically by a set of UML object designs (containing nodes and connectors).

8.8   CASE STUDIES SUMMARY

Table 8-2 lists the characteristics of the case studies.

TABLE 8-2.   *Case study characteristics.*

CASE STUDY	CHARACTERISTICS
ATM system software	Persistent objects with a binary association class as the core design pattern
	Interface design with the object manager and object adapter patterns
	Four-tier architecture with two layers (interface and persistent) in the ATM Central Server
Shared whiteboard	Object-oriented GUI with simple aggregation and composition
	Persistent objects in the form of byte array data
	Layer design with interface and control layers
	An aggregation architecture that forms a collaboration group with operational policies
	Two-phase evolution development with a rapid prototype in the second phase
	Relationship loop with an interface

CASE STUDY	CHARACTERISTICS
A rental business	Persistent object design with binary association class, collection manager, and container patterns
	Four-tier architecture for the SuperRent system
Access control lists	Two designs based on different core patterns (binary association class and relationship loop)
	Linkage to objects based on the handle-body pattern with a servant interface
Enterprise JavaBeans	EJB servers use object factory, servant class, and collection manager patterns to manage the life cycle of beans actively, with the overall goal of conserving system resources.

C H A P T E R   9

Answers
to Exercises

9.1 CHAPTER 1 EXERCISE ANSWERS

1-1. A detailed design for the Person class is presented in Figure 9-1.

Here, Hobby[*] indicates a variable-length collection (hobbies), which
in practice can be implemented by a certain collection class (for example, the HashTable in java.util) that supports indexing by a key (the
name of the hobby in this case). The get operations simply return the
relevant variables. The first addHobby operation takes a Hobby object
as input and adds it to the hobbies collection. The second addHobby
method creates a new Hobby object with the input hobbyName and
returns the object. (If we consider that the Hobby objects are managed

Person
name : String hobbies : Hobby[*]

<<constructor>>
Person(name : String)
  <<get operations>>
getName() : String
getHobbies() : Hobby[*]
  <<editing>>
addHobby(hobby : Hobby)
addHobby(hobbyName : String) : Hobby
removeHobby(hobbyName : String) : Hobby
removeAllHobbies()

FIGURE 9-1. *Answer to Exercise 1-1.*

by a Person object, then the second `addHobby` method should always be used to create Hobby objects.)

The `removeHobby` method removes a Hobby object from the hobbies collection and returns the object. The `removeAllHobby` method removes all Hobby objects from hobbies. Finally, one could add other operations like `changeHobby(oldHobby : String, newHobby : String)`, which removes an old Hobby object, and creates and returns a new one. However, such an operation can be easily constructed from the `add` and `remove` operations. We therefore leave them out of our design.

The detailed design for the Hobby class is presented in Figure 9-2.

Again, the `get` operations simply return the relevant variables. The `setName` operation sets the name of the hobby whereas `setPerson` sets the person attribute.

As you can see, because the multiplicity on the Person side is one, the operations in the Hobby class for the person attribute is very simple. On the other hand, the zero or more multiplicity (*) on the Person side maps to a set of editing functions that are standard for collections. These are the design patterns related to the multiplicity.

Note: In Figures 9-1 and 9-2, we used the UML *stereotype* notation, which is << ... >>. It indicates the usage intent of a group of operations (see Section 2.1).

1-2. The design with UML class notations in short form is presented in Figure 9-3.

The detailed design with UML class notations in long form is presented in Figure 9-4.

Hobby
name : String person : Person
<<constructor>> Hobby(name : String, person : Person)   <<get operations>> getName() : String getPerson() : Person   <<editing>> setName(name : String) setPerson(person : Person)

FIGURE 9-2. *Answer to Exercise 1-1.*

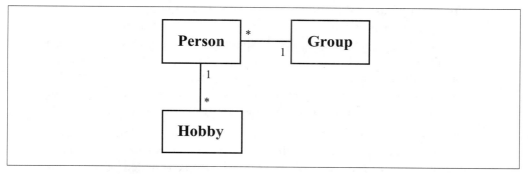

FIGURE 9-3. *Answer to Exercise 1-2.*

Group
name : String persons : Person[*]
<<constructor>> Group(name : String)   <<get operations>> getName() : String getPersons() : Person[*]   <<editing>> addPerson(person : Person) removePerson(personName : String) : Person removeAllPersons()

Person
name : String hobbies : Hobby[*] group : Group
<<constructor>> Person(name : String)   <<get & set operations>> getName() : String getHobbies(): Hobby[*] getGroup() : Group setGroup(group : Group)   <<editing>> addHobby(hobbyName : String) : Hobby removeHobby(hobbyName : String) removeAllHobbies()

FIGURE 9-4. *Answer to Exercise 1-2.*

The Hobby class is the same as before, which is a direct reuse. The Group-Person association is similar to the Person-Hobby one. For the Person class, we simply copy the Person-related attributes and operations from the previous Hobby class to the previous Person class (also renaming Person to Group in the copied material). Similarly, to construct the Group class, we copy the previous Person class, rename Person to Group, and then Hobby to Person. The result is basically our new Group class.

There is a difference between the new Group class and the previous Person class. There is no need for an `addPerson(personName : String)` operation because a Person object should have been created before adding it to a group. In other words, the Person objects are not subordinate to the Group objects.

1-3.   The design with UML class notations in short form is presented in Figure 9-5.

A square is a special kind of polygon with four points and four 90-degree angles. A polygon can have three or more points. A circle is a special type of ellipse. A ellipse uses two points (as its foci). The two foci coincide for a circle. A line has two end points. Thus the superclass Geometry Item can contain one or more points. We do not distinguish the weak and strong form of aggregation here.

We could have used the Point class in Polygon, Ellipse, and Line classes separately. In terms of data storage, this is not much different from the previous design. However, if we were to add some operations that are common for all Geometry Item objects, then letting the Geometry Item

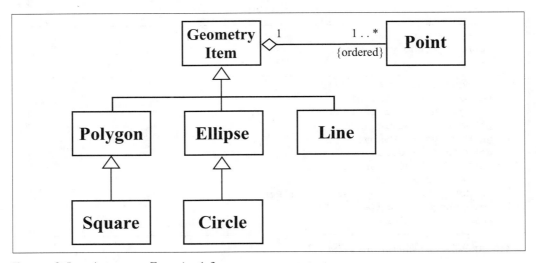

FIGURE 9-5.   *Answer to Exercise 1-3.*

class contain the points is most efficient. For example, we can have a move(dx, dy) operation that shifts all the points by dx in x and dy in y. Such an operation in the Geometry Item class can be inherited by all subclasses, thereby achieving maximal reuse for that function.

Another way of using points in Ellipse and Circle is to use four points to form a rectangle, which encloses the Ellipse or Circle object, as shown in Figure 9-6. In this way the size of the ellipse or circle is determined by the size of the enclosing rectangle.

1-4. Common operations that can be added to Geometry include

- draw(), which draws a geometric object on screen

- move(dx : Real, dy : Real), which shifts all the points by dx in x and dy in y

- rotate(angle : Double, point : Point), which is a rotation about the input point (which can be the center of the square, for example)

- reflect_x() and reflect_y(), which are reflections about the x- and y-axes respectively

Assuming we use four points to represent an enclosure for Ellipse and Circle, we can also have a scaling operation for the Geometry class:

- scale(scaleFactor : Double, point : Point), where the input point is the origin for the scaling.

Of these operations, only draw( ) is truly polymorphic because the drawing of pixels depends on the class. Specifically, the implementations of draw( ) are

- For Polygon and Square, connect adjacent points and the last to the first points by straight lines

- For Line, connect the two end points using a straight line

- For Ellipse and Circle, treat the four points as the corners of an enclosing rectangle and draw the ellipse or circle

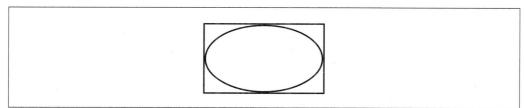

FIGURE 9-6. *A method of using points for ellipses and circles.*

All other operations can be implemented in the superclass Geometry, and it can be applied to all subclasses.

9.2   CHAPTER 2 EXERCISE ANSWERS

2-1.   (a) The detailed design for the UserManager class using Container as a servant class is presented in Figure 9-7.

(b) If the links between UserManager and User are bidirectional, we can maintain referential integrity by encapsulating all link manipulations in two core operations: addUser(username : String, password : String) and removeUser(user : User). All other operations should call these two instead of handling the links directly.

A simple design for the User class is presented in Figure 9-8.

In UserManager, the operation addUser(username : String, password : String) contains the following steps:

- Construct a new User object with User(username, password, userMgr) and assign it to User.

- Call users.add(user, username) and return the object User.

The operation removeUser(user : User) contains the following:

UserManager
users : Container
<<constructor>> UserManager()   <<get & query operations>> getUsers() : User[*] getUserCount() : Integer getUser(username : String) : User contains(user : User) : Boolean   <<editing>> addUser(username : String, password : String) : User removeUser(username : String) removeUser(user : User) removeAllUsers( )

FIGURE 9-7. *Answer to Exercise 2-1.*

User
username : String password : String userMgr : UserManager
<<constructor>> User(username : String, password : String, userMgr : UserManager)   <<get & query operations>> getUsername() : String   <<editing>> setUserManager(userMgr : UserManager) changePassword(password : String, newPassword : String) validatePassword(password : String)

FIGURE 9-8. *Answer to Exercise 2-1.*

- Call `user.setUserManager(null)` to delete the backward link (this is needed because in a more general case the User object may also be managed by another UserManager)

- Call `users.remove(user)` to delete the forward link.

The operation `removeUser(username : String)` contains the following:

- Call `users.get(username)` and assign it to User.

- Call `removeUser(user)` (instead of `users.remove(user)`).

2-2. The reasons for using Container as a servant class inside a collection manager class (delegation), as opposed to deriving the collection manager from Container, are the following:

- A collection manager behaves differently from a Container. Specifically, the manager creates the objects that it manages. If we derive the collection manager from a Container, then we can create objects separately and then add them to the collection, thereby breaking the desired behavior pattern.

- A collection manager may manage multiple collections, in which case the use of containers is necessary.

2-3. The class java.awt.Container is very rich and has many features not found in our Container. In particular, operations related to layout, event handling, display, and printing are not found in our Container. Moreover, the underlying collection in java.awt.Container is ordered (like an array), because components in a window must be displayed in a certain order. Our Container, on the other hand, uses name as the index. (Note: The following operations for java.awt.Container are based on Java Development Kit 1.1.6 and do not include deprecated ones from previous versions.)

The following operations are similar to those in our Container:

- **Basic container management**—getComponent(int), getComponentCount(), getComponents(), add(Component), add(Component, int), remove(Component), remove(int), removeAll(), and isAncestorOf(Component)

The get / add / remove operations are similar to those in our Container, except that an integer is used as the index to identify a component in the ordered collection of java.awt.Container. Thus, for example, add(Component) will add the component to the end of the collection. The isAncestorOf operation is similar to the contains operation except the former is recursive to all ancestor components.

The following operations are not found in our Container:

- **Container management with layout information**— add(Component, Object), add(Component, Object, int), addImpl(Component, Object, int), getComponentAt(int, int), and getComponentAt(Point)

- **Layout control**—doLayout(), getAlignmentX(), getAlignmentY(), getLayout(), getMaximumSize(), getMinimumSize(), getPreferredSize(), getInsets(), setLayout(LayoutManager), validate(), validateTree(), and invalidate()

- **Event handling**—addContainerListener (ContainerListener), processContainerEvent (ContainerEvent), processEvent(AWTEvent), removeContainerListener(ContainerListener), addNotify(), and removeNotify()

- **Display and printing**—paint(Graphics), paintComponents (Graphics), update(Graphics), list(PrintStream, int), list(PrintWriter, int), print(Graphics), and printComponents(Graphics)

2-4.   The Component and Container object diagram, and a sample picture for frames are presented in Figures 9-9 and 9-10 respectively.

Because both Component and Container are abstract classes, we follow the UML convention to show their names in italic type. (Missing

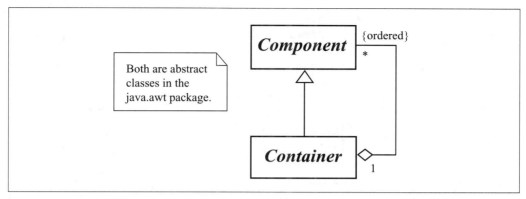

FIGURE 9-9. *Answer to Exercise 2-4.*

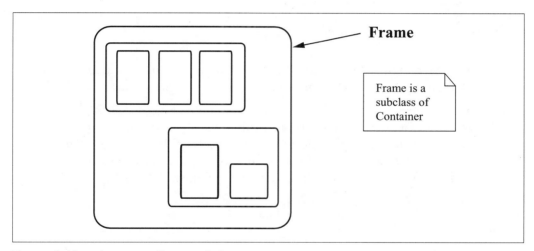

FIGURE 9-10. *Answer to Exercise 2-4.*

this subtle point would not cost you any points though.) The Container class, being a special type of Component, is an aggregate of zero or more components, which are contained by an ordered collection.

2-5.   The object diagram for the Menu family is presented in Figure 9-11.

The relationship between Menu and MenuItem is just the same as that between Container and Component in Exercise 2-4. MenuBar, on the other hand, contains one or more menus. CheckboxMenuItem is just a special type of MenuItem, which contains no submenus.

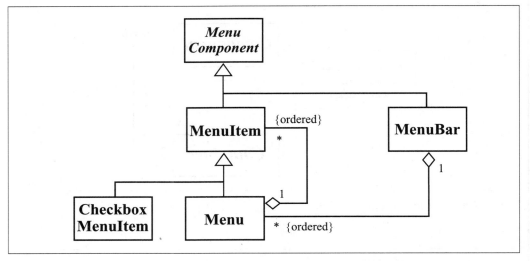

FIGURE **9-11.** *Answer to Exercise 2-5.*

This Menu family constitutes the menu bar and menus seen in any
Windows program, which may be used as the sample picture.

2-6. The detailed design for the directory hierarchy in Figure 2-3b is presented in Figure 9-12. Only basic attributes such as name, size, and
date are included for the File and Folder objects. Obviously, one can
treat Folder as a subclass of File because they share the same attributes
and operations except for the containers in Folder.

File
name : String size : Integer date : Date parentFolder : Folder

<<constructor>>
File(name : String, size : Integer, date : Date)
  <<get & query operations>>
getName( ) : String
getSize( ) : Integer
getDate( ) : Date
getParentFolder( ) : Folder
  <<editing>>
setName(name : String)
setSize(size : Integer)
setDate(date : Date)
setParentFolder(folder : Folder)

Folder
name : String size : Integer date : Date parentFolder : Folder files : Container subFolders : Container
<<constructor>> Folder(name : String, size : Integer, date : Date)   <<get & query operations>> getName( ) : String getSize( ) : Integer getDate( ) : Date getParentFolder( ) : Folder getSubFolders() : Folder[*] getFiles() : File[*] getFileCount( ) : Integer getFolderCount( ) : Integer getFile(name : String) : File getFolder(name : String) : Folder contains(file : File) : Boolean contains(folder : Folder) : Boolean   <<editing>> setName(name : String) setSize(size : Integer) setDate(date : Date) setParentFolder(folder : Folder) addFile(file : File) addFolder(folder : Folder) removeFile(name : String) removeFolder(name : String) removeAll( )

FIGURE 9-12. *Answer to Exercise 2-6.*

2-7. The detailed design for the Version objects, which form a linked list, is presented in Figure 9-13. The insert operation inserts the input Version object between the current one and the next one (which is null if the current one is the last object in the linked list). The remove operation takes away the current object from the linked list and joins the next object to the previous one. Note that the object reference "prev" is null if the current object is the first object in the linked list.

2-8. Because the links between nodes in the Node network of Figure 2-4a are bidirectional, we need to maintain referential integrity. We first

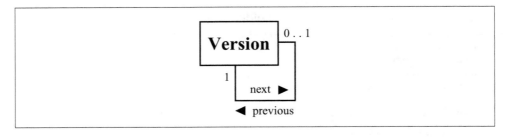

Version
label : String prev : Version next : Version
<<constructor>> Version(label : String)   <<get & query operations>> getLabel( ) : String getPrev( ) : Version getNext( ) : Version getFirst( ) : Version getLast( ) : Version getVersionCount( ) : Integer   <<editing>> insert(v : Version) remove( )

FIGURE 9-13. *Answer to Exercise 2-7.*

identify a set of core operations from those in Figure 2-5 as presented in Table 9-1.

Here, the right column shows the methods invoked on the input node to guarantee referential integrity. We have assumed that the

TABLE 9-1. *Set of core operations.*

CORE OPERATIONS	METHODS INVOKED ON INPUT ARGUMENT "NODE"
addUpstreamNode(node : Node)	node.downstreamNodes.add(this)
addDownstreamNode(node : Node)	node.upstreamNodes.add(this)
removeUpstreamNode(node : Node)	node.downstreamNodes.remove(this)
removeDownstreamNode(node : Node)	node.upstreamNodes.remove(this)

objects DownstreamNode and UpstreamNode have `add` and `remove` operations. Thus, the pseudocode for `addDownstreamNode()` is

```
addDownstreamNode(node : Node) {
    downstreamNodes.add(node);        // add node to the
                                      //    collection
    node.upstreamNodes.add(this);     // add backward
                                      //    link
}
```

Because we encapsulate all link manipulations in these core operations, if we use only these operations to add or remove links, we can ensure referential integrity. All other operations, such as

```
removeUpstreamNode(nodeName : String)
removeDownstreamNode(nodeName : String)
removeAllNodes()
```

should call these core operations to handle the links.

2-9.   For the forward containment loop in Figure 2-6b, the aggregation and inheritance diagrams after relationship fission are shown in Figure 9-14.

Class A contains multiple B, which is a special type of A and can contain B itself. An example is the Group-Secured Group design presented in Figure 9-15.

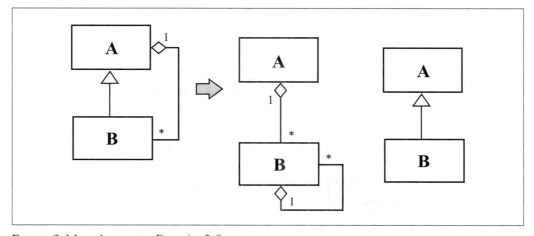

FIGURE **9-14.** *Answer to Exercise 2-9.*

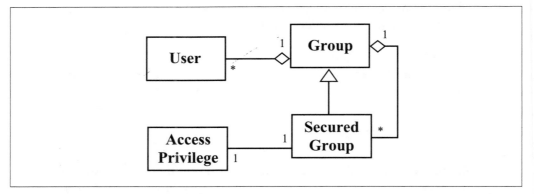

FIGURE **9-15.** *Aggregation and inheritance.*

The Group class contains multiple users and a set of secured groups. Each secured group has an access privilege (such as read, write, delete) and can contain multiple secured groups in addition to users. Thus Secured Group is a special kind of Group.

2-10. The aggregation diagram for the Menu class family in Exercise 2-5 is presented in Figure 9-16.

Note that the (abstract) class MenuComponent does not appear in this diagram.

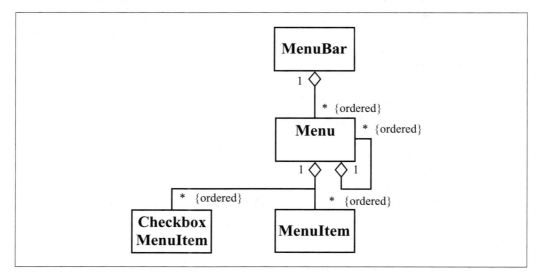

FIGURE **9-16.** *Answer to Exercise 2-10.*

2-11.   Instead of using inheritance (as in Figure 2-11), we may build a new relationship loop for the Secured classes. The SecuredFolder class may contain the original FolderItem class. The resulting structure is shown in Figure 9-17.

We may carry out relationship fission for each of the loops to obtain the aggregation diagram shown in Figure 9-18.

Notice that the aggregation from the SecuredFolder class to the FolderItem class yields the aggregation to the Folder class as well. Figure 9-18 confirms that a SecuredFolderItem cannot be contained by a regular Folder.

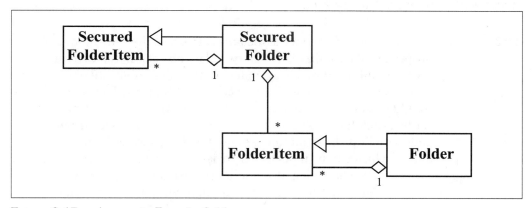

FIGURE **9-17.**   *Answer to Exercise 2-11.*

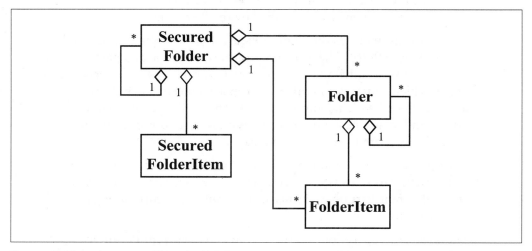

FIGURE **9-18.**   *Answer to Exercise 2-11.*

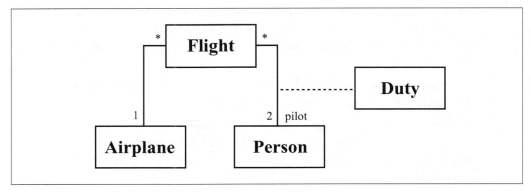

FIGURE 9-19. *Answer to Exercise 2-12.*

2-12.   (a) Each instance of a binary association class describes the unique properties of each link between two class objects. In the current problem, information encapsulated in the Flight object (flight number, time, and so on) is identical for both pilots. Thus Flight should not be an association class between Airplane and Person. Rather, each Flight object should be associated with one airplane and two pilots. Each pilot in a flight may have his/her own duties, which can be modeled as an association class, as shown in Figure 9-19. The design also implies that each pilot may serve in multiple flights (at different times though) with different duties.

(b) A committee can have three to five members (Person objects), each serving a specific post. A person can serve in zero to two committees, in a role specified by the Post object.

2-13.   We use the drawing on the right of Figure 2-22 to begin our detailed design (Figure 9-20). The attributes for Part are name and part number. For Property, the attribute is count. The Part class has a properties container, which contains a number of Property objects. Each Property object is linked with a component part. The parents container, on the other hand, contains a number of parent Property objects, each of which is associated with a parent part.

The operation getComponents( ) returns an array or sequence of component Part objects. Likewise, getParentParts( ) returns an array of parent Part objects (this array is null if the current object is a top-level part).

The clone( ) operation returns a clone of the current Part object, whereas cloneTree( ) returns a Part object containing a cloned tree of the current object's hierarchy (recursive operation).

```
                              Part
----------------------------------------------------------------
name : String
partNumber : Integer
properties : Container
parents : Container
----------------------------------------------------------------
  <<constructor>>
Part(name : String, partNumber : Integer)
  <<get & query operations>>
getName( ) : String
getPartNumber( ) : Integer
getComponents( ) : Part[*]
getParentParts( ) : Part[*]
getNumberOfComponents( ) : Integer
getNumberOfParentParts( ) : Integer
containsComponent(component : Part) : Boolean
findProperty(component : Part ) : Property
findComponent(name : String, partNumber : Integer) : Part
  <<editing>>
setName(name : String)
setPartNumber(partNumber : Integer)
addComponent(component : Part, count : Integer)
removeComponent(component : Part)
replaceComponent(old: Part, new: Part)
addParent(parent : Part)
  <<others>>
clone( ) : Part
cloneTree( ) : Part
```

FIGURE 9-20. *Answer to Exercise 2-13.*

The Property class (Figure 9-21) simply contains one parent part, one component part, and the property attribute.

The operation addComponent(component : Part, count : Integer) is a core operation for referential integrity. It first creates a new Property object with the current object as parent, the input Part object as component, and the count. (The Property constuctor also adds the new Property object to the parents container of the component Part.) The addComponent operation then adds the new Property object to the properties container.

Another core operation for referential integrity is removeComponent (component : Part). It first calls findProperty(component : Part) to get the corresponding Property object, which is then removed from the properties container of the current object. Finally, the Property

Property
parent : Part component : Part count : Integer
<<constructor>> Property(parent : Part, component : Part, count : Integer)   <<get & query operations>> getParent( ): Part getComponent ( ) : Part getCount ( ) : Integer   <<editing>> setParent(parent : Part) setComponent (component: Part) setCount(count: Integer)

FIGURE 9-21. *Answer to Exercise 2-13.*

object is also removed from the parents container of the component object.

The operation `addParent(parent : Part)` is not a core operation and should normally be called only by the Property constructor to ensure referential integrity.

A simple vehicle parts example illustrates the use of the Part and Property objects. Here the counts are given in parentheses. Only part names are shown:

- Sport car
  - ◆ Wheel (4)
  - ◆ Engine (1)
    - * Cylinder (6)
- Family car
  - ◆ Wheel (4)
  - ◆ Engine (1)
    - * Cylinder (4)

2-14. The object design of the file directory system with sharing (symbolic link) capability in short form is presented in Figure 9-22. The association class Property describes the link type (in other words, whether it is a primary link or a symbolic link).

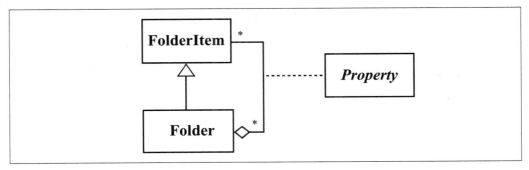

FIGURE 9-22. *Answer to Exercise 2-14.*

The object design can be drawn in an equivalent way, as shown in Figure 9-23 (with the added requirement that each pair of FolderItem and Folder uniquely determines a Property object).

The detailed design is presented in Figure 9-24. FolderItem is basically the same as the File class in Exercise 2-6, except now it has a parents container, which contains a set of Property objects. The operation `getParentCount( )` returns the number of parent Property objects.

The Folder class is a subclass of FolderItem (Figure 9-25).

The core operations for maintaining referential integrity are `addFolderItem(folderItem : FolderItem)` and `removeFolderItem(name : String)`. The key steps in `addFolderItem(folderItem : FolderItem)` conforming to the specified policy are the following:

1. Call `getParentCount()`.

2. If the result is zero, create a new Property object with the constructor `Property(this, folderItem, true)`—in other

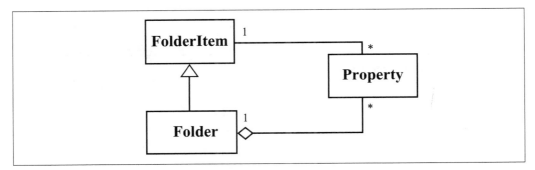

FIGURE 9-23. *Answer to Exercise 2-14.*

FolderItem
name : String size : Integer date : Date parents : Container
<<constructor>> FolderItem(name : String, size : Integer, date : Date)   <<get & query operations>> getName( ) : String getSize( ) : Integer getDate( ) : Date getParentFolders( ) : Folder[*] getParentCount( ) : Integer   <<editing>> setName(name : String) setSize(size : Integer) setDate(date : Date) setParentFolder(folder : Folder)

FIGURE 9-24. *Answer to Exercise 2-14.*

Folder
properties : Container
<<constructor>> Folder(name : String, size : Integer, date : Date)   <<get & query operations>> getFolderItems() : FolderItem[*] getFolderItemCount( ) : Integer getFolderItem(name : String) : FolderItem contains(folderItem : FolderItem) : Boolean findFolderItem(name : String) : FolderItem findProperty(name : String) : Property   <<editing>> addFolderItem(folderItem : FolderItem) removeFolderItem(name : String) removeAll( )

FIGURE 9-25. *Answer to Exercise 2-14.*

words, a primary link. Otherwise, call `Property(this, folderItem, false)`—a symbolic link.

Likewise, `removeFolderItem(name : String)` has the following steps:

1. Call `findProperty(name : String)` to locate the Property object (Figure 9-26).

2. If the Property object represents a primary link (isPrimary being true), call `getFolderItems()`. For each FolderItem object in the returned FolderItem array, remove the Property object from its parents container. Clear the entire properties container of "this" afterward.

3. If the Property object represents a symbolic link (isPrimary being false), call `findFolderItem(name : String)` to locate the FolderItem object. Remove the Property object from its parents container. Finally, remove the Property object from the properties container of "this."

2-15.   The XML object model for the Folder-File hierarchy is shown in Figure 9-27. The Folder and File classes are tagged Element. They correspond to the `<Folder>...</Folder>` and `<File>...</File>` elements respectively. We also include an Attribute class, which is of type <<Attr>> and represents an attribute of those elements (such as filename).

Property
parentFolder : Folder folderItem : FolderItem isPrimary : Boolean
<<constructor>> Property(parent : Folder, folderItem: FolderItem, isPrimary: Boolean)   <<get & query operations>> getParentFolder( ): Folder getFolderItem ( ) : FolderItem isPrimary( ) : Boolean   <<editing>> setParentFolder(parent : Folder) setFolderItem (folderItem: FolderItem)

FIGURE 9-26.   *Answer to Exercise 2-14.*

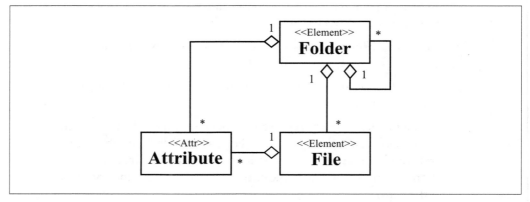

FIGURE 9-27. *Answer to Exercise 2-15.*

A sample XML file for the object follows. Note that files do not contain other elements. Thus they end with the special XML end tag.

```
<?xml version="1.0" standalone="yes"?>
<Folder name="JDK">
  <File name="license" size="6100"/>
  <File name="README" size="49000"/>
  <Folder name="bin">
    <File name="java.exe" size="5120"/>
    <File name="jre.exe" size="11200"/>
  </Folder>
  <Folder name="lib">
    <File name="classes.zip" size="879640100"/>
  </Folder>
</Folder>
```

As shown, an XML document typically starts with a top-level folder, going down to lower level folders and files. On the other hand, the Folder-File hierarchy can be reconstructed from the XML document.

2-16. Based on the aggregation diagram for the Menu class family in Exercise 2-5, we identify all classes to be of <<Element>> type (Figure 9-28). Each class is implied to contain a set of XML attributes (<<Attr>> objects).

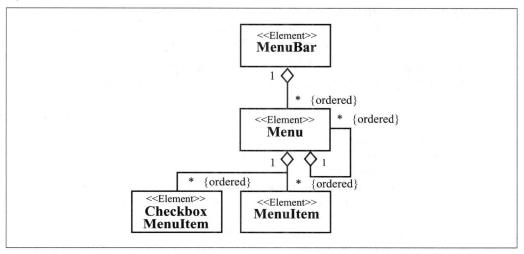

FIGURE 9-28. *Answer to Exercise 2-16.*

An example XML document for the File and Help menus follows. All menu items have their action. Some also have icons. The menu item of the special name #Separator signifies a separator.

```
<?xml version="1.0" standalone="yes"?>
<MenuBar>
  <Menu name="File">
    <MenuItem name="New…" icon="new.gif"
     action="newFile"/>
    <MenuItem name="Open…" icon="open.gif"
     action="openFile"/>
    <MenuItem name="Save" icon="save.gif"
     action="saveFile"/>
    <MenuItem name="Save As…" icon="saveAs.gif"
     action="saveFile"/>
    <MenuItem name="#Separator" />
    <MenuItem name="Exit" action="exit"/>
  </Menu>
  <Menu name="Help">
    <MenuItem name="Index" action="showIndex"/>
    <MenuItem name="Search" action="searchHelp"/>
    <MenuItem name="#Separator" />
    <MenuItem name="About…" action="showAbout"/>
  </Menu>
</MenuBar>
```

2-17. Because the Attribute class now has three attributes, we can no longer treat the class as an <<Attr>> type. Rather, it is promoted to be an <<Element>>, as shown in Figure 9-29.

The mapping of this new XML object model to XML tags is straightforward. An example similar to the one in the text is as follows:

```
<?xml version="1.0" standalone="yes"?>
<Catalog name="electronics">
 <Part name="resistorList">
  <Part name="resistor">
    <Attribute name="partNumber" value="123" unit=""/>
    <Attribute name="resistance" value="5.6"
     unit="Ohm"/>
    <Attribute name="power" value="0.1" unit="W"/>
    <Attribute name="length" value="12" unit="mm"/>
  </Part>
  <Part name="resistor">
    <Attribute name="partNumber" value="323" unit=""/>
    <Attribute name="resistance" value="12.6"
     unit="Ohm"/>
```

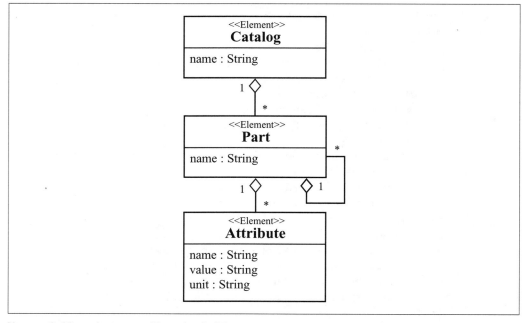

FIGURE 9-29. *Answer to Exercise 2-17.*

```
      <Attribute name="power" value="0.2" unit="W"/>
      <Attribute name="length" value="16" unit="mm"/>
    </Part>
  </Part>
  <Part name="capacitorList">
   <Part name="capacitor">
      <Attribute name="partNumber" value="13" unit=""/>
      <Attribute name="capacitance" value="12.5"
       unit="F"/>
      <Attribute name="voltage" value="30" unit="V"/>
    </Part>
  </Part>
</Catalog>
```

Compared with the old one, this new scheme offers a finer resolution in tagging the data, at the expense of more tags. To shorten the XML document, we may replace the element names with the values in the name attributes, as follows. The resemblance to the object model now becomes less obvious:

```
<?xml version="1.0" standalone="yes"?>
<electronics>
 <resistorList>
  <resistor>
    <partNumber value="123" unit=""/>
    <resistance value="5.6" unit="Ohm"/>
    <power value="0.1" unit="W"/>
    <length value="12" unit="mm"/>
  </resistor>
  <resistor>
    <partNumber value="323" unit=""/>
    <resistance value="12.6" unit="Ohm"/>
    <power value="0.2" unit="W"/>
    <length value="16" unit="mm"/>
  </resistor>
 </resistorList>
 <capacitorList>
  <capacitor>
    <partNumber value="13" unit=""/>
    <capacitance value="12.5" unit="F"/>
    <voltage value="30" unit="V"/>
  </capacitor>
 </capacitorList>
</electronics>
```

2-18. Besides the binary association class, we may identify the following patterns in Figure 2-18:

- **Shared object pool (Figure 2-27)**—Users share FolderItems with individual permission settings. FolderItems are managed by Folders.

- **Handle-Body (Figure 2-24)**—A user owns multiple FolderItems, which can be either a File or a Folder. Thus FolderItem is similar to Role in Figure 2-24.

- Others are the obvious containers, managers, and relationship loops.

9.3   CHAPTER 3 EXERCISE ANSWERS

3-1. For the Polygon-Point association in Figure 1-11, we use the standard class-table mapping to arrive at Tables 9-2 through 9-4, in which the primary keys are shaded.

TABLE 9-2.   *Point table.*

POINT_ID	X	Y
101	0.2	0.0
102	1.0	0.0
103	0.0	0.3
104	0.5	0.5

TABLE 9-3.   *Polygon table.*

POLYGON_ID	COLOR	ISFILLED
11	Red	False
12	Blue	True

TABLE 9-4.   *Polygon-Point link table.*

POLYGON_ID	POINT_ID	ORDER
11	104	3
11	102	2
11	101	1
11	103	4

Table 9-2 simply contains the primary key point_ID and the (x, y) coordinates. Table 9-3 simply contains the primary key polygon_ID and two additional fields as display attributes. Table 9-4 associates a polygon with its points. According to the multiplicity in Figure 1-11, each point can be associated with only one polygon, thus point_ID is the primary key in the link table. In addition, each polygon must have three or more points. The points must maintain a certain order so that you can draw the polygon by connecting consecutive points with lines (and the last point to the first one).

Thus, the database application must ensure the following:

- That the same polygon_ID appears at least three times in the link table
- That the order numbers in the link table for each polygon are complete and correct
- That the order of the points is preserved in the application

Because Table 9-4 shares the same primary key with Table 9-2, we could combine the two. However, this would not be a good practice because records in Table 9-2 may be used in other relationships. The Circle-Point relationship in Figure 1-11 is such an example.

3-2. The relational tables for the network of Node objects in Figure 2-4b are the Node table (Table 9-5), which has node_ID as the primary key, and the link table (Table 9-6; the distance values are made up), which has (up_node_ID, down_ node_ID) as the primary key.

3-3. The link table (Post) in Figure 3-8 does not satisfy the third normal form because the duty field depends on the name field, which is not a

TABLE 9-5. *Node table.*

NODE_ID	CITY	COUNTRY
1	Chicago	USA
2	Hong Kong	China
3	Los Angeles	USA
4	Macao	China
5	Tokyo	Japan
6	San Francisco	USA
7	Washington	USA

TABLE 9-6. *Node-Node link table.*

UP_NODE_ID	DOWN_NODE_ID	DISTANCE, KM
4	5	6,000
4	2	300
4	6	12,000
5	6	6,000
2	6	12,000
2	1	15,000
2	3	12,000
6	7	8,000
1	7	4,000
3	7	7,500

primary key. (This is easily detected by noting that some duty descriptions appear more than once.)

To make it compliant with the third normal form, we may extract the name and duty fields and create a separate Duty table with primary key duty_ID, as shown in Table 9-7. The name and duty fields in the Post table are then replaced by foreign key duty_ID. In terms of an object model, this indicates a one-to-one association between Post and Duty.

3-4.   The relational tables for the inheritance tree are shown in Figure 9-30.

TABLE 9-7. *Duty table.*

DUTY_ID	NAME	DUTY
1	Chair	Chairs meetings
2	Vice-chair	Supports the chair
3	Secretary	Takes minutes
4	Treasurer	Handles money
5	Head	Calls meetings
6	Member	Attends meetings
7	Co-chair	Helps the chair

A	
A_ID	A_type
1	A
2	B
3	B
4	C
5	C
6	B
7	B

B	
A_ID	B_type
2	D
3	B
6	D
7	E

D
A_ID
2
6

C
A_ID
4
5

E
A_ID
7

FIGURE 9-30.   *Answer to Exercise 3-4.*

Here we have ignored all attributes that may appear in the object model. To navigate to the D object with A_ID = 2, we do the following:

1. Go to table A, find the row with A_ID = 2 (probably through a query with other fields in that table). Pick up other desirable fields in table A.

2. Get the A_type value for that row, which is B.

3. Go to table B, find the row with A_ID = 2. Pick up the desirable fields in table B.

4. Get the B_type value for that row, which is D.

5. Go to table D, find the row with A_ID = 2. Pick up the desirable fields in table D.

3-5.   We follow the "one class/one table" approach to map the FolderItem-Folder relationship loop in the left part of Figure 2-7 to the tables in Figure 9-31.

The primary key in the FolderItem and Folder table is FI_ID. In the link table, it is (FOLDER_ID, FILE_ID), both of which are foreign keys. The following restrictions apply to the values of the foreign keys in the link table:

FolderItem				
FI_ID	type	name	size	date
1	Folder	Project A	6	1/2/1999
2	File	Status.txt	7300	8/1/2000
2	File	July.doc	55000	7/1/1999
4	File	March.doc	24000	3/1/1999
5	Folder	Reports	6	1/2/1999
6	File	January.doc	20000	1/15/1999

Folder-FolderItem Link	
FOLDER_ID	FILE_ID
1	2
1	5
5	3
5	4
5	6

Folder	
FI_ID	number of items
1	1
5	3

FIGURE 9-31. *Answer to Exercise 3-5.*

- FOLDER_ID cannot be the same as FILE_ID because a folder cannot contain itself.
- FOLDER_ID must come from the Folder table.
- Each FILE_ID value can only appear once because each FolderItem can have only one parent.

The following lists the steps for the query: Find all files under the Reports folder with names that match the pattern J*.doc.

1. Select the row from the FolderItem table with name equal to Reports and type equal to folder. Get the FI_ID of the row (which is 5 in our example).

2. Select all rows from the link table with FOLDER_ID equal to the previous FI_ID (5 in our example). Put them into a temporary collection.

3. For each record in the collection, use its FILE_ID to find the name in the FolderItem table. If the name does not match the pattern J*.doc, remove the record from the collection.

4. The temporary collection now contains the records that satisfy the query requirements. (The files July.doc and January.doc are returned in our example.)

3-6. First we notice that in the new Transaction table, a specific pair (supplier_ID, buyer_ID) can appear more than once. Hence, because of the candidate key requirement, the relationship involving the Supplier, Buyer, and Transaction classes can no longer be modeled by a binary association.

However, for each transaction_ID, there is only one supplier_ID and buyer_ID. The field supplier_ID is a foreign key to the Supplier table, and buyer_ID is a foreign key to the Buyer table. These foreign keys indicate binary associations between Supplier and Transaction, and between Buyer and Transaction. Thus we arrive at Figure 9-32.

These three classes and two associations map to five tables. However, because the multiplicity on the Supplier and Buyer sides is unity, the link tables have the same primary key as the Transaction table. They can then be absorbed into the Transaction table, yielding the three tables described in the exercise.

Note that the design in Figure 9-32 is the same as that on the right of Figure 2-21, except that the candidate key requirement is not needed because Transaction is not a binary association class.

Alternatively, we can maintain the old Trade class and extend it by adding a Transaction class. Each trade relationship between a supplier and a buyer is associated with multiple transactions, as shown in Figure 9-33.

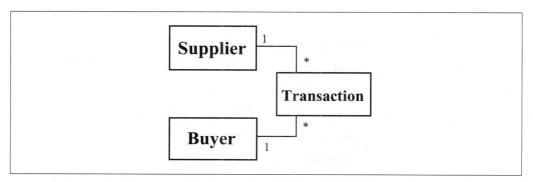

FIGURE 9-32. *Answer to Exercise 3-6.*

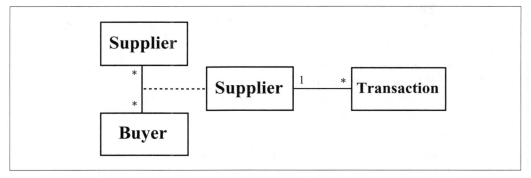

FIGURE **9-33.** *Answer to Exercise 3-6.*

One can show that this object design produces the same tables as those in Figure 9-31 in the following way. Note that by following the mapping rules in Table 3-2, the Trade table has (supplier_ID, buyer_ID) as the primary key. Now because the multiplicity on the Trade side is unity, the Trade table can be absorbed into the Transaction table, which has transaction_ID as the primary key. Thus again we are left with three tables.

3-7.   To normalize the table using the "object-oriented approach," we first identify the object classes. An assignment represents a link between a company and a consultant. A company can have multiple consultants, whereas a consultant can work for multiple companies. Hence, we arrive at the object-oriented design in Figure 9-34.

Next we map the objects to normalized relational tables using the standard approach. The results are shown in Tables 9-8 through 9-10.

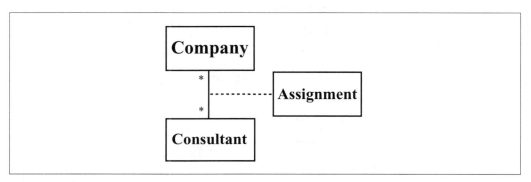

FIGURE **9-34.** *Answer to Exercise 3-7.*

TABLE 9-8. *Consultant table.*

CONSULTANT_ID	NAME	SOCIAL SECURITY NUMBER
101	John Smith	123-45-6789
102	Tom Chan	582-54-5528
103	Mike Brown	473-55-8721
104	Sue Lee	743-31-3782

TABLE 9-9. *Company table.*

COMPANY_ID	NAME	ADDRESS
1	ABCD	888 3rd Ave
2	IT.com	1 Main St
3	HiTech	7 State Rd

TABLE 9-10. *Assignment table.*

CONSULTANT_ID	COMPANY_ID	JOB	PERCENTAGE	HOURLY RATE
101	1	Database work	60	$55
102	1	Network setup	40	$70
103	2	Web design	100	$80
101	2	Database work	40	$60
104	2	Database work	100	$65
102	3	Network setup	60	$75

3-8. Comparison of a binary association and a ternary associaton (Table 9-11), assuming both mA, mB > 1. The differences are due to the fact that (b) is intrinsically a three-way relationship, although the multiplicity of L is one.

3-9. The two designs are not equivalent if either mA or mB is not *. The one on the right is more restrictive. This is because the multiplicity on the right is between A and B, rather than among three classes. For example, suppose mB = 3 and mA = *. Table 9-12 is allowed by the design on the left, but is disallowed by the design on the right.

3-10. (a) The persistent object design for the invoice is shown in Figure 9-35. We identify the core pattern as the association class

TABLE **9-11.** *Comparison of binary and ternary associations.*

STATE	FIGURE 3-42A	FIGURE 3-42B
Same	Each (A, B) pair is associated with one L object (the candidate key requirement).	Each (A, B) pair is associated with one L object (multiplicity equals one).
Same	The primary key of the link table is (A_ID, B_ID).	The primary key of the link table is (A_ID, B_ID).
Different	Each A is linked to mB B objects, with each link being associated with one L object. Similarly for B.	Each (A, L) pair is associated with mB B objects. Similarly for a (B, L) pair.

TABLE **9-12.** *Link table.*

L_ID	A_ID	B_ID	C_ID
1	a1	b1	c1
2	a1	b2	c1
3	a1	b3	c1
4	a1	b4	c2

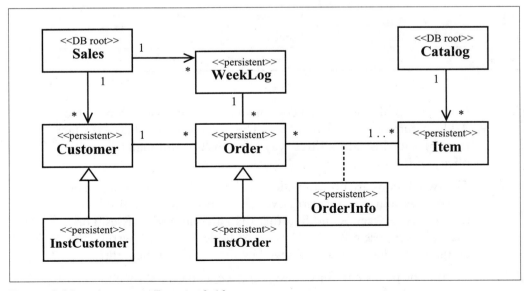

FIGURE **9-35.** *Answer to Exercise 3-10.*

OrderInfo between Order and Item. Each order may contain multiple items, whereas each item may appear in multiple orders. Hence the multiplicity in the design. The rest of the design is an extension of this core pattern.

A customer may have multiple orders. The subclasses InstCustomer and InstOrder are used to represent institutional customers and their orders. The class WeekLog is simply a container of all orders in a week, whereas Catalog is a root container of all items for sale. The other database root, Sales, contains a list of customers and weekly logs.

The essential attributes for these classes are listed in Table 9-13.

(b) To allow multiple shipments within an order, we may add a new class ShipmentInfo, which is associated with the OrderInfo class. All data related to a shipment (quantity shipped, subtotal, date) are now contained in this new class.

To track which sales representative handles which order, we note that an order is associated with a customer and a sales representative. Thus, we may simply add a SalesRep class under Sales, as shown in Figure 9-36.

Note that it may appear plausible to treat Order as an association class between SalesRep and Customer. This, however, is not appropriate because for a specific pair (SalesRep, Customer) there may be more than one Order.

TABLE 9-13. *Class attributes.*

CLASS	ATTRIBUTES
Customer	number, name, address, telephone
InstCustomer	department number, institution name
Order	number, date, credit card number, total price
InstOrder	purchase order number
Item	number, name, unit price
OrderInfo	quantity ordered, quantity shipped, subtotal
Sales	customer list, week log list
Catalog	item list
WeekLog	order list

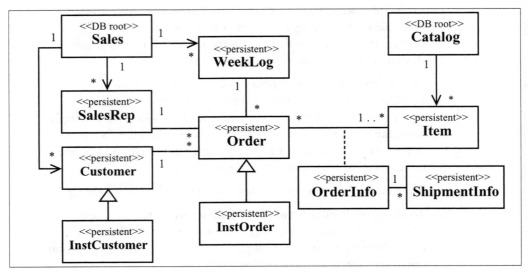

FIGURE 9-36. *Answer to Exercise 3-10.*

The updated attributes for these classes are listed in Table 9-14. Note that all subordinate quantities shipped should add up to the quantity ordered in an OrderInfo object.

Note that in the design in Figure 9-36, there is no shipment object. If we want to find all the items in a shipment, we need to

TABLE 9-14. *Updated class attributes.*

CLASS	ATTRIBUTES
Customer	number, name, address, telephone
InstCustomer	department number, institution name
Order	number, date, credit card number, total price
InstOrder	purchase order number
SalesRep	name, telephone
Item	number, name, unit price
OrderInfo	quantity ordered
ShipmentInfo	quantity shipped, subtotal, date
Sales	customer list, week log list, sales rep. list
Catalog	item list
WeekLog	order list

select all ShipmentInfo with the same date. To make this task easier, we may add a new class Shipment and let ShipmentInfo be the association class between Shipment and Item, as shown in Figure 9-37. This offers a clearer shipment concept at the expense of a more complex class relationship.

3-11. To map the binary associations to tables, we may follow the standard approach. First we list the courses and instructors in simple tables. The primary keys are course_ID and instructor_ID. Because the multiplicity for Course is one, we may use foreign key embedding in the Session table, which has session_ID as the primary key and course_ID as a foreign key. The association between Session and Instructor is captured by the Session-Instructor link table, with a primary key of (session_ID, instructor_ID). Because each session must have one or two instructors, a particular session_ID must appear once or twice in this link table. The tables are shown in Figure 9-38.

For the association between Session and Instructor, we may indeed use the technique of foreign key embedding. This works because the multiplicity on the Instructor side has a small upper bound (2). Hence we may have two additional fields in the Session table, each corresponding to an instructor, as shown in Table 9-15. Note that a zero value for instructor 2 indicates that there is no second instructor for the session.

Now the Session-Instructor link table is no longer needed. The elimination of one table helps improve the performance at the expense of degraded flexibility. If in the future there needs to be more than two instructors, then the table schema has to be changed. For the orginal

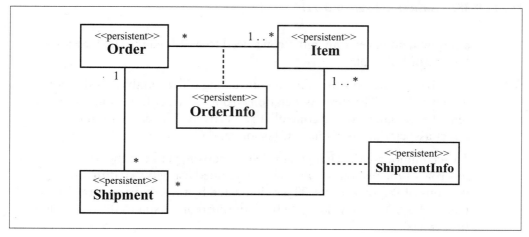

FIGURE 9-37. *Answer to Exercise 3-10.*

Course	
course_ID	title
Physics-101	Introduction to Physics
Math-102	Calculus II
Drama-401	Drama Theory
English-201	English Literature

Instructor		
instructor_ID	name	phone
1	John Smith	303-1234
2	Jack Brown	303-5678
3	Mary Lee	404-9876
4	Jane Long	404-4321
5	Tony Bond	703-5643

Session-Instructor Link	
session_ID	**instructor_ID**
1081	1
1081	2
7031	3
7032	3
4231	4
4031	5

Session			
session_ID	course_ID	schedule	classroom
1081	Physics-101	M1-2 & Th2-3	C-A31
7031	Math-102	T10-12	D-102
7032	Math-102	Th10-12	D-102
4231	Drama-401	F9-11	S-904
4031	English-201	W3-5	T-236

FIGURE 9-38. *Answer to Exercise 3-11.*

approach, however, only more rows need to be added into the Session-Instructor link table.

3-12. The object design for the general contracting office database is shown in Figure 3-39. The three associations from Contract to Person represent client, manager, and controller respectively. The database root has direct associations to Contract, Person, and Company.

To accommodate the change of role in a person, yet keep the previous role of the person, we may set up a linked list between different versions of Person objects. This is indicated by the self-association in Figure 9-39. You may navigate from the current person to the next role (if it exists).

TABLE 9-15.   *Session table.*

SESSION_ID	COURSE_ID	SCHEDULE	CLASSROOM	INSTRUCTOR 1	INSTRUCTOR 2
1081	Physics-101	M1-2 & Th2-3	C-A31	1	2
7031	Math-102	T10-12	D-102	3	0
7032	Math-102	Th10-12	D-102	3	0
4231	Drama-401	F9-11	S-904	4	0
4031	English-201	W3-5	T-236	5	0

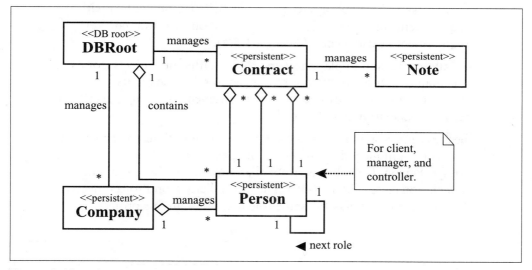

FIGURE 9-39.   *Answer to Exercise 3-12.*

Converting the design back to tables, we need only one additional table. This "RoleLink" table (Table 9-16) has the pair (current, next) as the primary key. The pair links one person to his/her next role.

3-13.   The static side of the company's work environment is well captured by the design. That is, the company manages a collection of Persons, each having a supervisor (except for the President). The job description for each person is captured by the association class Job.

On the dynamic side, however, things are more subtle. First, the company has a collection of projects, which in turn manage one or more tasks. Second, a person can play more than one role, and a role may involve more than one person. These are all consistent with the requirements.

TABLE 9-16. *RoleLink table.*

TABLE	FIELDS (primary key in bold)
RoleLink	**current** (=> person_ID)
	next (=> person_ID)
	effective_date

However, the design treats Task as a binary association class between Role and Person. Thus a person in a specific role can only be involved in one task (which belongs to one project). This is in conflict with the requirement statements. (See the discussion on the candidate key requirement near the end of Section 1.5.4).

To allow a person to play the same role in different projects (for example, manager of those projects), we need to relax the binary association, particularly the candidate key requirement. This suggests that a ternary association may be needed.

Because a person may play the same role in more than one project, a task is not uniquely determined by the pair (Person, Role), but by the triplet (Person, Role, Project). We therefore model Task as a ternary association class (Figure 9-40). The multiplicity * on Project means that a person may play the same role in more than one project.

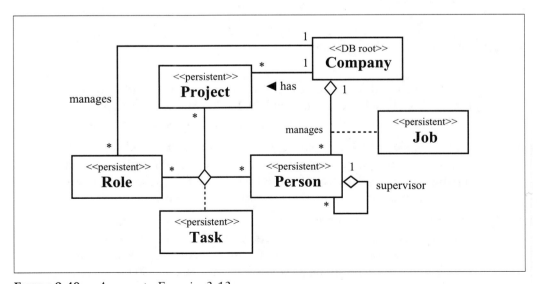

FIGURE 9-40. *Answer to Exercise 3-13.*

Table 9-17 helps illustrate the improved design. The rows with "!" were not allowed in the original design because other rows with the same (person_ID, role_ID) exist.

3-14.   From the team score table we find that a Team object is uniquely specified by the triplet (man, woman, year). In other words, the triplet forms the primary key for the table. Because in (a) each team is uniquely identified by the pair (man, woman), we may immediately rule it out.

In design (b), on the other hand, each team is associated with one triplet. But a triplet does not uniquely specify a team. Thus, a pair (man, woman) may form two teams in a given year, which is not allowed.

Finally, design (c) uses the triplet as the primary key, which allows a pair (man, woman) to form teams in different years and prohibits a person from joining more than one team in any year. Hence (c) is the correct design.

We may also analyze this problem as follows. Design (a) allows a person to form teams with *different* partners in different years, but the same pair can form a team for only one year. Thus, for instance, the Tom-Jane team in 2002 is not allowed under design (a) because they already were a team in 2001.

Design (b) relaxes this constraint and allows a specific pair (man, woman) to form teams in different years. However, the relaxation is overdone because the same pair may now form more than one team in a given year.

Design (c) tightens this to suit just what we need.

TABLE 9-17.   *Task table.*

PROJECT_ID	PERSON_ID	ROLE_ID	TASK_DESCRIPTION	
A	Mary	Manager	Project management	
A	John	Developer	Server-side development	
A	Tom	Developer	Web page design	
B	Mary	Manager	Project management	!
B	John	Developer	Database development	!
B	John	Tester	System testing	

9.4 CHAPTER 4 EXERCISE ANSWERS

4-1. The abstract classes in the Java Abstract Windowing Toolkit package (java.awt) are Component, Container, and MenuComponent.

4-2. The dependency between the packages is shown in Figure 9-41.

4-3. For the draft object design in Figure 4-11, the irreducible patterns are as described in the text:

- **Backward relationship loop**—Between the classes Module and Network

- **Object managers**—Network and Node managing Link objects

- **Binary association class**—Link as the association class for (Node, Module) and (Network, Module)

The backward relationship loop yields a compositional hierarchy. A Network object may contain multiple Node objects and other subnetworks. The association class Link specifies the connection between two Module objects. The links may be interpreted as unidirectional (data always flowing from one module to another) or as bidirectional. Each link is managed by a module that creates the link.

An example of the hierarchical network structure with unidirectional links is shown in Figure 9-42.

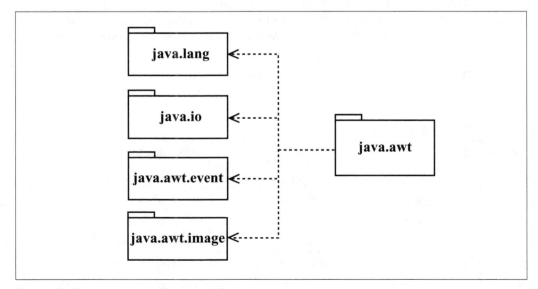

FIGURE 9-41. *Answer to Exercise 4-2.*

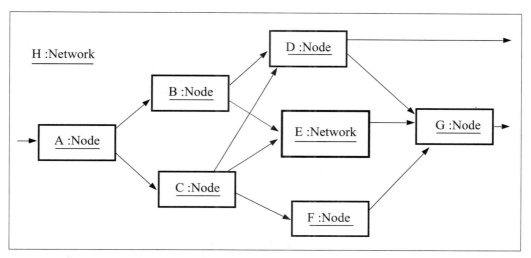

FIGURE 9-42. *Answer to Exercise 4-3.*

Here the parent network H contains six nodes and one subnetwork. The links are shown as lines with arrows. For each node or network, there are incoming and outgoing links. The network E may contain multiple nodes or even subnetworks.

The parent network H itself may also have external incoming and out-going links, besides the internal ones that connect to nodes A, D, and G. Such a network may be used in modular computation in which each node performs certain mathematical operations or data processing.

The class Link can also be viewed as an association class between Node and Network. However, an ambiguity exists regarding which one manages the Link objects. Because both Node and Network classes have the association class Link, we may bring this relationship one level up to their superclass. This simplifies the design considerably and avoids redundant and ambiguous links. It also enables greater reuse of code that manages the Link objects. The modified design is shown in Figure 9-43.

The modified design clearly shows the recursive association class pattern (see Section 2.5.2), in addition to the backward relationship loop. (The design is now structurally identical to the one in Figure 4-6.)

4-4. Unfortunately, neither of the students got it right. Student (a)'s design shows that a library owns a collection of books and a borrower can

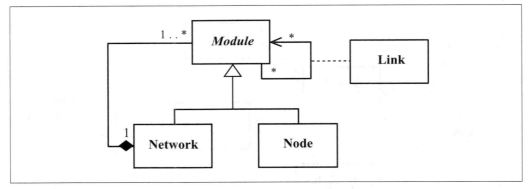

FIGURE 9-43.   *Answer to Exercise 4-3.*

borrow a number of books. However, the Book object is not a logical place to hold the loan information (such as due date, fine, and so on). Student (b), on the other hand, treated a loan as a binary association between a borrower and a library. The loan object is separate from the book, which is an improvement over Student (a)'s design. In this sense design (b) is better than (a).

There is, however, a flaw in (b). As implied by a binary association, each pair of Borrower and Library objects uniquely identifies a loan. However, a borrower can borrow more than one book from the same library, which means that the Loan object is not uniquely determined by the pair.

To improve the design, let us step back a bit and ponder the Loan object. A loan is actually *uniquely* determined by three objects: a Borrower, a Library, and a Book. Thus, we can use a ternary association class as the irreducible pattern for our design. Regarding multiplicity, we know that for each loan, a (borrower, book) pair can only be associated with one library, and each (library, book) pair with one borrower. This gives rise to the design in Figure 9-44.

Because the ternary association has a multiplicity of one, it degenerates into binary associations. In particular, the primary key for Book is the same primary key for the Loan association, which means there is a one-to-one link between Loan and Book. Thus, the design is as shown in Figure 9-45.

This is very similar to Student (a)'s design, except that the class Loan is used to encapsulate information about a loan. The Book objects simply form a collection managed by a library.

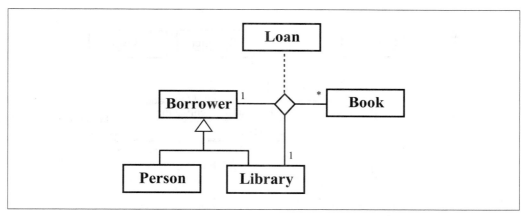

FIGURE **9-44.** *Answer to Exercise 4-4.*

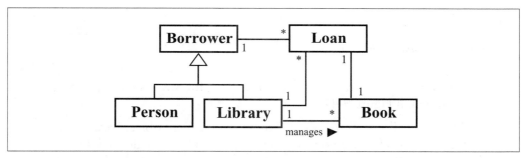

FIGURE **9-45.** *Answer to Exercise 4-4.*

9.5 CHAPTER 5 EXERCISE ANSWERS

5-1. Let us call the trade manager class TradeMgr. The operation addTrade() is represented by the sequence diagram in Figure 9-46. An actor invokes the addTrade() operation of a TradeMgr object with all the parameters needed for constructing a Trade object. The TradeMgr then creates a Trade object, with a constructor that sets up references to the pair of input Supplier and Buyer objects. The constructor also calls the addTrade() operations of both Supplier and Buyer, with trade collections that are inserted with the new Trade object. This establishes the links from the Supplier and Buyer objects back to the Trade object. Finally, the new Trade object is added to the trade collection in TradeMgr before the control returns to the caller. Note that before the new Trade object is created, the Supplier and Buyer objects already exist.

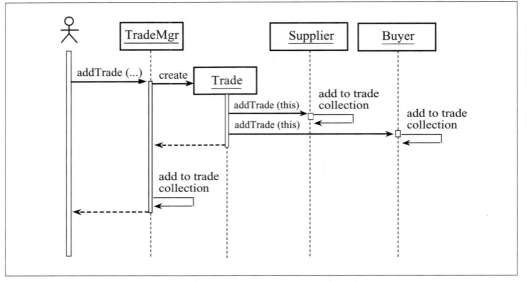

FIGURE 9-46. *Answer to Exercise 5-1.*

The other core operation, `removeTrade()`, follows a similar pattern, as shown in Figure 9-47.

After the call, the Trade object becomes an orphan object because there is no object reference pointing to it. The object will be deleted during garbage collection.

5-2.   The sequence diagram for the operation `addComponent(component:Part, count:Integer)` in the Part class of Figure 2-22 is shown in Figure 9-48. Note that the operation `addParent(parent:Part)` is called by the constructor of the Property class.

5-3.   The mapping to Java for the Part and Attribute structs follows. An IDL struct is mapped to a public final Java class with the same name. There is a null constructor and a constructor for all member variables in the class.

```
// Attribute.java
package pdm;
public final class Attribute {
   public java.lang.String name;
   public double value;
   public java.lang.String unit;
   public Attribute() {
   }
```

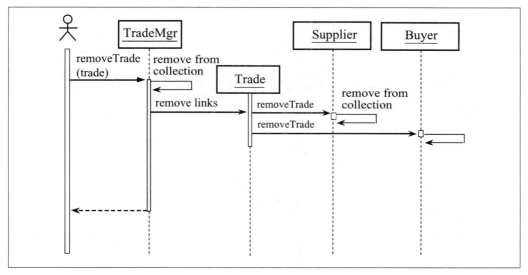

FIGURE **9-47.** *Answer to Exercise 5-1.*

```
      public Attribute(java.lang.String name, double value
                       java.lang.String unit) {
   this.name = name;
   this.value = value;
 }
}


// Part.java
package pdm;
public final class Part {
  public java.lang.String name;
  public pdm.Part[] components;
  public pdm.Attribute[] attributes;
  public Part() {
  }
  public Part(
    java.lang.String name,
    pdm.Part[] components,
    pdm.Attribute[] attributes
  ) {
    this.name = name;
    this.components = components;
    this.attributes = attributes;
  }
}
```

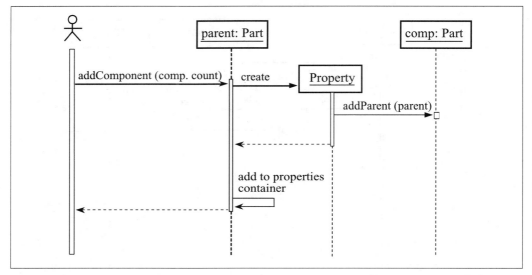

FIGURE 9-48. *Answer to Exercise 5-2.*

We note that there are additional helper and holder classes generated from an IDL compiler. The helper classes define some static methods for manipulating the data in the structs.

5-4. Let us explore what the construct implies. According to Figure 2-21, the construct may be drawn as that shown in Figure 9-49.

Because the interface LinkIF cannot contain any attributes, the associations from A and B are unidirectional. Thus, although we can define operations such as getA() and getB() in the interface LinkIF, the object references to A and B can only appear in the implementation

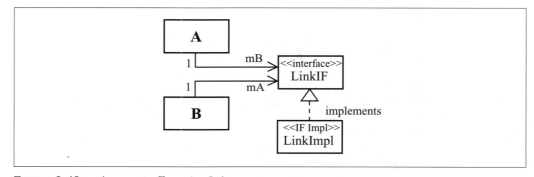

FIGURE 9-49. *Answer to Exercise 5-4.*

object LinkImpl. This discrepancy shows that LinkIF does not encapsulate *both* the link properties and the operations on them. Hence, LinkIF does not play the role of an association class.

A solution is to use an abstract class in place of the interface LinkIF. The object references to A and B can then be part of the abstract class.

5-5.   The sequence diagram for the `draw()` operation in the decorator pattern is shown in Figure 9-50. The `draw()` operations of the objects in the linked list are invoked in a chain.

Instead of using the decorator pattern, one may use class inheritance to extend the behavior of TextArea. For example, we may have a subclass TextAreaWithScroller that puts scroll bars around the text area. This approach, however, is too rigid because the extra functionality in the TextAreaWithScroller subclass can only be applied to a text area. The decorator pattern uses a servant class to replace inheritance (see Section 4.2), so that classes such as Scroller and Border can be applied to other Component objects.

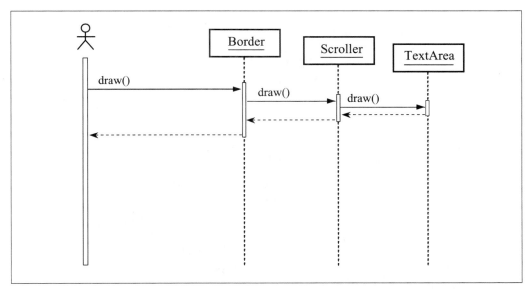

FIGURE 9-50.   *Answer to Exercise 5-5.*

9.6 CHAPTER 6 EXERCISE ANSWERS

6-1. The IDL file for a general service factory is as follows. Note that two exceptions are defined as well:

```
module factory {

  exception ServiceError {
    string message;
  };

  interface Service {
    string getName();
    any performService(in any a) raises (ServiceError);
  };

  exception FactoryError {
    string message;
  };

  interface ServiceFactory {
    Service create();
    Service find(in string name) raises (FactoryError);
    void remove(in string serviceName) raises
               (FactoryError);
    string showAll();
  };
};
```

The design in short form of the URL service factory is shown in Figure 9-51.

Note that ServiceFactoryImpl and ServiceImpl are abstract classes. Their detailed designs are given in Figure 9-52. The hash table in ServiceFactoryImpl is used to map a name to a service object. (Certain implementation details have been omitted. For example, a member variable for a BOA object in the ServiceFactoryImpl class is needed when deactivating service objects.) The specific classes for the URL service are shown in Figure 9-53. The class URLServiceFactoryImpl implements the operation performService, which was omitted in ServiceFactoryImpl.

6-2. The sequence diagram for the Timer and its Listener in Figure 6-10 is shown in Figure 9-54. An example of closing a Dialog window is used. Main represents a main program object.

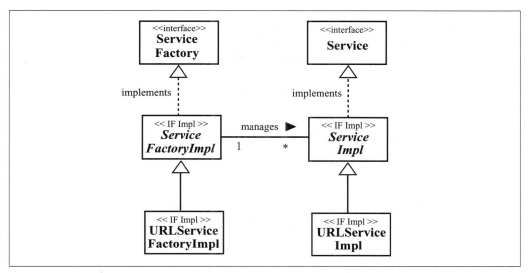

FIGURE 9-51. *Answer to Exercise 6-1.*

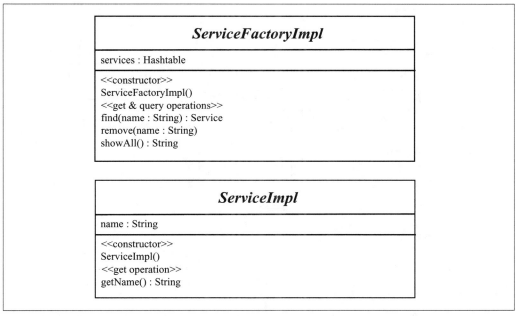

FIGURE 9-52. *Answer to Exercise 6-1.*

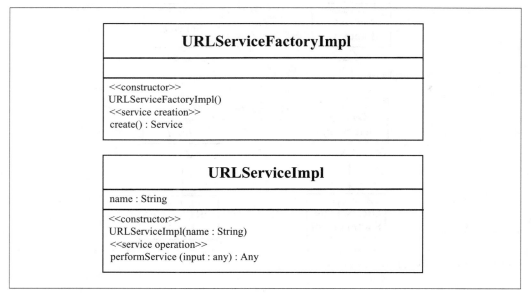

FIGURE 9-53. *Answer to Exercise 6-1.*

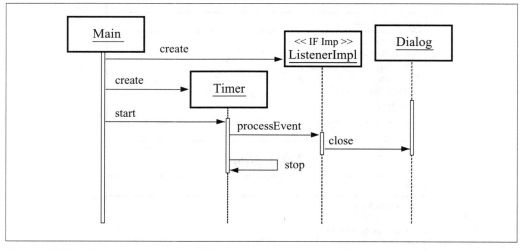

FIGURE 9-54. *Answer to Exercise 6-2.*

6-3.   The sequence diagram for the chat room application is shown in Figure 9-55. After each chat user signs on, the chat room adds the ChatUser object to a collection, thereby establishing a link to the ChatUser object. Later, when a chat user sends a message to the chat room, it then can step through the collection and invoke the

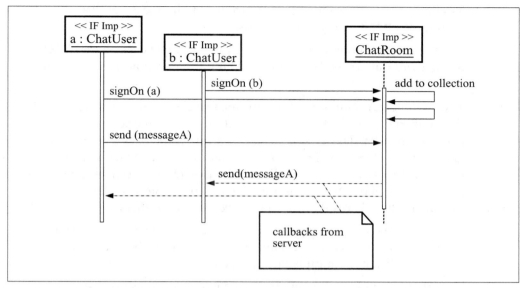

FIGURE **9-55.** *Answer to Exercise 6-3.*

callback (send) operation of each ChatUser object. This sequence is typical of direct push events.

6-4. A design diagram for a SAX application including the basic interfaces and their implementation classes is presented in Figure 9-56. Here, ABCParser is a particular implementation of an XML parser. MyHandler is a class that implements both the document and error

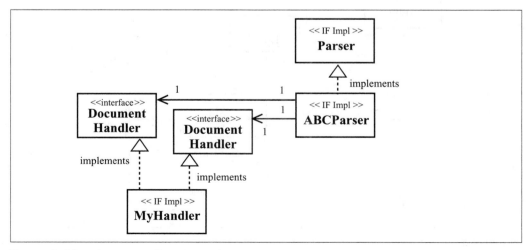

FIGURE **9-56.** *Answer to Exercise 6-4.*

handlers. The links from ABCParser to the handlers are established at runtime by calling the `set` methods.

The sequence diagram in Figure 9-57 shows a simple event-based XML parsing without errors. We include a Main program object that sets up and starts the parsing.

6-5.   The design diagram in short form for the five classes and interfaces is shown in Figure 9-58. This is an indirect push event model stemming from Figure 6-9a. The most interesting feature is the backward containment loop from AWTEventMulticaster to EventListener, which form a chain of event listeners. Each AWTEventMulticaster object contains two listeners. One is a user implementation object, such as MyPanel. The other is the link to the next pair of listeners.

The Button class has an object reference to an AWTEventMulticaster object that processes action events sent from buttons. Note that each listener can listen to multiple buttons, hence the * multiplicity.

Note that event processing in this design is synchronous because AWTEventMulticaster does not hold any event data.

In the sequence diagram (Figure 9-59), only concrete classes are involved. Button is the event supplier and MyPanel is the consumer. The MyPanel object invokes the method `addActionListener` in the Button class, which calls the `add` method in AWTEventMulticaster. Assuming that there is only one listener, the MyPanel object is

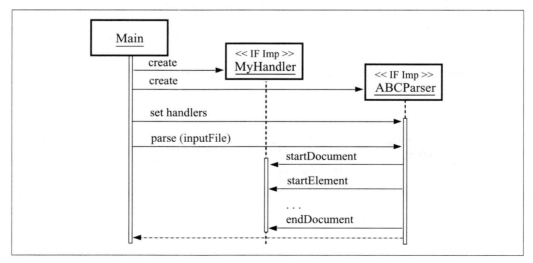

FIGURE 9-57. *Answer to Exercise 6-4.*

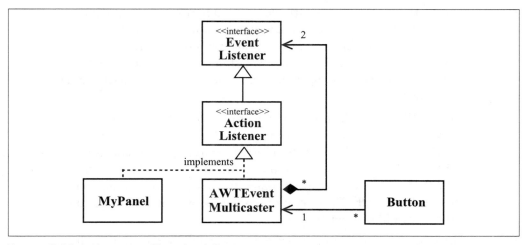

FIGURE 9-58.   *Answer to Exercise 6-5.*

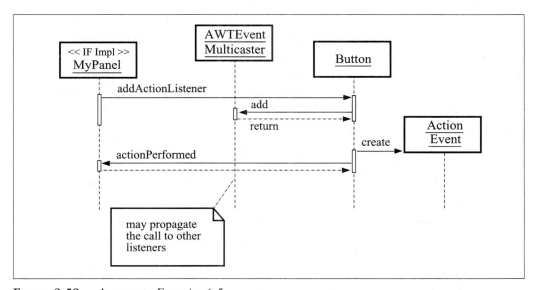

FIGURE 9-59.   *Answer to Exercise 6-5.*

returned by the add method and is subsequently pointed to by a member variable of the Button object.

If there were more listeners, they would be linked by a chain of AWTEventMulticaster objects, which propagate the `processEvent` calls to all listeners.

6-6.   The XML object model is exposed through four interfaces (Figure 9-60). All the interface classes have names ending with IF. The superclass ContentIF defines some operations common to both its subclasses ElementIF and TextIF. The `get` sibling operations return the previous or the next sibling content interface that belongs to the same parent Element.

ElementIF follows the object manager pattern in Figure 6-4. The operations `addText`, `addElement`, and `addAttr` create the corresponding objects. The operation `getElementsByName` returns an array of ElementIF with the specified name and in the same order as they are in the Element. The operation `insertBefore` inserts and then returns the new ContentIF. The operation `replaceContent` replaces and then returns the old ContentIF.

6-7.   The sequence diagram in Figure 6-17 is expanded to include multiple views, shown in Figure 9-61. Only two views are shown. All views are registered as listeners to the model object (the registration process is not shown). When the model data change, the model will notify all the views, which in turn may retrieve relevant data to update their displays.

6-8.   We modify the diagram in Figure 6-28 by including the complete MVC pattern in each client component and by adding a central coordinator to synchronize all clients. The corresponding static design in short form is shown in Figure 9-62.

The client component contains a complete MVC pattern. The server component has a Hub interface and its implementation. The Model and Hub objects form a callback interface pattern similar to that of Figure 6-12.

The association from Model <<IF Impl>> to the Hub interface allows a user to register a Client and send updates to the Server, which in turn uses the backward links to broadcast the updates to all client components. A sequence diagram with two clients is shown in Figure 9-63. (We have omitted the details within each client.)

6-9.   The RMI object tree for interface A is shown in Figure 9-64. The Remote interface is the top-level interface for all RMI objects. Users define the interface A and its implementation class A_Impl. This object tree is very similar to the one for CORBA server objects in Figure 6-19. The abstract class Remote Server plays the role of Skeleton in CORBA, whereas Unicast RemoteObject is similar to A_Impl_Base in Figure 6-19. However, there is no TIE approach in RMI, as in CORBA.

ContentIF

<<get & query operations>>
getParentElement() : Element
getPreviousSibling() : Content
getNextSibling() : Content
isAnElement() : Boolean

ElementIF

<<get & query operations>>
getName() : String
getContents() : Content [*]
getFirstContent() : Content
getLastContent() : Content
getContentCount() : Integer
getContentsBetween(start : Integer, end : Integer) : Contents [*]
getElementsByName(name : String) : Element [*]
containsContent(content : Content) : Boolean
hasContents() : Boolean

<<edit operations>>
addText(text : String) : Text
addElement(name : String) : Element
addContent(content : Content) : Content
insertBefore(newContent : Content, ref Content : Content) : Content
replaceContent(new : Content, old : Content) : Content
removeContent(content : Content) : Content
removeAllContents()

<<get operations for attributes>>
getAttrValue(name : String) : String
getAttr(name : String) : Attr
getAttrs() : Attr [*]
getAttrCount() : Integer
containsAttr(attr : Attr) : Boolean
hasAttrs() : Boolean

<<edit operations for attributes>>
addAttr(name : String, value : String)
addAttr(attribute : Attr) : Attr
removeAttr(name : String)
removeAllAttrs()

(*continued*)

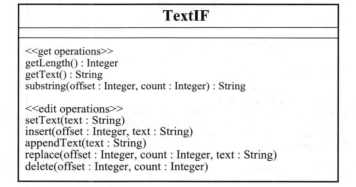

AttrIF

<<get operations>>
getName() : String
getValue() : String

<<edit operations>>
setValue(value : String

TextIF

<<get operations>>
getLength() : Integer
getText() : String
substring(offset : Integer, count : Integer) : String

<<edit operations>>
setText(text : String)
insert(offset : Integer, text : String)
appendText(text : String)
replace(offset : Integer, count : Integer, text : String)
delete(offset : Integer, count : Integer)

FIGURE 9-60. *Answer to Exercise 6-6.*

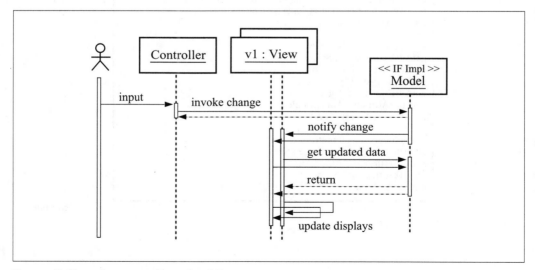

FIGURE 9-61. *Answer to Exercise 6-7.*

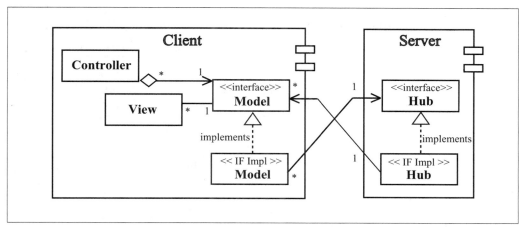

FIGURE 9-62. *Answer to Exercise 6-8.*

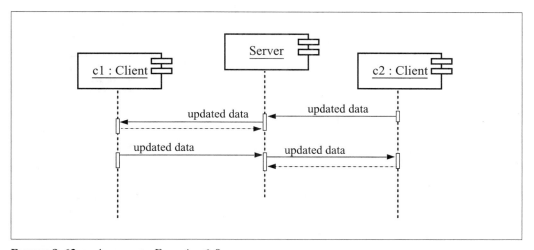

FIGURE 9-63. *Answer to Exercise 6-8.*

After the class A_Impl is implemented, the RMI compiler scans it to generate the A_Impl_Stub in the inheritance ladder shown in Figure 9-65. This stub is used by the client to invoke the operations on the remote server object (A_Impl). Note that the stub implements the interface A so it has all the remote operations of A. Again, this inheritance ladder is very similar to Figure 6-25. (Note that in Java 1.2 or higher there is no Skeleton class.)

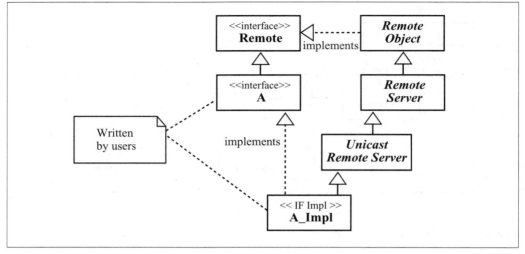

FIGURE 9-64. *Answer to Exercise 6-9.*

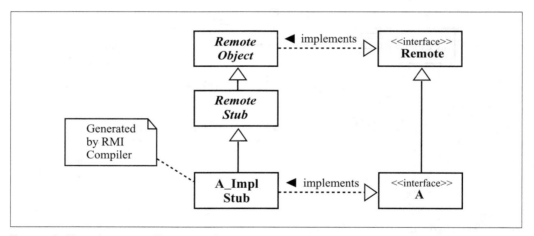

FIGURE 9-65. *Answer to Exercise 6-9.*

9.7   CHAPTER 7 EXERCISE ANSWERS

7-1.   A four-tier architecture with a cluster of Web servers is shown in Figure 9-66. The gateway Web server (ws0) collects real-time statistics from the clustered Web servers. When a client connects to the gateway Web server, it redirects the client to a specific Web server in the cluster according to the current load of the servers. (For example, the least loaded one is selected.)

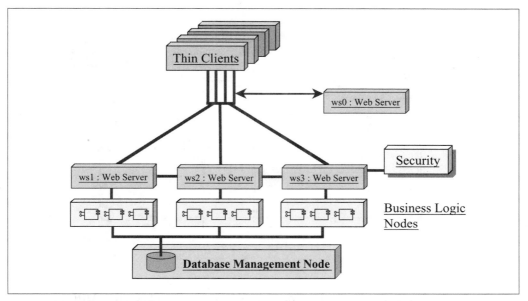

FIGURE 9-66. *Answer to Exercise 7-1.*

Each Web server in the cluster has one Business Logic node connecting to a single Database Management node. Because each Web server in the cluster is directly accessible to all Web clients, a security check must be performed at each server. This is done by a common Security node.

A sample sequence diagram is shown in Figure 9-67.

The advantages of this architecture are the following:

- By balancing the load among a cluster of servers, the system can handle a large number of concurrent clients.

- It is easy to expand the system by adding more servers. It offers a high degree of availability because of the redundant servers. Defective servers can be replaced in real time.

- It enables enterprise-level integration, typically by connecting the business logic tier with other enterprise systems.

The limitations of this architecture are the following:

- Multiple mirror Web servers and Business Logic nodes need to be maintained.

- The Security node is used by all clustered Web servers. It may become a bottleneck for the overall performance.

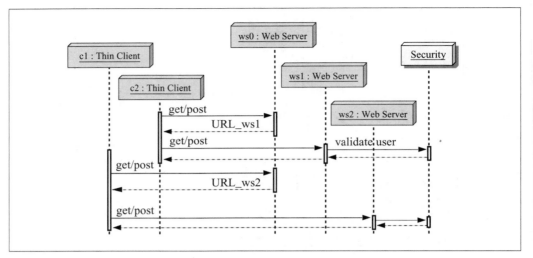

FIGURE **9-67.** *Answer to Exercise 7-1.*

- Several communication protocols (such as HTTP, CORBA/IIOP, and SQL) are involved between the client/server pairs, requiring a wide range of expertise in implementing the system.

7-2. The sequence diagram in Figure 5-16 is refined in Figure 9-68 to include interaction with objects in the interface and persistent layers of the ATM Central Server. (The DailyLog object is omitted from the diagram.) Note that before a SessionImpl object is created, a persistent Session object already exists. The latter serves as the servant object to the former.

Also, all interactions with persistent objects must be enclosed in synchronized transaction blocks. This prevents an execution thread from crossing the transaction boundary of another one. For example, the following synchronized transaction block encloses the addSession operation on an ATMManager object:

```
synchronized (DBManager.TOKEN) {
    DBManager.beginUpdateTransaction();
    ...
    mpATMManager.addSession(...);
    DBManager.commitTransaction();
}
```

Here, DBManager is a generic utility for database management. Its attribute TOKEN is used as a lock for synchronization. The variable

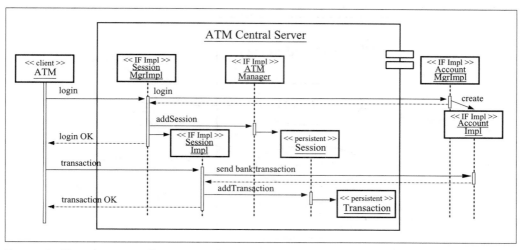

FIGURE 9-68. *Answer to Exercise 7-2.*

mpATMManager is an object reference to an ATM Manager object. The begin and commit calls identify the transaction boundary.

7-3.   An example use case for the administration of the ATM Central Server is adding new bank information to the server (Figure 9-69).

Use Case: Adding new bank information
Actor: An administrator for the ATM Central Server
Description: This use case describes the scenario of adding new bank information to the server.
Typical course of events:

ACTOR	SYSTEM
Connects to the ATM Central Server securely.	Gives a prompt.
Enters information for a bank. Input data include name and card prefix number of the bank.	Stores the bank information in the database.
Repeats the same for other banks. Ends the process when done.	

FIGURE 9-69. *Answer to Exercise 7-3.*

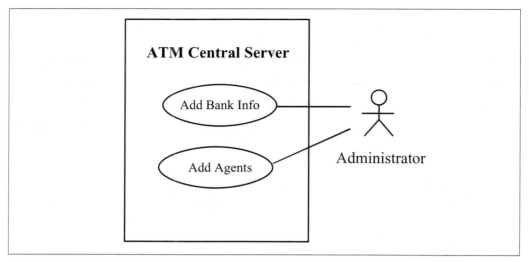

FIGURE 9-70. *Answer to Exercise 7-3.*

Other processes, such as adding new agents to the server, are similar. The corresponding use case diagram is shown in Figure 9-70.

7-4. The full design in long form for the persistent objects in Figure 7-27 (except the class Internet) is shown in Figure 9-71. Most of the operations are straightforward copies from the collection manager or binary association class patterns.

ATMManager
adminPassword : String bankInfos : Container sessions: Container dailyLogs: Container agents: Container
<<constructor>> ATMManager( ) ATMManager(adminPassword)   <<get & query operations>> getBankInfos() : BankInfo[*] getBankInfoCount() : Integer getBankInfo(prefix : Integer) : BankInfo getBankInfo(name : String) : BankInfo contains(bankInfo : BankInfo) : Boolean   getSessions() : Session[*] getSessionCount() : Integer   *(continued)*

```
getSessionsBetween(timeA : Time, timeB : Time) : Sessions [*]
contains(session : Session) : Boolean

getDailyLogs() : DailyLog[*]
getDailyLogCount() : Integer
getDailyLog(date : Date) : DailyLog
contains(dailyLog : DailyLog) : Boolean

getAgents() : Agent[*]
getAgentCount() : Integer
getAgent(id : String) : Agent
contains(agent : Agent) : Boolean

  <<editing>>
addBankInfo(name : String, prefix : Integer, serverName : String)
  : BankInfo
removeBankInfo(name : String)
removeBankInfo(prefix : Integer)
removeBankInfo(bankInfo : BankInfo)
removeAllBankInfos( )

addSession(startTime : Time, card : Card, agent : Agent) :
Session
removeSession(session : Session)
removeAllSessions( )

addDailyLog(date : Date) : DailyLog
removeDailyLog(date : Date)
removeDailyLog(dailyLog : DailyLog)
removeAllDailyLogs( )

addAgent(agent : Agent)
removeAgent(id : String)
removeAgent(agent : Agent)
removeAllAgents( )
```

(*continued*)

BankInfo
name : String prefix : Integer serverName : String cards : Container

<<constructor>>
BankInfo(name : String, prefix : Integer, serverName : String)
  <<get & query operations>>
getName() : String
getPrefix() : Integer
getServerName() : String
getCards() : Card[*]
getCardCount() : Integer
getCard(number : Integer) : Card
contains(card : Card) : Boolean
  <<editing>>
addCard(number : Integer, name: String, accountNumber: Integer) :
  Card
removeCard(number : Integer)
removeCard(card : Card)
removeAllCards( )

Card
number : Integer name: String accountNumber: Integer sessions : Session [*]

<<constructor>>
Card(number : Integer, name: String, accountNumber: Integer)
  <<get & query operations>>
getNumber() : Integer
getName() : String
getAccountNumber() : Integer
getSessions() : Session[*]
getSessionCount() : Integer
getSessionsBetween(timeA : Time, timeB : Time) : Sessions [*]
contains(session : Session) : Boolean
  <<editing>>
addSession(session : Session)

(continued)

Session
startTime : Time endTime : Time card : Card agent : Agent transactions : Transaction [*]
<<constructor>> Session(startTime : Time, card : Card, agent : Agent)   <<get & query operations>> getStartTime() : Time getEndTime() : Time getCard() : Card getAgent() : Agent getTransactions() : Transaction[*] getTransactionCount() : Integer getTransaction(time : Time) : Transaction contains(transaction : Transaction) : Boolean   <<editing>> addTransaction(time : Time, content : String) : Transaction endSession(endTime : Time)

Note: There is no `removeTransaction` operation because transactions should not be removed once added.

Transaction
time : Time content : String
<<constructor>> Transaction(time : Time, content : String)   <<get & query operations>> getTime() : Time getContent() : String   <<editing>>

Note: There is no `editing` operation because a transaction should not be changed once created.

(continued)

DailyLog
date : Date sessions : Container
<<constructor>> DailyLog(date : Date)   <<get & query operations>> getDate() : Date getSessions() : Session[*] getSessionCount() : Integer getSessionsBetween(timeA : Time, timeB : Time) : Sessions [*] contains(session : Session) : Boolean   <<editing>> addSession(session : Session)

Note: There is no removeSession operation because session should not be removed once added.

Agent
id : String name : String sessions : Container
<<constructor—none since it is abstract class >>   <<get & query operations>> getId() : String getName() : String getSessions() : Session[*] getSessionCount() : Integer getSessionsBetween(timeA : Time, timeB : Time) : Sessions [*] contains(session : Session) : Boolean   <<editing>> addSession(session : Session)

Note: There is no removeSession operation because session should not be removed once added.

(continued)

ATM
location : String
<<constructor>> ATM(id : String, name : String, location : String)   <<get & query operations>> getLocation() : String   <<editing—none except those inherited >>

Cashier
branch : String
<<constructor>> Cashier(id : String, name : String, branch : String)   <<get & query operations>> getLocation() : String   <<editing—none except those inherited>>

FIGURE 9-71. *Answer to Exercise 7-4.*

7-5.   Variations of the Web-based application in Figure 7-6. For requirement 1, the data for the Applet are known at startup. Thus we can include the data within the HTML page (which contains the link to the Applet). For requirement 2, however, we need to either pull or push data from the server. Here we pick the pull approach. There are two designs, each using a different way to communicate with the server.

First, we may use the same WebServer to hold the data in a predefined URL. The Applet may pull data from the URL periodically. This design uses the same WebServer to handle the data. However, the data must be serialized to fit the HTTP format. They are therefore no longer object oriented. The corresponding sequence diagram is shown in Figure 9-72. (The dashed link between the HTML page and the Applet indicates that the Applet is transported together with the page.)

Second, we may use a separate DataServer to hold the data. The Applet may pull data from the DataServer periodically using IIOP (CORBA). This allows us to have a fully object-oriented interface. The corresponding sequence diagram is shown in Figure 9-73. (The dashed link between the HTML page and the Applet indicates that the Applet is transported together with the page. Also, the connection between the Applet and the DataServer may be constrained by certain security policies.)

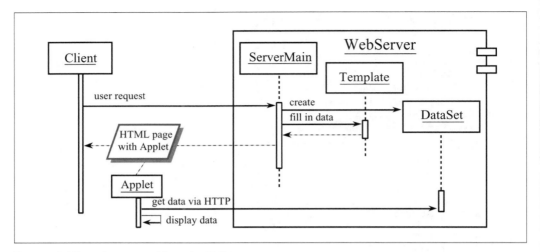

FIGURE 9-72. *Answer to Exercise 7-5.*

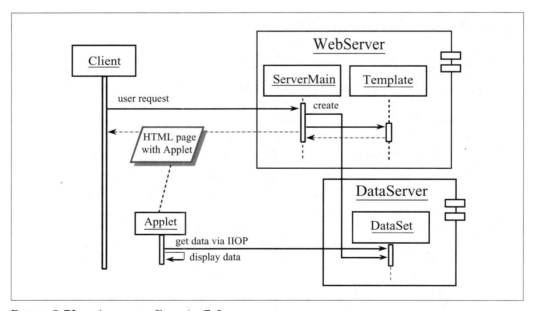

FIGURE 9-73. *Answer to Exercise 7-5.*

The architecture diagram for the first design is the same as the usual client/server systems. The architecture diagram for the second design is presented in Figure 9-74, which has two connectors with different communication protocols between the client and the server.

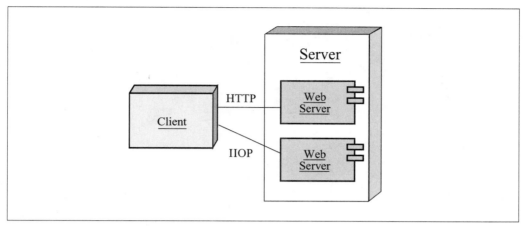

FIGURE **9-74.** *Answer to Exercise 7-5.*

Quick References for Object Designers

The images in Figure A-1 show some selected UML notations.

The images in Figure A-2 show different class relationships expressed in UML.

The sequence diagram in Figure A-3 shows the dynamic relationships between instances of classes in UML.

The sample statechart diagram in Figure A-4 summarizes the states of a system or an object, along with the transitional events between states. State 2 contains two nested states.

Table A-1 lists the core patterns and references in the main text for various practical applications, which are identified by their topics.

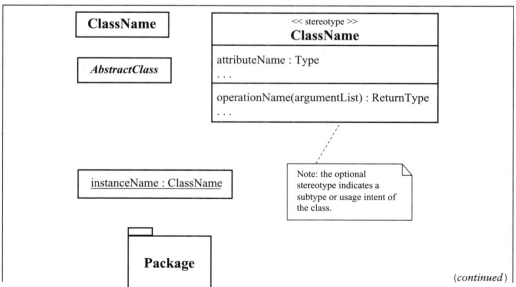

(*continued*)

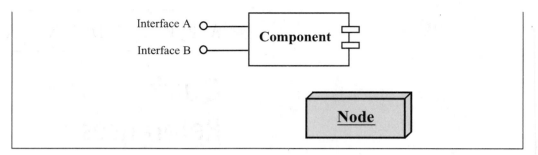

FIGURE A-1. *UML notations.*

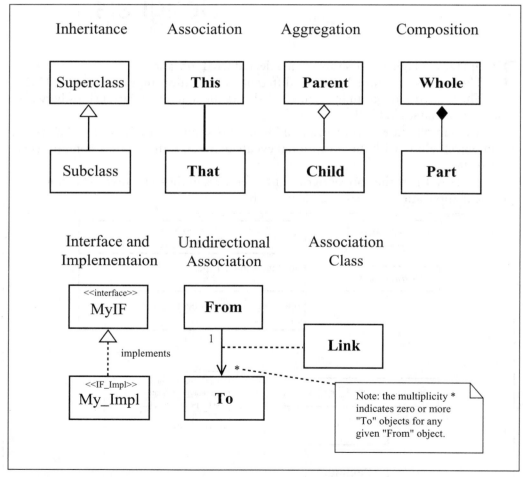

FIGURE A-2. *UML class relationships.*

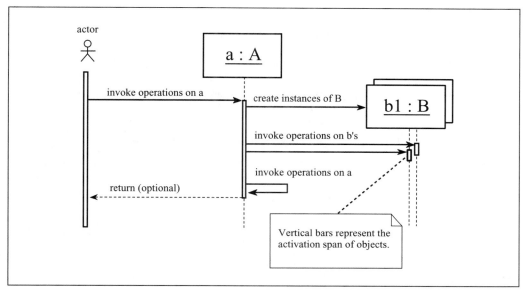

FIGURE A-3. *UML sequence diagram.*

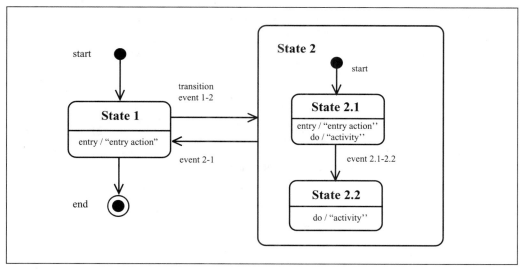

FIGURE A-4. *Sample statechart diagram.*

TABLE **A-1.** *Core patterns and referernces.*

TOPICS	CORE PATTERNS	REFERENCES
Account manager and account interface	Object manager interface	Figure 6-31
Access control lists	Binary association class and relationship loop with forward containment	Section 2.12
Callbacks from server objects	Servant interface with push events	Figure 6-12
Cash card transaction with ATMs	Binary association class	Figure 2-33, Figure 3-21
Catalogs of parts and attributes	Dynamic schema	Figure 2-26
Catalog and part interface	Layered architecture	Figure 7-10, Figure 7-11
Chat room	Servant interface with push events	Figure 6-12, Exercise 6-3
Class scheduling on university campuses	Degenerate ternary association class	Figure 3-13, Figure 3-14
Collaboration group with message exchange	Relationship loop with interface	Figure 6-39, Figure 6-42, Figure 6-43, Figure 6-44
Collaboration group with image sharing	Relationship loop with interface, inheritance ladder, layered architecture	Figure 7-30, Figure 7-34, Figure 7-35
Components and containers	Two-tier relationship loop	Exercise 2-4
Components and parts with attributes	Double relationship loop	Figure 2-12
CORBA client stubs	Inheritance ladder	Figure 6-26
CORBA objects	Servant class	Figure 6-21, Figure 6-22
Enterprise JavaBeans	Object factory, servant class, and collection manager	Figure 7-41
Event-based parsing of XML documents	Servant interface with push events	Exercise 6-4
Files and folders	Two-tier relationship loop	Figure 2-6
Folders with symbolic links	Two-tier relationship loop with binary association class	Exercise 2-14
Geometric objects	Servant class and inheritance	Exercise 1-3
Hierarchical networks and nodes	Two-tier relationship loop, recursive binary association class	Exercise 4-3
Job assignment (formal)	Binary association class	Exercise 3-7

TOPICS	CORE PATTERNS	REFERENCES
Mapping of objects to tables	Binary association class	Figure 3-5, Figure 3-6
Mapping of objects to tables	Ternary association class, multiple binary associations with joint multiplicity constraints	Figure 3-8, Figure 3-10
Mapping of objects to tables	Degenerate ternary association class	Figure 3-12
Mapping of objects to tables	Inheritance tree	Figure 3-16
Menus and related items	Two-tier relationship loop	Exercise 2-5, Exercise 2-10
Model-View-Controller	Servant interface with both push and pull events	Figure 6-16, Figure 6-17, Exercise 6-7
Network of nodes	Recursive binary association	Figure 2-4a
Orders and sales	Binary association class	Exercise 3-10
Parts and attributes with classification	Dynamic schema	Figure 2-25
Part hierarchy with properties	Recursive association class	Figure 2-22
Projects in companies	Ternary association class	Exercise 3-13
Rental to members and tracking of rental items	Binary association class, collection manager, and container	Figure 3-25
Schedule/room assignment	Binary association class	Figure 3-14
Session manager and session interface	Object manager interface and object adapter	Figure 6-37
Session manager and session in a layered architecture	Object manager in interface and persistent layers	Figure 7-28, Exercise 7-2
Subscription and notification service	Servant interface with asynchronous push events	Figure 6-14, Figure 6-15
Timer and simple event pushing	Servant interface with push events	Figure 6-10, Exercise 6-2
Trade between buyers and suppliers	Binary association class	Exercise 3-6
User group with security	Two-tier relationship loop	Exercise 2-9
User permission in file systems	Binary association class and two-tier relationship loop	Figure 2-18
Web-based applications	Thin clients with object IDs	Figure 7-5
Web-based applications	MVC framework	Figure 7-6
Wrapper for legacy code	Object wrapper	Figure 6-2
XML document (well formed)	Two-tier relationship loop	Figure 2-29

Sample Code Reference List

Tables B-1 through B-7 list the directories of the code samples for the chapters. Also listed are the corresponding figures and/or exercises. To download the most updated sample code, please see the online resources section in the Preface of this book.

TABLE B-1. *Chapter 1 sample code.*

DIRECTORY NAMES (UNDER CHAPTER 1)	FEATURES/PATTERNS	REFERENCE FIGURES/EXERCISES
Person	Simple object	Figure 1-1
Trade	Simple object	Figure 1-2, Figure 1-3, Figure 1-4
Person-Hobby	Binary association	Figure 1-7 (see Exercises 1-1, 1-2)
Polygon-Point	Aggregation (ordered)	Figure 1-8, Figure 1-11
Committee	Ternary association	Figure 1-9, Figure 1-10
Car-Part	Aggregation	Figure 1-11
Circle-Point	Composition, servant class	Figure 1-11, Figure 1-12
Person-User	Simple inheritance, polymorphism, object substitution	Figure 1-13, Figure 1-14

TABLE B-2. *Chapter 2 sample code.*

DIRECTORY NAMES (UNDER CHAPTER2)	FEATURES/PATTERNS	REFERENCE FIGURES/EXERCISES
UserManager	Collection manager	Figure 2-1
Container	Object container	Figure 2-2
Node	Self-association	Figure 2-4, Exercise 2-8
Folder	Relationship loop (backward containment)	Figure 2-7, Exercise 2-6
Version-Revision	Relationship loop (no containment)	Figure 2-8, Exercise 2-7
Item-Group	Relationship loop (with leaf node)	Figure 2-10
Trade	Binary association class	Figure 2-17, Figure 2-20
Person-Role	Handle-body pattern	Figure 2-24
Category-Part	Dynamic schema	Figure 2-25
Catalog-Part	Shared object pool	Figure 2-27
XML	XML object model	Section 2.9.2, Exercise 2-17

TABLE B-3. *Chapter 3 sample code.*

DIRECTORY NAMES (UNDER CHAPTER3)	FEATURES / PATTERNS	REFERENCE FIGURES/EXERCISES
Person-Hobby	Persistent objects, collection manager	Figure 3-2b
University	Persistent objects with binary association class, collection managers, and container	Figure 3-14
Person-Citizen	Persistent objects with inheritance	Figure 3-15, Figure 3-19

TABLE B-4. *Chapter 4 sample code.*

DIRECTORY NAMES (UNDER CHAPTER4)	FEATURES/PATTERNS	REFERENCE FIGURES/EXERCISES
Content	Abstract class, template method	Figure 4-1
Movable	Interface and implementation	Figure 4-3

TABLE B-5. *Chapter 5 sample code.*

DIRECTORY NAMES (UNDER CHAPTER5)	FEATURES/PATTERNS	REFERENCE FIGURES/EXERCISES
pdm	Interface definition	Figure 5-9, Section 5.6, Exercise 5-3

TABLE B-6. *Chapter 6 sample code.*

DIRECTORY NAMES (UNDER CHAPTER6)	FEATURES/PATTERNS	REFERENCE FIGURES/EXERCISES
User	Object adapter	Figure 6-3
Factory	Object factory and manager	Figure 6-4, Figure 6-5
Bank	Servant interface, interface handle-body pattern	Figure 6-8
Timer	Simple event pushing	Figure 6-10
Observer	Observer pattern	Figure 6-11
ChatRoom	Server callback	Figure 6-12
Event	Subscription and notification	Figure 6-14
MVC	Model-View-Controller	Figure 6-16
Admin	Inheritance ladder	Figure 6-19

TABLE B-7. *Chapter 7 sample code.*

DIRECTORY NAMES (UNDER CHAPTER7)	FEATURES/PATTERNS	REFERENCE FIGURES/EXERCISES
pdm2	Layering with servant objects (full-exposure approach)	Figure 7-10

Features of Object-Oriented Languages

Table C-1 compares the object-oriented features of different programming languages.

TABLE C-1.   *Comparison of programming language features.*

FEATURE	JAVA	C++	VISUAL BASIC	SMALLTALK	ADA	EIFFEL
Class, polymorphism (dynamic binding), single inheritance	Y	Y	Y	Y	Y	Y
Interface	Y	N	Y	N	N	N
Garbage collection	Y	N	Y	Y	N	Y
Strong class type checking	Y	Y	N	N	Y	Y
Prohibition of multiple inheritance	Y	N	Y	Y	Y	N

Y = yes; N = no.

References

[Astrahan et al. 1976] Astrahan, M. M., et al. "System R: A Relational Approach to Database Management." *ACM Transactions on Database Systems* 1976; 1(2): 97–137.

[Booch 1994] Booch, G. *Object-Oriented Analysis & Design with Applications.* 2nd ed. Reading, MA: Addison-Wesley, 1994.

[Bretl et al. 1989] Bretl, R., et al. "The GemStone Data Managementt System." In: Kim, Won, and Frederick Lochovsky, eds. *Object-Oriented Concepts, Databases, and Applications.* New York: ACM Press, 1989: 283–308.

[Cattell 1991] Cattell, R. G. G. *Object Data Management: Object-Oriented & Extended Relational Database Systems.* Reading, MA: Addison-Wesley, 1991.

[Cattell 1993] Cattell, R. G. G. *The Object Database Standard.* San Francisco, CA: Morgan Kaufmann Publishers, 1993.

[Cattell & Barry 1997] Cattell, R. G. G., and D. Barry. *The Object Database Standard: ODMG 2.0.* San Francisco, CA: Morgan Kaufmann Publishers, 1997.

[Codd 1970] Codd, E. "A Relational Model for Large Shared Data Banks." *Communications of the ACM* 1970; 13(6): 377–387.

[Codd 1990] Codd, E. "Mastering the Art of Database Fusion." *Datamation* October 15, 1990; 36(20): 61–64.

[Coplien 1992] Coplien, J. *Advanced C++ Programming Styles & Idioms.* Reading, MA: Addison-Wesley, 1992.

[Date 1986] Date, C. J. *A Guide to the SQL Standard.* Reading, MA: Addison-Wesley, 1986.

[Date 1995] Date, C. J. *An Introduction to Database Systems.* 6th ed. Reading, MA: Addison-Wesley, 1995.

[Diederich & Milton 1989] Diederich, J., and J. Milton. "Objects, Messages, and Rules in Database Design." In: Kim, Won, and Frederick Lockovsky, eds. *Object-Oriented Concepts, Databases, and Applications.* New York: ACM Press, 1989: 177–197.

[D'Souza & Wills 1999] D'Souza, D. F., and A. C. Wills. *Objects, Components, and Frameworks with UML: The Catalysis Approach.* Reading, MA: Addison-Wesley, 1999.

[Ellis & Stroustrup 1990] Ellis, M. A., and B. Stroustrup. *The Annotated C++ Reference Manual.* Reading, MA: Addison-Wesley, 1990.

[Fishman et al. 1989] Fishman, D. H., et al. "Overview of the Iris DBMS." In: Kim, Won, and Frederick Lochovsky, eds. *Object-Oriented Concepts, Databases, and Applications.* New York: ACM Press, 1989: 219–250.

[Fowler et al. 1997] Fowler, M., and K. Scott, *UML Distilled: Applying the Standard Object Modeling Language.* Reading, MA: Addison-Wesley, 1997.

[Gamma et al. 1995] Gamma, E., et al. *Design Patterns: Elements of Reusable Object-Oriented Software.* Reading, MA: Addison-Wesley, 1995.

[Goldberg & Robson 1989] Goldberg, A., and D. Robson. *Smalltalk-80: The Language.* Reading, MA: Addison-Wesley, 1989.

[Heinckiens 1998] Heinckiens, P. *Building Scalable Database Applications: Object-Oriented Design, Architectures, and Implementations.* Reading, MA: Addison-Wesley, 1998.

[HTTP and HTML] Specifications for HTTP and HTML can be found at http://www.w3.org/.

[ISO 1986] ISO Standard 8879:1986—Standard Generalized Markup Language (SGML), which can be obtained at http://www.iso.ch/.

[Jackson 1991] Jackson, M. S. "Tutorial on Object-Oriented Databases." *Information and Software Technology* 1991; 33: 4–12.

[Jacobson et al. 1992] Jacobson, I., et al. *Object-Oriented Software Engineering: A Use Case Driven Approach.* Reading, MA: Addison-Wesley, 1992.

[Kim et. al. 1989] Kim, W., et al. "Features of the ORION Object-Oriented Database System." In: Kim, Won, and Frederick Lochovsky, eds. *Object-Oriented Concepts, Databases, and Applications.* New York: ACM Press, 1989: 251–283.

[Larman 1998] Larman, C. *Applying UML and Patterns: An Introduction to Object-Oriented Analysis & Design.* Upper Saddle River, NJ: Prentice Hall, 1998.

[Liskov 1987] Liskov, B. "Data Abstraction and Hierarchy." In: *OOPSLA 87. Addendum to the Proceedings.* New York: ACM Press, 1987: 17–34.

[Monson-Haefel 2000] Monson-Haefel, R. *Enterprise JavaBeans*. Sebastopol, CA: O'Reilly & Associates, 2000.

[Mowbray & Ruh 1997] Mowbray, T., and W. Ruh. *Inside CORBA: Distributed Object Standards and Applications*. Reading, MA: Addison-Wesley, 1997.

[OMG/CORBA 1999] The CORBA specification and related information are available at the Object Management Group Web site: http://www.omg.org/.

[OMG/IDL 1999] The Java-IDL Language Mapping Specification "formal/99-07-54" is available at the Object Management Group web site: http://www.omg.org/.

[Orfali et al. 1995] Orfali, R., et al. *The Essential Distributed Objects Survival Guide*. New York: John Wiley & Sons, 1995.

[Otte et al. 1995] Otte, R., et al. *Understanding CORBA*. Upper Saddle River, NJ: Prentice Hall, 1995.

[Page-Jones 2000] Page-Jones, M. *Fundamentals of Object-Oriented Design in UML*. Reading, MA: Addison-Wesley, 2000.

[Roman 1999] Roman, E. *Mastering Enterprise JavaBeans and the Java 2 Platform. Enterprise Edition*. New York: John Wiley, 1999.

[Rosenberg & Scott 1999] Rosenberg, D., and K. Scott. *Use Case Driven Object Modeling with UML: A Practical Approach*. Reading, MA: Addison-Wesley, 1999.

[Rumbaugh 1988] Rumbaugh, J. "Controlling Propagation of Operations Using Attributes on Relations." *OOPSLA '88 as ACM SIGPLAN 23* 1988; 11: 285–296.

[Rumbaugh 1991] Rumbaugh, J, et al. *Object-Oriented Modeling and Design*. Upper Saddle River, NJ: Prentice Hall, 1991.

[Sessions 1996] Sessions, R. *Object Persistence: Beyond Object-Oriented Databases*. Upper Saddle River, NJ: Prentice Hall, 1996.

[Stonebraker 1976] Stonebraker, M. "The Design and Implementation of Ingres." ACM Transactions on *Database Systems* 1976; 1(3): 189–222.

[UML 1997] The specification for the Unified Modeling Language is available at http://www.rational.com/uml. The most recent update is version 1.1, September 1997. The UML specification there consists of two parts: (1) UML semantics, a metamodel that specifies the abstract syntax and semantics of UML object modeling concepts; and (2) UML notation, a graphic notation for the visual representation of UML semantics. It also describes the mapping of the graphic notation to the underlying semantics.

[Weiser & Lochovsky 1989] Weiser, S. P. and F. H. Lochovsky, "OZ+: An Object-Oriented Database System." In: Kim, Won, and Frederick Lochovsky, eds.

Object-Oriented Concepts, Databases, and Applications. New York: ACM Press, 1989: 309–340.

[XML 1998] Extensible Markup Language (XML) 1.0, REC-xml-19980210, February 1998. The XML specification is available at http://www.w3.org/. Also, XML frequently asked questions are at http://www.ucc.ie/xml/.

Index

Also Available from Addison-Wesley

Fundamentals of Object-Oriented Design in UML

Meilir Page-Jones

With the recent introduction and widespread adoption of the UML, programmers are now equipped with a powerful tool for expressing software designs. *Fundamentals of Object-Oriented Design in UML* shows aspiring and experienced programmers alike how to apply design concepts, the UML, and the best practices in OO development to improve both their code and their success rates with object-based projects. Readers will come away with a better understanding of object-oriented concepts and of how to design and develop the high-quality software their clients need.

0-201-69946-X • Paperback • 480 pages • ©2000

Use Case Driven Object Modeling with UML

A Practical Approach
Doug Rosenberg and Kendall Scott

Learn a streamlined approach to UML modeling that includes a minimal but effective set of diagrams and techniques you can use to get from use cases to code quickly and efficiently. *Use Case Driven Object Modeling with UML* provides practical guidance that shows developers how to produce UML models with minimal startup time, while maintaining traceability from user requirements through detailed designing and coding. The authors present clear, proven methods for driving the object modeling process forward.

0-201-43289-7 • Paperback • 192 pages • ©1999

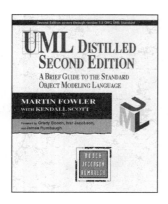

UML Distilled, Second Edition

A Brief Guide to the Standard Object Modeling Language
Martin Fowler and Kendall Scott

The award-winning first edition of *UML Distilled* was widely praised for being a concise guide to the core parts of the UML and has proved extremely successful in helping developers get up and running quickly. *UML Distilled, Second Edition,* maintains the concise format with significantly updated coverage of use cases and activity diagrams, and expanded coverage of collaborations. It also includes a new appendix detailing the changes between UML versions.

0-201-65783-X • Paperback • 224 pages • ©2000